MW00479929

THE HOLY GHOST HAS A FUNNY BONE!

by

Robert Hitt Neill

To "David Ross"
Enjoy the Joy!
Robert Hitt Neill
"Uncle Bob"
3/24/05

THE HOLY GHOST HAS A FUNNY BONE!

Copyright 1997 & 2010 by
Robert Hitt Neill

Cover artwork by
Margaret Moss Furr Barnett
184 Main Street
Ridgedale, MO 65739

Design Assistance provided by
John Irwin & Dedra Dorris & Mark Weilenman

All Rights Reserved

Manufactured in the United States of America

Printed by Lightning Source, Inc.

ISBN # 1-879034-22-0

Other Books by Robert Hitt Neill:

THE FLAMING TURKEY

GOING HOME

DON'T FISH UNDER THE DINGLEBERRY TREE

HOW TO LOSE YOUR FARM IN TEN EASY LESSONS &
COPE WITH IT

THE VOICE OF JUPITER PLUVIUS

BEWARE THE BARKING BUMBLEBEES

THE JAKES

THE BAREFOOT DODGERS

MS KAROTALES

compiled & edited:

THE MAGNOLIA CLUB

OUTDOOR TABLES AND TALES

Brownspur Books
PO Box 6
Stoneville, MS 38776
roberthittneill.com

This Book Is Dedicated To:

Betsy Neill, *of course*

Joe and Susan Street

Mike and Frances Bedford

Table of Contents

Chapters 12 thru 18 are reprinted in part in a companion book entitled MS KAROTALES, which is a fund-raiser for the Kairos International Prison Ministry.

The Religious Experience

Almost any religious book should probably begin with the author's own religious experience: i.e., a testimony, in good evangelistic terms. Well, this author wants the world to know that he has had a Religious Experience; several of them, in fact. And enjoyed the heck out of them. Or, the Heaven out of them, to be more accurate.

I am not sure how many denominations follow the practice of holding prayer meetings on one night of the week, usually Wednesday night. I belonged to a church that not only had this weeknight prayer meeting, but also hosted a potluck fellowship supper before prayer time. Everybody would bring a dish, two or three couples would be in charge of setting up tables and silverware, and a fine time would be had by all. Good food and good fellowship is certainly not a prerequisite for good prayer: any combat veteran can tell you that; but I can't imagine that it hurts anything, either.

The meat at these affairs is usually ninety percent fried chicken, which is plumb fine with me. One preacher even told me that he knew he had been called into the ministry when he developed this unquenchable craving for fried chicken, though I'm not sure that's asked on the entrance examination for most main-line Protestant seminaries.

Matter of fact, I wouldn't give a plugged nickel for any Bred-In-The-Bone Southern man, woman, or child who couldn't eat their weight in fried chicken whenever the occasion calls for it. With their fingers, too. Being Raised Right, I not only know how to use a knife and fork, I even know which side of the plate they go on. But we all know certain things are to be eaten with one's fingers: fried chicken, crawfish, quail, spareribs, and hot peppers, among others.

One couple who hailed originally from Louisiana always brought a quart jar of homegrown hot peppers; not the kind that burns your mouth, but the kind that cleans your sinuses and breaks your forehead out in a light sweat. I love peppers like that, and on this one particular Wednesday night, was last in line to be fed, being the host deacon. But the ladies had miscounted on the silverware, and someone had gotten the fork out of the pepper jar to eat their supper with.

Well, so what; I was going to eat them with my fingers anyway. I reached down into the juice and got three or four peppers for my plate, and moved on down the line. I did find some silverware, but I ate my chicken and peppers with my fingers, having been Raised Right.

Since I had been last in line, the preacher started the prayer list while I was still eating. Finishing supper just as prayer time began, I pushed my plate back, leaned my elbows on the table, and cupped my face in my hands. Sometime during the second or third prayer, I moved my thumb and forefinger to the bridge of my nose and gently pressed the inside corners of my eyes, where the tear ducts are located. This was a subconscious type routine, for I was trying to concentrate on prayer.

My eyes began to sting and water.

Unthinkingly, I wiped the tears away, which seemed to cause more stinging and increased the flow. I began to sniffle and again wiped my eyes with my fingers. My concentration on prayer was beginning to suffer, for tears gushed from my eyes like the waters must have when Moses whanged the rock with his rod. My wife handed me a handkerchief. The lady on my other side patted my shoulder. The deacon across the table muttered "Praise the Lord!" and shoved me a clean napkin. His wife began to weep herself, only her tears were for joy, not pain.

Suddenly, I remembered the peppers! Even though I had used a napkin after I ate, enough pepper juice remained on my fingers to create a wellspring from my tear ducts. But what could I do about it now? Getting up and making my way through the tables during prayer time was unthinkable. I cheated and peeked, hoping I wouldn't get struck by lightning, but there was not a glass containing water or tea within reach, so I couldn't wash my hands and flush out my eyes.

Other people were also cheating, I noticed. They had to see who the Spirit was getting aholt of. Embarrassed to have caught them peeking, as well as to have been caught peeking, I ducked my head back into my hands, compounding the problem even more. By now, I needed a crying towel, and the tear-jerking was spreading to other tables as well. The preacher began to snuffle over his prayer list, but I don't think he ever peeked. However, I do suspect that he went rather hurriedly through the last third of the list.

It was a very empathetic church. Thank the Lord that the prayer meeting was cut short that night because so many folks were moved to their own tears by my so very obvious Experience. I was hugged a lot on my way to the kitchen to wash my face, hands, and eyes. People talked about it for weeks, and it sparked a real revival amongst the regular Wednesday night crowd.

I have never had another Religious Experience quite like that one.

And, I learned to eat peppers with a fork.

Obviously, there have been much more serious Religious Experiences in my life, down deep in my heart where pepper juice cannot be blamed. Had to be Jesus, and I praise the Lord that we've had a long walk with Him, through church music, youth work, Sunday School teaching, and the wonderful warm times with family and friends. Yet it's also been a lot of fun -- good, clean, Christian fun. It's my personal conviction that we too seldom recognize, at least publicly, that Christian service can not only be inspiring, but it can at times be a barrel of laughs, without losing our Spiritual perspective.

People often miss church because they have plans that involve fun and enjoyment. What if we could convince them that Christianity, too, can be fun, without losing any of its meaning?

Of course, for the younger generation, church and fun often mean discipline is coming just as soon as services are over. I'm speaking from a boy's standpoint, and at that age, not necessarily a Christian boy. Simply boys whose parents brought them to church as a matter of course, sometimes when the preacher would just as soon they would be elsewhere.

I watched from the back row in the choir recently as a daddy toward the rear of the sanctuary finally stood during the sermon and escorted his young son out the door. It didn't look like a call of nature, from where I sat; more like a disciplinary matter. I knew how the youngster was feeling at that point; most boys have had the experience, and it ain't exactly Godly.

When I was growing up, there were several of us boys about the same age who all attended the same church on a regular basis, though -- truth be known -- that was our parents' fault: if it had been left up to a vote of just boys and the preacher, once a month would have sufficed. It was said that the preacher did his best work during deer and turkey season, when our fathers had us boys in the woods on several consecutive weekends.

The Boy Pew alternated between the front row, right up under the preacher's eyes, to the back row, where the preacher wasn't as liable to be distracted and we didn't feel so "under the gun," so to speak. A couple of our daddies were in the choir, and over the years got very proficient at shooting daggers from their eyes right by the preacher's ear, whenever we'd get something really interesting going on the front row during the sermon. We learned that a really good daggering session would invariably mean a licking after church that Sabbath, but the other side of that coin was next-week banishment to the back row, to give the preacher a shot at concentrating on sermon delivery. If the preacher lost his place more than three times during a sermon, we could all expect lickings by all six daddies and two uncles, sometimes within the sanctuary, but it also meant back row seats for nearly a month. Perhaps it was worth the price.

We were on the back row one warm Sunday during the early spring, between deer season and turkey season, and had spent the intermission after Sunday School playing marbles outside. I don't guess boys play marbles any more, and words like "taw" and "lag" and "cats-eye" and "steelie" will soon disappear from the English language. I think it was Ed Wood who had cornered all our marbles that morning (come to think of it, I guess it is a little bit like gambling, isn't it?), and had both pockets full of his round winnings. Of course, the rest of us gave him no credit for extra skill; we laid it all to the new steelie taw he had used.

Which he still had clenched in his fist where we sat, having been sent to the rear for a week for some deed. About halfway into the sermon, Ed began to gloat, patting his pockets and admiring his taw. But he shouldn't have kissed it.

Kissing marbles makes the smooth slickness even slicker.

His new steelie taw slipped from his hand.

The church had carpets down the aisles; nice, soft, thick, silencing carpets. But we weren't sitting on the aisles. Under the pews were hardwood floors, which slanted downward from the back row toward the pulpit. The new steelie taw hit and rolled slowly -- and audibly -- all the way down to the base of that pulpit, stopping right beneath the preacher's feet. In retrospect, it doesn't seem possible that it could have rolled freely that far without hitting someone's foot, for the church was filled that day. Must have been Divine Intervention.

To give him credit, the preacher never lost his place, though he did wince quite visibly. Big Dave in the choir got that dagger look which we all knew so well. The back row, in preparation for what we knew was coming, began to slip our Sunday School books into the seat of our britches, for padding. If Ed hadn't had his pockets stuffed full of marbles, we'd have all gotten by with a lick or two from our own daddies.

For in shoving a youth study of Habakkuk into his pants, he dislodged half a pocket of marbles, including my orange cat's eye, which I know I'd have won back at school Monday. Another dozen marbles hit the floor and began rolling toward the pulpit. This time, the preacher did lose his place. A dozen or so marbles rolling down a hardwood floor will do that to many ministers. I have since wondered if such distractions shouldn't be covered in seminary training.

It was an all-daddies plus uncles session, in the sanctuary!

And we were back on the front row the next Sunday. They even frisked us first.

Boys, it has been my experience that playing marbles for keepsies anywhere close to a church is a sin. I know that ain't specifically covered in the King James version, but trust your old Uncle Bob on this one, okay?

Make a Joyful Noise!

Big Robert was a Presbyterian, so we went to that church for my early years. But Miss Janice was an Episcopalian, so when she joined a group to form a small Episcopal Mission in town, we went there mostly, since they needed warm bodies. Betsy's daddy was Catholic and her mother was Methodist, so she went some to each, and we were married in the Lexington Methodist Church by its minister, Crawford Ray, and our Presbyterian preacher, Sam Patterson, in a joint ceremony. It must have took, since we've been together for nearly half a century so far.

Point is, we had experience in four different denominations. When we returned from the service (Navy Chaplains are essentially non-denominational) we settled down back home and began attending the Presbyterian Church, where I sang in the choir and was elected a deacon.

It's no secret that most church organizations have had their troubles over the past couple of decades. Several denominations actually had schisms, the Presbyterians being one of those, during the time we were attending. Betsy and I decided to seek a more peaceable fellowship, since neither of us was particularly Bred-In-The-Bone, as noted. For several months we attended other churches in town, and settled on the First Baptists. There were two more Baptist congregations in town, but they were Locational Baptists, not Numbered Baptists. Since we didn't live in their locations, we preferred to be Firsts. I don't think it makes any difference who's a First in Heaven, though. Really.

So, we began attending the First Baptist Church on a regular basis, yet we were careful not to jump into anything -- once bitten, twice shy, you know. But I did want to sing, wherever we settled, and there were no membership requirements for the choir, especially since there wasn't but one regular bass already in attendance. I -- or my voice, rather -- was welcomed with open arms into the choir.

It IS very much a close-kept secret, however, that denominations sing different songs. I had already learned that Presbyterians and Episcopalians, even in the same town, don't sing off the same book, except for "Onward, Christian Soldiers," "Lead On, Oh King Eternal" (and I think the schools have all community churches practice that one for graduation), "Jesus Loves Me," and most Christmas Carols. I knew from attending church in Lexington while courting Betsy that Catholics and Methodists followed the same rule, and it was pretty obvious that Hill Churches didn't sing songs I had learned in the Delta, though I wasn't at the time sure I could blame that on denominationalism. I am sure now, however.

Point is, people, that when you get upset with your present church, you need to realize that if you switch you may have to start all over again learning the hymnbook. If you cannot think of another single reason to bury the hatchet anywhere but in a fellow Christian's back, your Uncle Bob has just now given you a real good one!

Ten years later, when I was occasionally asked to lead the congregational singing, I'd have to either pick Presbyterian hymns that Baptists knew, or else spend hours at the church during the week re-learning the Baptist hymns -- for I could only sing those in the bass line. There ain't no way one can lead the congregational singing in a co-educational church singing the bass line. Take my word for it. We did a lot of "Jesus Loves Me" during those couple of years, since the preacher

13

balked at singing "We Three Kings of Orey and Tar" in the summertime.

Worse than that, all my practice time during the week trying to learn the melody of Baptist hymns led to community rumors that the piano player and I were having an affair. Thusly accused, I pointed out that there were three different ladies playing the piano at various times during three weekly services. The accommodating rumor-mongers obligingly expanded their stories to include all three ladies, who, to give them credit, were sure good-looking and personable enough to tempt any non-Bred-In-The-Bone song leader. When the rumors went from trying to guess which lady WAS involved to trying to guess whether any of them were NOT involved, we went back to regular choruses of "Lead On, Oh King Eternal" and "Jesus Loves Me." It was getting close to graduation anyway.

Give me a church any time, for proficiency in spreading rumors! Even the preacher's wife isn't spared -- or maybe that should be, especially the preacher's wife. We got a new preacher one year, and they hadn't been here but a couple of months when the rumor sprang full-grown into being, that Frances and I were having an affair. Once we got it stomped out, we found that it had followed a rather logical succession during two consecutive Sabbaths.

We have a large, two-bedroom guest house, and when Mike and Frances moved here after seminary, they stayed out in the "Store" (we had moved and remodeled the old plantation general store) for a couple of months while home-shopping. Their two boys were about the ages of our children, and we grew to be the closest of friends, and have stayed thataway for decades.

However, I was recovering from major knee surgery that summer, and the joint was swollen and bandaged; there was no way I could wear long pants until it healed, so for nearly six months I wore shorts and cut-off jeans. Understandably, I didn't attend church much during those months. Everyone knows the Lord frowns on attending services in shorts, right? I had to be content to limp around the church in shorts during the week helping organize the music, until I could get suit pants on again.

And that day finally came. I limped into Sunday morning services for the first time in months, and obviously, one of the common questions was, "How do you like having the preacher's family out there all this time?"

I confessed that I loved it, and then opened my mouth to voice an observation that occurred to me -- when I should have kept it to myself. "You know," I laughed, "I guess this is the first time Frances has seen me with britches on!" Of course, she was in hearing range, and we all had a chuckle. But the seed had been planted, unbeknownst to us.

And it sprang into full bloom the next Sunday when we had a duet. She and I had run over the song a final time in the music room between Sunday School and church, and as we finished, I noticed that she had lipstick on one front tooth. "Hold still," I said, pulling out my handkerchief. "You don't have time to go look in a mirror." I leaned close and wiped the lipstick off of her tooth, just as one of the head deacons stuck his head in the door to tell us church was starting.

By that afternoon, it was all over town!

Thank the Lord, the ones who laughed the hardest were Mike and Betsy! And Susan, the piano player who had witnessed it.

Incidentally, Mike ended up separating Susan and me during any service in which he was preaching. As song leader and pianist, she and I were in the habit of sitting together on one side of the sanctuary by the piano after the special music. He would preach his sermon, then she and I would take our places to lead the invitational hymn. Only problem was, we couldn't keep our mouths shut when he made a mistake. Which preachers occasionally do, in spite of what you may have heard.

I guess it began back when he was doing the parable of the vine and the branches. Mike used a tomato plant as his illustration, declaring that, once the branch is torn from the main vine, it ceases to grow. I was a farmer, and Susan's husband Joe was also one. She looked at me and mouthed, "Sure it will root and grow, if it just gets water, won't it?" I nodded emphatically, and began to tick off other branches which would root when taken from the main vine. Mike lost his place in the sermon that morning.

One Sunday soon afterward, he was preaching on David and Jonathan, and mentioned Mephibosheth; except he got his "tang tongueled," as one preacher used to put it, and called him "Messhibopheth." Susan looked at me for confirmation, and I nodded and mouthed "Mephibosheth." She stifled a chuckle and mouthed back, "Messhibopheth." I grinned real big. Only thing was, the audience caught our expressions, as well as Mike's mispronunciation. Snickers changed to chuckles and coughing, and Mike lost his place again, tracing the looks to Susan and me. It was the first time I had been moved in church since the marbles incident when I was a kid!

The choir was fairly small back when I first started to sing Baptist, and there were only two of us basses who came regularly. Choir practice was at 6:00 Wednesday night, and since I was farming, I usually made it by the skin of my teeth, still in my work clothes and without supper. The other bass had a government nine-to-five job, so he was always clean and fed before choir. And he always ate onions for supper on Wednesday night.

Now, I had a horrible experience with onions in my youth and cannot stand the things. This is a Religious Book, so I'd rather not get into any of the gruesome details; suffice it to say that it involved a football field ankle deep in wild onions and a guard who was seventy-five pounds heavier than I was. Also seven inches taller and five years older. I ate my lifetime quota of onions that night, if I never eat another.

This other bass was a wonderful singer. He opened his mouth wide to enunciate the words, had good breath control, and in general was pretty enthusiastic about the songs we practiced. Problem was, he sat next to me.

If you were Raised Right, you don't just go up to somebody and say, "your breath stinks of onions!" I tried a few subtleties like, "Have hamburger on your onions tonight?", but the guy never seemed to catch on. I began to recruit more basses for the choir on the premise that the more basses, the less chance I'd have to sit next to this friend. My efforts did lead to a new rule in the Choir Directors' Handbook, to the effect that the better looking the altos are, the easier it is to recruit basses. So it worked to some extent, but not every week. Finally, I had a Revelation From God, and found the solution.

My brother and I had been fishing that day (rule number one for farmers: do what you can when you can; and when you can't, go fishing!) and we were running short of time when we came back through town. Instead of going to the house to change, I just had Beau drop me at the church for choir. As usual, there was only one other bass there; and once again, he had eaten onions for supper.

We had been through the first couple of songs when I shifted around in my chair and felt an uncomfortable lump in my back pocket. The third song started, one that had a tricky bass part to it. My onion-breathing companion was a better musician than I was, so I had to sit extra close to him in order to get my notes right. We even sang off the same book. His breath hit the book held in front of us and rebounded into my face. I shifted again and felt the lump once more. It had been part of our boat lunch that we had not eaten: a flat can of sardines.

Inspiration struck! I've always believed it was Divine.

I excused myself between songs, stepped into the next room, which was the church kitchen, opened my sardines, and gobbled them down. I even drank the juice. There were not going to be any halfway measures. This would either kill or cure. I returned to my seat in the bass section, as confident as a David with a smooth flat slick river rock.

Oh, how I sang that night! I would not use my own book, but turned to read with my comrade. My enunciation, my enthusiasm, my breath control, could not have been better. I aimed each note to pass right by my friend's nose, only occasionally ricocheting a high note off of the song book and back into his face. He began to take on a greenish cast, and two altos in front of us excused themselves and left.

This continued through a half-dozen songs, and then he finally capitulated.

"Listen," he pleaded, unable to look me in the face, "if you won't eat any more sardines on choir nights, I won't eat any more onions!"

Though Gene and I attend different churches nowadays, I sat down to supper in another church with him last month, and he chuckled as he declared, "I didn't have onions tonight!"

The Lord works in mysterious ways.

Let me pause here to point out that the English language is sometimes confusing. The term "Bass" or even "Big-mouth Bass" might mean one thing to a guy in a fishing boat on a Southern lake, and another thing entirely to a church congregation. It's even pronounced differently, though spelled exactly the same. We are now discussing the Religious Bass, which rhymes with "First Base."

And why not rhyme it with "Second" or "Third" Base, you might ask?

Well, that type question was apparently asked by a newcomer to the choir as we were headed to the sanctuary one Sunday morning. One of my fellow Religious Basses was quick to answer him: "Well, God is a Bass. Says that in the Bible."

"And He's got a black Labrador," I added helpfully.

"And He's Southern, too," Trent declared as we walked

through the church door.

"Yeah, if you was to get to Heaven and ask for a 'Pop,' God would tell you right quick, 'Boy, I'm gonna pop you upside the head if you don't talk right!' If you want something to drink, you ask for a Coke, like it says in the Bible." This was delivered by the initial Religious Bass, but further theological enlightenment from Dwayne was cut off by the accompanists starting the prelude as we entered the sanctuary.

Please don't be offended. We were not being disrespectful to our Heavenly Father. He is Mighty and Holy, yet also Warm and Loving. He is All Powerful, yet He is also a Friend: a hug or handshake when you need it. He created the awesome universe we sometimes sit up on the roof and marvel at on clear nights here at Brownspur, yet He also created the mosquitoes that finally ran us inside the other night when we were marveling at the Milky Way.

There's a quote on my bulletin board by William Inge: "I have never understood why it should be considered derogatory to the Creator to suppose that He has a sense of humor!"

I agree. After all, He created the giraffe and the rhino, the bumblebee and the platypus, the ostrich and the jellyfish. When we originally excavated our Swimming Hole, we discovered two-foot-long, thick-as-my-arm legless salamanders as deep as ten feet in that blue clay, and I can just picture my Heavenly Father chuckling (in a deep bass chuckle) as we tried to figure out what in the world those things were, and what they were doing that deep in Delta clay!

When we, as little children, first try to picture God our Father, we usually begin with the image of our earthly fathers, and expand from there. It boggled my young mind that God could be bigger than Big Robert, but it was at least a start.

The tragedy today is that so many children do not have that awe-inspiring image of an earthly father to begin with. In the Kairos Prison Ministry that Betsy and I both work in, we've learned that only 5% of men in prison in America had a positive

19

father figure in the home. These men have a hard time picturing their Heavenly Father, much less understanding His Love for them. A tragedy.

So it bothers me not that Dwayne's image of God involves Him singing Bass. My image of Heaven is a hammock slung between a bay magnolia and a gardenia bush, both in eternal full bloom, close to a cypress arbor with bumblebees buzzing around it, with good-looking angels (image of Betsy here) serving me mint tea and lemon meringue pie. A quote from Richard Bach's *ILLUSIONS* springs to mind: "Imagine the universe beautiful and just and perfect. Then be sure of one thing: your Heavenly Father has imagined it quite a bit better than you have!"

Better than bay magnolia fragrance, bumblebees buzzing, and lemon pie? Wow!

My point here is that it's okay to have a mental image of Heaven, and of your Heavenly Father -- assuming, of course, that you have made arrangements for your post-mortem travel to such a Place, to meet such a Being face to face.

The sad thing is that so many have no concept atall of a loving, joyous Heavenly Father.

Looks like when one has sung in the choir for two or three decades, even though he may have never had any formal musical training, he would acquire some degree of musical knowledge just by osmosis, right? That ain't necessarily so.

In preparation for a spring convention, and a couple of speaking and book-signing engagements each side of it, I had secured from the choir director a tape of the Easter Cantata music. While I had been singing for years on a non-professional basis, I had never figured out reading music. Following the ups and downs on the bass cleft is fairly easy, but starting out on a Cantata, I need to crip along with a good strong bass or alto alongside. Since the trip was going to take me away for several critical practices, playing the tape during the drives would help me to prepare for the Cantata. I snagged a little pocket-sized tape player with a set of earphones right before we left, and plugged in on long Interstate stretches.

Toward the end of a three-thousand-mile, seven-state tour, I was getting pretty confident on the Easter music. It did seem a tad longer than most Cantatas I have sung, but was pretty enough that the congregation ought to be able to hold still for it. And I flat had the notes in the bass line down pat, as well as the words and timing. I'd be singing lead bass on this Cantata.

We were on the final lap toward home with several kids in the van -- we had met up with our daughter's school drama group in Winston-Salem, where they had just won the Southeastern Theater Competition, and had agreed to let B.C. and some of her friends ride home with us instead of on the school bus. When the conversation lagged somewhat, I decided to plug in again. One of the kids in the back offered me his jam box when I asked someone to hook me up. I poked the earphones in my ears as he started the tape and adjusted the volume. My fingers began to tap in time on the steering wheel. A different time than I had been practicing.

"It's on Fast Forward," I said, motioning to slow it down.

"No, it isn't," he replied.

I had Betsy check Scott's recorder to see what the problem was with the speed. She couldn't find anything wrong. Then Scott checked my little player on one of his tapes. Blood, Sweat, And Tears sounded like the Mormon Tabernacle Choir!

"Uncle Bob, sounds like your batteries are weak," he said.

During almost three weeks, three thousand miles, and seven states, I had diligently learned and practiced singing the thirty-minute Easter Cantata -- in fifty-two minutes!

Well, at least I had the words and notes down. One of these days I intend to learn how to read music, but it's tough to teach an old dog new tricks.

Not every church does an Easter Cantata, but it's obviously in the Bible somewhere that everyone must do a Christmas Cantata. Even if you're one of the Most High Hallowed Brethren of the One-And-Only Denominational Congregation, for this one season of the year we can all sing the same songs together. Having grown up in two different denominations, and then experiencing three more into adulthood, I'd bet there ain't a dozen similar songs in those five hymnals, with the exception of Christmas Carols. At this time of the year, we can all sing and listen to familiar stuff. And I once found a confirmation of this Christmas music in the singing of it.

Two decades ago I experienced several months of dizzy spells, and the various medical authorities looked at everything from stem to stern, as the saying goes, without solving the problem. (Turns out I was badly anemic, but it was over a year later when we finally found that out.) The fall that it was so bad, I gave up squirrel and duck hunting, because looking up made me fall over backwards. Sometimes I'd have to get Betsy or Christie to come to town and get me, when I'd have a spell and didn't feel safe driving myself home. Then standing for more than a few moments began to give me problems, and it looked like I was going to have to give up singing, right when Cantata time arrived.

At that time, we had a mixed sextet at church, which did a lot of singing hither and yon around the state. Engagements were lined up for months in advance, and since most of our music was memorized, it was decidedly inconvenient having a dizzy bass. I even considered taking a barstool along for a prop, but that was quickly ruled out, it being a Baptist church group. Most basses sway a little anyway when singing, but I was swaying a LOT! Finally, I had to "face the music": I was going to have to give up singing, it looked like; and soon.

Just after I had made that decision, there was an

engagement at another church somewhere, and I had to try to tough it out. However, just before we took the stage, I could feel a spell coming on. "I can't do it," I whispered to the alto who always stood on my right, and who also knew the problems I was having.

Dianne was of "the show must go on" persuasion, and had a temporary solution: "Hold your mike in your left hand, and I'll hold mine in my right. If you feel yourself starting to go, just jerk on my robe with your right hand, and I'll slip my left arm around behind you and hold you up while we sing."

There was a song several years ago that went "Lean on me, when you're not strong, and I'll. . . help you carry on." Perhaps it wasn't meant as a church song, but the concept works in church, believe me.

Just as I had feared, I felt myself going over in the middle of the third song, and jerked on the robe, as instructed. While these spells destroyed my equilibrium, nothing else was affected, and a good bass can sing flat on his back if he has to. But the supporting arm was there immediately after the jerk, and we finished the performance without further incident, though there were some funny looks from the choir members behind us during the program. One could tell that their minds were not particularly purified prior to Christmas; but then, that's what the carols are for, right?

We had several more performances during that Christmas season in which I had to have support, though I was accused at times of being a hypochondriac!

There was also a period of several months when Dianne had to let me keep my right hand on her left shoulder while we sang. I had crushed the hand in a cotton gin accident, and it took three years to rehab it to the point where I could shake hands again. Anyone who had suffered a serious injury to an extremity knows how painful it is when blood runs to the wound, and I had to keep it elevated; even a sling wasn't high enough. We sang for almost six months with my bandaged hand atop her shoulder, even at practices. "Learning to Lean," "Leaning On the Everlasting Arms," and "Lean On Me" were songs with a special meaning for me. And the mainmost message of the music is that there is Someone who is there to lean on when you need Him.

This singing group performed many times over the years, and there was one performance in a neighboring church when I had a real crisis with one of the sopranos, I thought.

We arrived at the church on time, but as so often happens, the meeting was running long. Seeing that we were going to be delayed for a while, we picked a break before a hymn and filed into the sanctuary. I let the ladies precede me into a pew, shut the door behind us, and sat down on the end next to the outside aisle.

Time dragged on, and our leader leaned over to whisper something to us. Seeing a couple of the others look at their watches and nod, I nodded also, figuring we weren't going to have time to do our song. Since I'm deaf in one ear, and the rest knew that, I assumed they'd tell me anything important.

At long last, the final report was given, and the preacher arose to intone, "Let us pray." Obediently, I lowered my head, closed my eyes, and rested my chin on my crossed arms to join his prayer.

He was doing some jam-up good praying, too, getting licks in for the Sunday School teachers and the youth leaders, as well as for the sister churches scattered about. I was really catching his spirit, when I felt this hand laid gently on my thigh.

It had to be a lady's hand; there were no men close enough.

She squeezed my leg tenderly.

Oh, boy. The lady sitting next to me was a striking blonde, whose husband was out of town on an extended business trip.

Once again, the hand caressed my thigh: was it my imagination, or had it moved higher?

Forsaking the prayer from the pulpit, I silently besought my own Divine advice: "Lord, this beautiful girl has for some reason begun squeezing my thigh during a time when there are no live Christian witnesses, because they've all got their eyes closed. What must I do? LORD! SHE JUST SQUEEZED AGAIN!!"

I normally have low blood pressure, but if this prayer was going to go on much longer, I was in real trouble!

I am a man ignorant in the ways of women. Betsy has been the only Love of my Life, and I've never been tempted otherwise. Yet I had never been approached during a prayer like this before!

All kinds of questions flashed through my mind, none conducive to a deeper prayer life, especially the one that asked, "If she was ugly, would you leave her hand on your leg?"

I gritted my teeth, decided to risk a peek, and opened one eye to see what was going on.

All the other ladies in the group were standing, waiting to file out of the pew to line up and sing right after the prayer. They were all glaring at me, especially the blonde who was squeezing my leg to get me to either stand to let them by, or to stand and move out to join them. I arose with a sigh.

Fortunately, the prayer lasted long enough for me to cool off and collect my wits before we sang.

Later, when I confessed my impure thoughts, the lady in question remarked, "Well, you DID have this startled expression on your face! But why in the world would you think I was coming on to you in the middle of prayer in church, for goodness sakes?"

I considered. "So, if the situation were reversed, what would you have thought if I had laid my hand on your thigh and squeezed several times?"

She never hesitated atall: "If you had, I'd have KNOWN you were coming on to me!"

Blatant, undisguised, sexual discrimination. In church,

too!

I was even more nervous than that when I first began my church singing career, but thanks to an observant preacher, I got over it. While speaking in front of an audience has never bothered me, singing did, at first. This pastor saw that I was nervous when we were waiting backstage for a performance, and pulled me off to the side.

"Son, you know what the great Gospel singer Ethel Waters said one time when someone asked her if she was nervous?" he asked me.

I knew I was caught. "No, Sir," I admitted, knees knocking.

"She said, 'Naw, I ain't nervous; 'cause God don't sponsor flops!' Son, you just keep the right sponsor, and you'll never have to be nervous in front of folks," he advised.

What a simple solution! I walked out on that stage a new man, and sang my heart out. Afterward, I cornered James and thanked him. "So that's what you think about every time you get up to preach or sing!" I marveled.

He pursed his lips and considered. "Yeah." Then added, grinning, "Plus, I always make a last-second check to be sure my fly is zipped!"

Good advice from a pro!

The Sonshine House

After singing in the Baptist choir for two full years, we decided to join the church -- after all, I knew the songs now. Within another year or so, I got elected deacon, and was assigned the chairmanship of the Youth Committee. Thereby began probably the most memorable period of our lives.

There followed a decade during which we were in charge of the church youth programs, and it was wonderful! We all went places, saw things, did things, and generally had more fun than most folks think should be allowed in church or church work.

Running a church youth program is fairly simple: get the good-looking girls, and the rest of it will fall into place. We did that, shoved a Bible at some of the older kids, and then just hung on for the ride. That may be a little simplistic, perhaps, but with a good set of kids it works. The rules are to keep it spiritual, have food and fun, and don't let a couple elope on your watch. The latter was sometimes our biggest concern.

During the Easter Season one year, we had a special service on our farm at Brownspur. A.L. Neal had made a rough-hewn cedar cross about five feet tall that we used for a "Take up your Cross" symbolism. The idea was to have a moving sermon in the pasture around a big bonfire (the night was nippy, and it was too early for mosquitoes), then to string out the kids about ten steps apart all the way across the pasture. The furtherest youngster picks up the cross and carries it to the next kid, then kneels and prays that he or she will have the strength to take up the Cross and follow it. The Cross goes from one youngster to the next in this manner, with the ones who have already handled it following. It has to be done in complete silence, except for the one doing the praying each time. The last kid stands the Cross in a hole close to the warmth of the fire, and the service is then concluded by a few remarks from the leader. It is a very moving ceremony, if done correctly.

Which it was the night I am thinking of. So moving, in fact, that I barely noticed a couple of cars creeping by on the blacktop road at the far side of the pasture. After the service ended, of course, we had hot dogs and marshmallows, and everyone was in a wonderful mood for Easter when we broke up and went home.

That next week was dry, and we were planting cotton, as busy as beavers on the farm. On Monday, I had observed that some of the tractor drivers were sort of walking on eggs, as the saying goes, but that was not too unusual for Mondays. We had a couple of guys who always tread softly and ate antacid pills regularly after weekends anyway. But when the situation continued through Wednesday, I began to get concerned. By Friday, the whole bunch was tiptoeing around like they were afraid of their own shadows and while I was absolutely impressed at their efficiency, I couldn't help but wonder what had caused the change in attitude.

I mean, they even anticipated my thoughts: "Herbert, did you check the. . . ."

"Yes Sir! I checked the oil, the transmission fluid, the anti-freeze, and topped it off with diesel. The battery water is fine, the wheel bearings are tight, and the air filter is clean. I aired up the tires, brushed the terminal connections, and. . . ."

"Okay, okay!" I'd interrupt. "Go to the. . . ."

He'd be on his tractor before I could finish. "Yes Sir! I'm headed for the south side of the cemetery cut, and if I finish

28

that, I thought I'd skip lunch and start in the newground. Don't worry about me!"

I mean, it was weird! Nice, but weird. A front was coming through on Friday night, so I paid off at the end of that day. As Bumpy took his check, he eyed me and cleared his throat. Thinking I had figured his time wrong, I looked up. "Anything wrong?" I asked, noticing that all the hands were standing there listening nervously. Big Bumpy was always the spokesman.

"Well," the foreman hesitantly began, rolling his eyes, "Er, we was wonderin'. . . er, well, we just. . . er. . . look; we wanta know if y'all was gonna have another one-a them cross burnin's out here this weekend?!"

My first inclination was to fall out laughing and tell the truth, but then I remembered how much work we had done that week.

We finished planting cotton before I 'fessed up!

A.L. had made that cross for the opening of the Sonshine House, which was our Youth Center for years. A widow who lived across the street had willed her home to the church when she died, and it sat vacant for a while, until someone had the great idea of making it a youth center. I approached the pastor, and he okayed the idea, on the condition that the youth do most of the remodeling themselves. His thinking was that the kids would take care of it better if they actually had a stake in it. It would also be easier to get the deacons to approve what expenditures were necessary, if we were doing the work ourselves.

The teenagers pitched in with an enthusiasm that no one had foreseen. They scrubbed, swept, vacuumed, washed, mopped, trimmed, everything! Items showed up from homes: chairs, a pool table, a ping-pong table, volleyball net uprights, kitchen utensils, pictures, everything needed for a youth center. James had been right: they did the work, then took care of it. Finally the day came when it was ready for occupancy. A committee of girls and boys chose "The Sonshine House" for a name, and A.L., whose son Gene was my first appointed Youth Leader, presented us with the cross, which was to be hung over the front door.

That was the first cross walk I had ever witnessed, and I honestly don't know who thought it up. But it worked! The kids lined up along the sidewalk and passed the cross from one to the next, praying for each other as they went. Tommy and I had screwed a big eye-screw into the gable rafter that afternoon, and the last boy to receive the cross was to climb the ladder and hang it over the doorway. It was poor planning on our part not to foresee that getting the heavy cross fifteen feet up the ladder was going to be a chore for two grown-ups.

The Lord will provide, right?

Charles was the last boy in line; it wasn't planned that way, he just was. He was a short, well-built high school sophomore, and he never hesitated, nor looked for assistance. He grasped that heavy, five-foot cross and began to climb the extension ladder, which bent under his weight. Tommy and Gene reached to steady the ladder, but the emotion of the moment forbid anyone asking Charles, "Do you need any help?" Up the ladder he went. About halfway, he swayed precariously for a moment, then steadied, somehow gained confidence, and moved on up. He had to go almost to the top rung to reach the eye-screw, did so, hung the cross, and turned around. It was then that he nearly fell, but recovered. But instead of fright, surprise was the emotion his face showed.

He later explained: "I started up the ladder before I realized how heavy the cross was, and how hard it was going to be to climb that old ladder while holding it. Then, about halfway, I felt Someone place their hands against my back, holding me steady. With that support, it was a cinch to finish the climb, stretch up, and hang the cross. But then, when I turned around, there was no one behind me! Yet I had felt the Hands!"

Another case of "Lean On Me" made for a memorable Sonshine House opening!

One Christmas season we took the youth caroling, and the group of two dozen kids with Betsy and me to chaperone called on several different houses of folks we knew, also stopping at houses randomly. Why we picked the old rundown house on the corner escapes me.

At the first carol, the porch lights went on, and an older lady appeared at the door. She was bent and somewhat gnarly, if you'll pardon the expression. She shuffled with the aid of a cane, and seemed to be close to a hundred years old, at least. As we sang, another lady stepped out, obviously a paid companion.

After several carols, the older lady spoke to the other, who beckoned me forward and invited the whole kit and caboodle in for hot chocolate. Since it was a cold night, we accepted.

The gnarly old lady shuffled to a seat as the kids trooped in, and her companion went to heat water. We all introduced ourselves, though it was obvious that our hostess could scarcely hear it thunder. Soon the hot chocolate was served, along with some little teacakes, which the kids made short work of.

When everyone was served, the old lady motioned to her companion, who helped her out of her chair and across the room to a grand piano. We were apparently going to be caroled-to ourselves. I smiled indulgently, as did some of the kids, wondering what those knotted, arthritic fingers could do on "We Three Kings of Orey and Tar," when we seriously doubted she was capable of "Chopsticks." I signaled the kids to be polite and pay attention, since she had been nice enough to feed us.

The walking cane clattered to the floor as the old lady settled feebly onto the bench, steadied by her companion. One of the boys snickered faintly, and I aimed a mock kick at him. A girl rolled her eyes as the crippled fingers struck a discord while pushing back the keyboard cover. "Five minutes and we're outa here," I signaled to the group behind the bent back.

Then the old lady began to play.

What a rush of sound poured from that grand piano!

This was music! Classical music!

She played "Oh, Holy Night," and we could hear the angels singing. She played "Oh Come, Oh Come, Emmanuel," and those big bass notes vibrated our breastbones. She played "The Hallelujah Chorus," and the whole house shook. "She played "Silent Night" so softly that we could actually hear the baby Jesus breathing gently as He slept, and none of us dared breathe ourselves, lest we should awaken Him. We sat entranced.

As she played, a strange thing happened: the old lady's bent back smoothed and straightened, her gnarly hands flew nimbly over the keyboard, the wrinkles on the back of her neck slowly disappeared as her head rose until she was focusing on a Heaven far out beyond the closed window, where a Star shone and the angels sang along with her flying fingers.

When the chords ceased, we sat spellbound, awestruck, staring at the artist's back as she leaned gracefully away from the keyboard and her hands floated caressingly above the ivories. No one moved.

Then our hostess seemed to slump forward slightly. Her hand shook as she reached for the cane her companion leaned to offer her. The arthritic fingers closed around the stick as she swung on the piano bench to face her audience.

"Thank you for coming," she croaked.

I finally broke the spell by standing abruptly. "We've got to be going, Ma'am. It's late. We didn't mean to stay this long. Thank you for playing." We'd been there an hour.

Her eyes glistened as the kids filed by to touch her hand. "Merry Christmas," she wished us as we left her home.

No one broke the silence as we walked slowly back to the Sonshine House. No one trusted their voice to speak.

We never had problems rounding up a caroling party

after that Christmas!

Nowadays, many church youth activities are centered around a specially-built gymnasium-type building where the kids share in wholesome activities ranging all the way from sports tournaments to movies to singalongs to sermons. This is a great concept; gets the youngsters together concentrating on healthy, vigorous, moral activities at prices they can afford. That is, after their families' pledges have satisfied the mortgage on the new Family Life Center. This sure beats having the kids on the streets at night, though. Yet, sadly, it is an idea beyond the means of many churches in rural areas.

Smaller churches these days (and all churches in days gone by) have to rely on the ability of their youth leaders to come up with activities to keep the kids interested and involved. Some of these activities involve some travel, for obviously the recreational facilities in small towns cannot satisfy the continual needs of an active youth program. Since this travel must be done when the youth are not in school, it must be planned for summertime and during school holidays. The Christmas holidays are a favorite time for church youth trips.

One fall, someone came up with the idea of going on some kind of trip for the Christmas holidays. I disremember where to or what kind; maybe a ski trip or something like that. Whatever, it required money, so several fund-raising proposals were suggested. The most popular suggestion finally turned out to be a Christmas-tree-cutting project.

This might not sound like too much of a problem to most congregations. But remember, evergreen trees are not native to all parts of the South. When Christmas comes to the Mississippi Delta, Delta folks must go elsewhere for Christmas trees.

All the arrangements were made, including transportation for the kids to and from the hills fifty miles away where the cedars grew; transportation back to the Delta for the trees; some kinfolks' farms to cut cedars from; chaperones; saws and axes; and publicity for the sale date upon the return of the cutting party. So on a beautiful December Saturday, off to the hills went our little Delta church's young folks.

Now, not all the young'uns were from this particular church. Several of the bunch were from other area churches, since most youth groups aren't too strict about denominationalism -- that fight usually comes when you get grown. I will here repeat my own observation that whichever local denomination can boast the most good-looking girls at any given time is the one that has the most potentially successful youth program; at least until that particular group of girls graduates, and then another church may take over. Anyway, in our town back then, the Non- Bred-In-The-Bones were just as much a part of the youth activities as the Bred-In-The-Bones, and they cut just as many trees that day in the hills.

The tired but happy party returned late that night, and a couple of days later everyone gathered for the big Christmas Tree Sale. One of the most active members of our group was a shy, pretty girl from another church; her name isn't important here, but she had the most beautiful green eyes.

The sale went pretty well that afternoon, and by dusk the kids had made about enough for their trip. Crowds of people had been through the parking lot where the trees were displayed, as well as the church itself, which had been left open for access to the bathrooms, phones, and drink machines inside. I was outside when three of the girls approached me. Green-eyes was weeping silently between Ann and Lia.

"What's wrong?" I asked.

"Uncle Bob, somebody went into her purse and stole her Christmas money out of her billfold," was the reply.

"Maybe it's just misplaced. Maybe you left it at home," I offered, clutching at straws.

"No, sir," Green-eyes wept. "I got some change for the drink machine out of it earlier and put it back. All the girls'

34

purses were in the choir room."

Dumb me. That was next to the drink machines, the same room with the phone, and on the way to the bathrooms. "Anybody else lose anything?" I mentally kicked myself for not suggesting locking up purses. But I don't carry one myself; besides, who would steal out of a church?

"No, sir," came the answer. "But nobody else had so much money."

I don't remember how much it was. Seems like a couple hundred dollars that Green-eyes had earned baby-sitting so she could buy Christmas presents for her family and friends. Too much for anybody to have stolen, especially from a church.

We organized and hunted high and low. Some of the boys searched the trash cans. Police were called. Preachers were called. There was no sign of the missing money. Green-eyes cried on my shoulder while I searched for the words to comfort her.

Then a delegation of the youth approached us, all smiles. "We found your money!" one of the boys said, handing Green-eyes a wad of cash.

The sobbing girl flipped through the stack of fives and tens. She shook her head. "I had a fifty and some twenties." She tried to hand it back. "This is from the Christmas Tree money. This is for the trip."

"The trip isn't that important, as far as Christmas goes; but your friendship with us is part of what Christmas is all about," one of the girls smiled. "We've voted to throw a Christmas party for the older folks with some of the money, and maybe send some to the orphans' home."

"I can't take this . . . ." Green-eyes choked to her smiling friends, but I reached out and gently closed her hand over the bills.

"Yes, you can," I said softly, and wiped my eyes with my other hand. It was the best church youth trip we never took.

One of the first long trips we organized with the church youth was to Eureka Springs, Arkansas, where the whole town puts on an all-summer-long production of the famous Passion Play. I have never been to Oberramagau, Germany, where the same thing has been done for probably centuries, but I cannot imagine that theirs could be more moving than the Arkansas play. And if it is, could I understand the language? I'll stick closer to home, thank you.

We made these trips several times over the years, and they sort of run together for me now. I wish I had kept a diary, but even if I had, it would have probably burnt up in our house fire, so what would have been the use? But there was one trip when our bus driver got involved with the kids' chatter and missed seeing the leading car turning off the Interstate. We watched in horror as the bus sped on, realizing that it would take so long for us to turn around and get back on the highway that we'd never catch him. Charles Jacks was driving the bus, and he had a heavy foot, but we had to try.

The Lord will provide, right?

The chase car hadn't been back on the Interstate more than ten miles when it was blue-lighted. The Arkansas Highway Patrolman had never been so quickly surrounded by so many really good-looking Mississippi women before, that was obvious. He listened, took in the situation swiftly, and ran back to his car to get on the radio. I mean, he didn't even give us a ticket! Now, whether that was because he was a Christian, or a native of Eureka Springs, or just overcome by the beauty before him, I cannot say. I do know that he got results in a hurry.

Charles said his heart sank when, twenty miles down the Interstate, he saw the flashing blue lights behind him. A glance at the speedometer showed that he might have been exceeding the limit just a teeny weeny bit, but Patrolmen usually cut any bus a little slack, especially church buses. For the first time in seven hours, all the teenagers were silent. Would they be arrested? The Patrolman approached, looking stern behind the sunglasses. Charles cut the key off and stepped to the ground.

"Anything wrong, Officer? We weren't going but a few miles over the limit. I'm sorry. I was just. . "

"Sir, when's the last time you saw your guide car?" the Patrolman interrupted.

"Oh, my Lord!" Charles realized that his wife and the parents of several of the kids aboard the bus must have been involved in an accident, and he had driven right past. "Is it bad? Who's hurt?"

The officer removed his shades and grinned. "Calm down, they're all okay. . ." There was a cheer from the listening bus passengers. "But they're on the way to the Eureka Springs Passion Play and wondered whether you wanted to go there too? Your turnoff was about thirty miles back! Do you want me to guide you back there?"

Charles didn't get a ticket either. But he did drive the limit the rest of the trip.

On our initial trip to the Passion Play, we had seats about a third of the way up in the stands built into the side of the mountain, a natural amphitheater. Possibly the most moving part of the play is when Herod tells his soldiers to scourge the bound Christ. At the order, one of the men turns to Jesus, mockingly calls "Hail, King of the Jews!" and swings from the heels, knocking the Lord sprawling in the dirt.

Gene, my Youth Leader, who later became a youth minister himself, was sitting in an aisle seat, and at this blow sprang forward and rushed down the steps, fists clenched. Another boy and I gave chase and caught him just before he vaulted the rail to join the fight -- on the side of Right, of course! We jerked him back, and he struggled briefly until Wesley shook him out of the powerful spell. "Gene! It's only a play; snap out of it!"

Gene looked around wide-eyed, for by now we three were the center of attention: even Christ, Herod, and the soldiers were prepared to call for reinforcements. Our warrior took a deep breath and confirmed for all within hearing his intentions: "Man! I was gonna whup them turkeys for hittin' Jesus!"

We were later told by the natives that it's not uncommon for such interruptions at this particular point in the Play. One of Herod's soldiers said he was once almost cold-cocked by an elderly lady in the first row who leaned out and whammed him across the helmet with her umbrella, yelling "Leave him alone!" in most unladylike fashion. While we talked, I noted that the soldiers whom Gene was attacking bare-handed were all carrying real swords -- perhaps for their own protection?

Any youth minister worth his salt has had to lead his group through such life-threatening experiences, and not always against the devil without. Sometimes it's the devil within. We had one kid who courted death at the hands not only of his own church companions, but also the visiting retreat evangelist. Actually, the culprit was that ole Demon Rum -- or, Demon Vodka, to be more exact about it.

This young man smuggled in a fifth of vodka rolled up in his new mummy sleeping bag. It has been my experience through the years that if a girl smuggles a bottle on a retreat, then one of the other girls will always find out about it and report it; or at least, our girls did that with me. I appointed Youth Leaders for every function we ever had, and they always did the job right. As noted before, the grownups' main problem was to keep young love from blooming into an elopement on my watch.

An aside here: maybe it's a tribute to the kids we worked with, or maybe it was their parents' upbringing, or maybe the Lord was watching out for us, or maybe I was just too ignorant to know what to look for -- but we never, ever, suspected any of our kids of getting into any sexual trouble; never, ever, even considered that a threat. The danger was not illicit sex, but too-early marriage, as far as I was concerned. I literally sweated bullets on a few couples to get them graduated before they eloped. But those who paired up on our watch all made it through the cap-and-gown stage, and the ones who wed are still thataway happily, as far as I know.

Come to think of it, there was one other time when we feared there might be a killing at the Sonshine House because of boy and girl relationships. One young man was caught dating not two, not three, but FOUR girls involved in Sonshine House activities! When the girl whom he ended up marrying later compared notes with the other three -- whom he didn't marry! -- then Ann, Lia, Big Lisa, Little Leesa, Tricia, Pitt, and the boys joined in the speculation, I seriously doubted his survival for a few days.

But back to Demon Vodka and a threatened early death for a young victim to D.V.: this kid was enamored of a certain girl in the group, and was determined to woo and win her -- seems like for a prom, or something that was coming up soon. When she turned him down yet again, he gave her final warning: if she wouldn't go with him, he was going to get skunk-drunk at the youth retreat. Understand that I gained some of this knowledge weeks later, second hand. One recalls the old saw, "Like a fly on the wall." When a certain grownup stays around a group of kids as much as I did, they begin to accept him -- not as one worthy of their confidence, but more like a harmless block of wood; an end table, perhaps.

The boys, unlike the girls, hardly ever reveal such plans. Now, perhaps that's because the boy smugglers simply don't take anyone into their confidence, while girl smugglers make that mistake. I ain't throwing rocks; just making an observation, sexist as it may be. Sorry. Point is, I had no idea that there was a fifth of vodka along on our retreat until that sucker was down to the last jigger. True to his word, the boy had indeed gotten skunk-drunk; drunk as Cooter Brown; drunk as a boiled owl; three sheets in the wind and the fourth one flapping. Whatever expression one wants to use in this case, it would have applied.

And as youth minister and head chaperone, I didn't have a clue until he tossed his cookies in the middle of a campfire service! "Tossed cookies" being a quite literal description, considering that we had just served plates of them for refreshments.

My evangelist was a big, clean-cut young man who played college football for one of our state schools. I never went wrong by contacting one of the nearby Fellowship of Christian Athletes chapters when I needed a special speaker, and I had used this kid before. Bill had been recommended to me by an MSU coach with whom I had played high school football, Charlie Garrett. Bill Maxey had a good relationship with our group.

However, this relationship did not extend to charity and understanding when his remarks were interrupted in the manner in which they were now interrupted. Any groundwork we had laid for this retreat seemed to have been upchucked upon and thusly obliterated. Myself, my two male youth leaders, and the football player descended upon the youngster in the clutches of Demon Vodka.

Yet before we reached him, another girl in the group -- not the one he had courted so assiduously, but a young lady who operated out of love, mercy, sympathy, Good Samaritanism, and several other wonderful Christian attributes temporarily quite noticeably absent from the characters of her youth minister, evangelist, and both male youth leaders -- jumped forward to gently wipe the face of her drunken comrade with a damp cloth. As we males watched anxiously, for we couldn't wait to get our hands on him, the girl cleaned him up somewhat, cooed over him, and generally made him feel that at least one somebody present cared whether he lived and was loved.

Under her ministrations, the boy managed to survive more-or-less chug-a-lugging a whole fifth of vodka; there hadn't been a jigger left in the bottle when I threw it into the woods.

Her demonstration, in retrospect, was the most valuable

and lasting lesson to come out of that particular retreat. For once she had insured the boy's survival, it fell to our lot to sober him up -- the aforesaid male leaders, I mean. Since he was going to have to spend the rest of the night in our (boys) half of the retreat group camp, we wanted him cleaned and de-stunk, and preferably unable to urp on anyone, especially ourselves.

To that end, we investigated the showers. This was a winter retreat, and it was cold outside; the hot water pipes are always the first to freeze, and they had done so. Anyone who needed to shower was condemned to doing so in cold water, nor was there a heater in the bathroom. "Condemned" was a quite appropriate word there, come to think of it.

If anyone atall needed a shower, it was a guy who had tossed his cookies -- all over himself. No one else wanted to have to smell that all night either, cooped up together in a small room with bunk beds. Besides, this was a Christian retreat; no one belonged to be drunk on it, especially from a Baptist youth group. A cold shower would therefore probably have been dictated even if there had been hot water available.

The temperature in the bathroom being what it was, no one else intended to shower anyway. Well, come to think of it, neither did the showeree; matter of fact, he did utter some weak protests, but he was in no condition to resist four strong men, two of whom had played college football, for I played at Ole Miss away back when. He was stripped of his stained clothing, and shoved unceremoniously into the shower stall, wherein the icy water was already flowing.

I'm not sure I have ever seen a quicker job of sobering up. The kid was quite vehement about wanting out of the shower, and he didn't stutter or slur whatsoever. However, the visiting evangelist had the adjacent bunk and wanted to make durn sure that there was no danger of him getting barfed on in the middle of the night. I sent the youngest of the youth leaders for towels while the other three of us held the stall door closed against the stone-cold sober and faintly blue youngster who was

41

emphatic about having finished his shower.

His teeth chattered like castanets when we finally let him out and dried him off. The blue tint apparently was not something that could be washed off in a cold shower, nor could it be dried off, obviously, for we tried. Nude, blue, dry, and sober, he was finally inserted into his mummy bag, which was zipped all the way up, not even leaving an arm out. He was in for the duration, and was absolutely sober for the rest of the retreat, which he survived thanks to the Christian girl who saved him from the evangelicals.

I'd hate to give the impression that only boys engage in this type behavior. One of the most meaningful Passion Play trips we ever embarked upon had an ominous beginning: before the cars even left the church, two of the girl youth leaders approached me to report that one of the young ladies had packed a bottle in her suitcase. Did I mention that our group always had youth leaders who got the job done? Ann and Joy and I went off to the side for a quick prayer about it. Then, since room assignments had not been made, I simply put the bottle and its owner into a room with these two leaders and a couple of others, and instructed them to not mention the potential problem to anyone else, especially the chaperones. We retreated. In spades.

When we returned to the church four days later, the bottle had never been mentioned, nor had the seal been broken on it. I'm not sure if you are familiar with the term "hot-boxed" as it may be used in a Christian connotation, but one young lady certainly was after that. Using military terms, if the opposite of "Youth Retreat" is "Charge" then this girl was charged up. She never knew what hit her, but it did the job.

That next week the preacher cornered me. "I hear Mandy took a bottle on the retreat," James commented with a hint of suspicion.

"She sure did," I agreed.

"Well, what'd you do about it?" he asked after a pause.

"Prayed. . .and put her in the room with Ann, Joy, and Lia," I grinned. "They took care of it fine."

My pastor stood considering a moment, then shook his head and walked away, declaring, "Well, if it ain't broke, don't fix it!"

I still consider that unbroken bottle seal to be a symbol of one of the most successful youth leadership demonstrations I ever saw. And I didn't do one cotton-picking thing about it; it was those girls, who cared that one of their comrades not do wrong.

Other adults recognized how outstanding these Leland kids were, too. We rented several rooms at a Eureka Springs motel one year, and to save money, I assigned as many as six kids to a room, although I had to assure the motel owner that there'd be no damage. Yet after we checked in, the lady told me she'd like to listen in and watch the kids in a few of their morning and evening devotions, which I'd assigned to different ones before the trip, as usual. After that trip, the motel owner called me, scaring me into thinking that there might have been some damage, but that wasn't the purpose of her call.

"Are y'all coming back later this summer for another youth retreat?" she asked.

"Yes, Ma'am, we usually try to go in the spring and fall," I replied.

"Well, here's my deal: I want you to stay here, you can have the whole motel for no extra charge, with one condition you must agree to," she declared.

What was going on? I asked what the condition might be.

"I want my two teenage grandchildren to accompany your group for the retreat," she said. "If they can grow up like the kids you brought up here, I'll be a happy grandmother!"

We stayed there several times over the years, and once held there the most meaningful Communion service I've ever attended. I had asked Ann and Cheryl to bake some loaves of homemade bread, and Big Lisa and Pitt to bring bottles of grape juice (Baptists, remember?). I believe it was Frank and Walter who led the devotion that evening, and the girls served the bread that they had baked, with the grape juice they had brought – all of which we had prayed over – to the kids and chaperones seated on the floor around the motel room. It was moving!

One of those young ladies taught me a lesson one Wednesday night after prayer meeting. This girl had been through a lot of bad stuff in her life already, but some of the kids had encouraged her to come to the Sonshine House services, in its early stages. She came to most youth functions for months, never saying much. She'd do her jobs, when she was assigned cleanup duty, kitchen duty, or whatever. At that time, I had not put her in charge of devotionals or made her a youth leader or house manager for the month. She was coming along, though.

One night after prayer meeting, as the other kids were cleaning up and preparing to close up to go home, she approached me tentatively. "Uncle Bob, I want to become a Christian; I want to give my heart to Jesus."

"Well, fine," I replied. "You've been coming here long enough to know what you need to do, right?"

"Yes, Sir."

"Well, what do you say we come up here tomorrow afternoon after school and go talk to the preacher?"

"No, Sir, I want to do it right now."

"You sure? Here? Now?"

"Yes, Sir." She was quite firm about it.

The kids had enclosed a small back screen porch to make a private prayer room. To get away from the noise of the others, I suggested we go out there. To tell the truth, however, I wasn't really keen about doing this right at the time. Not that I doubted her experience atall; it was physical problems on my part.

I had torn up a knee years before playing ball, and

44

sometimes now it would get swollen and painful, until I finally went to the doctor and let him run this huge blunt needle up behind my kneecap to draw off the bloody fluid a few times over a period of a couple of weeks. That left knee was almost to the critical stage, and I had decided to have it drained again soon. Kneeling to pray would be painful, I knew.

When we reached the prayer porch, I again hesitated. "You know, we'd probably do better to go see the preacher tomorrow."

Her lips were set resolutely. "No, Sir. Right now."

Sighing painfully, I knelt, in decidedly unChristian manner. "Okay, let's get it over with," I grunted. We bowed our heads.

And waited. And waited. My knee was swelling by the second; I could feel it. Finally I opened my eyes. "What's wrong?" I asked impatiently.

"I just can't find the words," she agonized.

"Fine." I began to try to rise. "Let's just go see the preacher tomorrow."

"No, Sir! I want to do this now. Please?"

"Well. . ." My knee was sure hurting. "Tell you what: I should have thought of this. I'll pray first, that you'll have the strength and courage to do what needs doing. Bow your head."

I prayed; I disremember what I said, but I said it pretty quickly, because my knee felt like it was on fire behind the kneecap. I got finished, amened, and waited.

Nothing.

A tad angry, I looked up again. "Now what?"

She was weeping a little, silently. "I just can't get the words out, Uncle Bob."

My joint sounded like a bowl of Rice Krispies as I began to rise in relief. "That's okay with me. I'll call the preacher and we can see him after school." I groaned as I put weight on the injured leg.

"Oh, please, Uncle Bob. I need to do this now, you

know that." She grabbed my hand and pulled me back to my knees as tears of pain flooded my eyes.

I grimaced in pain and frustration. "Okay. Tell you what: you've been to a wedding, right? We'll do it like that. I'll say what I think you need to say, and you can just repeat after me. Think you can do that all right?"

"Oh, yes, Sir. Thank you, Uncle Bob." She bowed her head and closed her eyes, hands clasped.

My knee was about to kill me, but I gritted my teeth and began the first sentence of what I deemed necessary for a poor but persistent sinner to say to obtain forgiveness and salvation. I recall hoping that we weren't keeping Jesus waiting on His knees if one of Them was as swollen and painful as mine was.

I finished a sentence and waited for her to repeat it.

Nothing.

"Arrgghh! What in the heck is wrong now!??" I gasped in pain and impatience.

The girl looked at me with tears in her own eyes. "Uncle Bob," she choked, and pounded me with one of the basic tenets of Christianity, sore knees or not, "I got to do this all by myself."

And she did. We knelt there for another forty-five minutes, and my knee quit hurting, and she said what she needed to say: never more than three or four words at one time, and always agonizingly, as if they were being dragged out one by one. But it changed her life. She became one of the youth leaders in enthusiasm, outreach, and responsibility.

And taught a grownup a lesson he should have known already.

One thing I've learned over the years: Truth is where one finds it, and the Lord can use a teenager just as easily as He can use an old, crippled-up deacon.

Or, He doesn't have to use either one; He can just speak through them, when they realize they ain't got sense enough to say what needs saying.

This same girl was involved in a prayer meeting one night a couple of years later when we were finishing up the Wednesday night service with a special prayer for someone's grandmother, and about fifteen of the Youth Council had stayed late for a few minutes. These kids believed in prayer, and had even been known to pray for dogs, cats, and horses, which didn't set too well with some of the deacons who alternated as chaperones.

One of them accosted me after he had attended a youth prayer service one Wednesday night. "Those kids prayed for a horse and somebody's dog tonight," he informed me hotly.

I wasn't Bred-In-The-Bone, so I wasn't sure which way to jump on this rather obvious theological question that I hadn't been smart enough to recognize needed asking. "And. . .?" I prompted the deacon.

He was right huffy about it. "A DOG! And a HORSE!" He stomped off, tossing back, "Take me off the chaperone list!"

I still ain't found in the Bible where it says that the Lord cannot heal sick dogs and horses, nor that it's a sin to ask Him to do that. But then, I ain't Bred-In-The-Bone, as noted before.

Nor did I mention it to the kids. Some things you don't need to learn until you're an adult, in my humble opinion.

Anyway, no one present the night I'm thinking of believed that The Lord wasn't capable of helping the grandmother in question. The Youth Council and I were kneeling (my knee was okay that week) in a circle on the living room rug, holding hands and praying around the circle. When we finished, Walter exclaimed, "Uncle Bob, right in the middle of the prayers I looked up, and Jesus was standing in the circle! He was holding His hands out, He had a gentle smile on His face, and I really felt like He was approving of what we were doing."

Now, I've got sense enough to know that just because I don't see something, doesn't mean that someone else hasn't seen something. But I'm cautious about such things, and didn't want

47

to talk about it then, since it was getting late, and a school night. "Fine," I said casually, "I DIDN'T see Him, but I felt like He was approving, too. Now, let's lock up and go home."

At 1:30 that morning, my phone rang. It was another of the boys who had been in the prayer meeting, and he was upset. "Uncle Bob, I've been praying and reading my Bible, and I want to have a vision, too: I want to see God. But I can't!"

This was Divine Inspiration, because I ain't this smart.

"Jon," I said, "put the phone down, go into the bathroom, look in the mirror, and come back and tell me what you saw."

In a few moments he was back, sounding somewhat unsure. "I did that."

"And. . . ? What'd you see?" I prompted.

"I didn't see anything," he said, still unsure.

"Wait a minute: you looked in a mirror and didn't SEE anything atall?!"

"Well. . . I just saw me."

"And what are you?" This was being driven home to me as well as Jon.

"Well. . . I'm just a boy. . . a kid. . . an ordinary person." I could tell he was catching on to where I was heading.

I said, "Jon, the way most people see God is in ordinary people."

"Yes, Sir. You're right! Thanks, Uncle Bob." He hung up, apparently happy as a clam.

But it's a lesson worth learning, even if we learn it from a kid. . . an ordinary person.

We have a God who can part the seas, but I sailed a lot of this earth's seas in the Navy, and I not only never saw one parted, I never talked to anyone who had.

We have a God who can move the mountains, yet I've been over a lot of mountains that I wish had been moved, but they weren't. Not one single mountain.

We have a God who can do all these wonderful things,

48

but most people never see the seas parted, never see the mountains moved, never even see God standing in the middle of a teenagers' prayer meeting.

The way most people see God is through ordinary people.

Like you and me, maybe.

The Brownspur Olympics

There came a time when the Baptist Powers That Be decided that it is NOT a sin for men and women to study the Bible together. Toward that end, we were asked by the Nominating Committee to teach a Couples Sunday School Class, for many of the younger couples in the church had come up through the youth program. Since we felt that we could not effectively do both, we put the choice to the Nominating Committee and they picked someone else to do youth work -- which ain't really work atall, as I pointed out before. More like fun. Being as how we had enjoyed so much Christian fun for a decade, we naturally followed the same philosophy in the Couples Class, which grew from nine on the roll to sixty-two in less than three years, without raiding other classes.

Obviously, outreach was the name of the game. Everyone outreached to their friends, family, and neighbors. They went out into the highways and hedges, so to speak.

Which brings up an interesting observation, and I must emphasize that it's only an observation, and it's my observation. Therefore, it may be wrong, and I ain't gonna fight about it, okay? I'm just going to lay it out there for consideration.

The Southern Baptists -- and here, I'm talking Denominationally, not Numbered or Locational Baptists -- skated by for a lot of years avoiding all the struggles and schisms which were plaguing other denominations. Then we began undergoing some troubles along that line that I believe can be directly attributed to successful Baptist outreach programs.

Betsy and I are a prime example of a couple becoming to some extent dissatisfied with their church situation, and responding in a positive way to the outreach of friends in another church. And we weren't the only ones, by a long shot. In our Couples Class, for instance, we had folks with backgrounds that were Presbyterian, Episcopalian, Catholic, Methodist, Pentecostal, Church of Christ, Numbered Baptist, Locational Baptist, Hardshell Baptist, Softshell Baptist, and Lutheran. We didn't cull, in other words. When some theological question came up in class, almost any viewpoint one can imagine got discussed, even Mormon and Mennonite, for I had good neighbors who belonged to those denominations and I sought out their input, just so we'd know how other folks think.

My point is that, when other denominations lost members, Baptist churches did a great job of recruiting folks who were unchurched during those years, with the result that now our denomination suddenly realizes that it has a large percentage of members who are not -- perish the thought -- Bred-In-The-Bones. Maybe we, speaking here as a Baptist, did too good a job of outreach back then, perish the thought.

It is my belief that any theological question is kind of like the present four-way stop at the edge of town. If four drivers all arrive at the same time, and are asked to describe their views, one will say that he's headed south, looking toward Rebel Gas; another will say he's headed west, right before going under the railroad overpass; another will say he's headed east, having just gone under the railroad underpass; and the last will say that he's headed north, going right into town passing by the liquor store.

They will all be correct, as they see the situation from their limited viewpoints, those views being colored by where they've come from. In theological questions, most of our opinions are formed by where we've come from, in our past routes with people, churches, denominations, and spiritual experiences. Just because someone doesn't agree with my view, doesn't necessarily mean that they are wrong. It just means they see things differently than I do, since they came from another direction. Maybe we should shy from dogmatism, at least until we understand where the other folks are coming from.

That's my two cents worth, anyhoo.

When we were teaching that Couples Class, I had the town supplying me on a monthly basis with the names and addresses of newcomers to our area, from the new billings for electricity. Usually I'd make a preliminary call on these families, then turn the name over to another class member for followup. I have since come to the recommendation that class visitation should be done by a couple.

One afternoon between five and six I was making some calls, and stopped at the home of a recently moved-in resident. I rang the doorbell and waited on the porch. Inside, I could hear the television going, so I knew someone had to be home. Patiently, I rang again, humming "Bringing in the Sheaves."

I had just decided that either the doorbell was broken, or that the couple didn't want to be disturbed, and had turned to leave, when I heard the doorknob click. "I was taking a shower," a woman's voice announced as I pivoted back toward the door.

Truer words had obviously never been spoken. The young lady had not taken time to dry completely as she rushed to greet probably her first visitor in their new home. She was toweling her hair as I spoke, "I'm from the church. . . ." and then stopped as I read the message emblazoned across her damp tee shirt, which had also obviously been hurriedly pulled on without benefit of interfering lingerie.

"Great!" she exclaimed enthusiastically. "Come on in. My husband will be back in an hour or so, and we're going to be looking for a church home. My name is. . . ."

But I was already headed for the steps, saying, "Yessum, I know. Tell him I said Howdy, and I'll be back tomorrow. I'm late for supper, but my card's in the door screen. Bye," and I raced off -- rudely, I'll admit.

You've probably guessed it. Her tee shirt was from Wendy's. And across its wet front it proclaimed a message that was the hamburger chain's motto at the time. Such a motto is terribly distracting on the front of a pretty lady's wet tee shirt!

Mislabeling things as a teacher once disrupted our class right before Easter one year. We were studying in II Corinthians about the relationship between our earthly bodies and our potential Heavenly bodies when I experienced what I thought was a Divine Revelation.

Betsy and the kids were still getting dressed for Sunday School and I was sitting out on the screen porch with a last cup of coffee, feeling well-studied-up on the lesson. During the week, I always tried to read the prescribed scripture in a different version of the Bible and a different commentary each morning, so that by Sunday, I knew what all the smart people who write books thought about that particular passage. One had to be on his toes to teach this Couples Class by that time; one of their collective joys was to catch the teacher out on a limb and proceed to saw it off. Everyone participated, and the church had moved us several times to different rooms both because we were growing and were noisy. It was discussion, in spades.

As I sat on the porch drinking my coffee, I realized that the daffodils in the back yard were in beautiful, bountiful bloom. Then I glanced down next to my chair to see Betsy's wicker basket of gardening stuff, in which were several old dirty dried-up bulbs she had yet to plant. Inspiration struck!

I raced out back and picked as many daffodils as I could hold in both hands, then ran back to find a large vase. Stuffing the flowers into the vase, I ran a little water into it, then headed to put them in the car, stopping to grab one of those bulbs as I passed. The rest of the family was finally ready, and off we went to our Sunday School, me in particular brimming with anticipation.

A couple of our class had lost parents recently, and the lesson lent itself to emotion that day. I skillfully built it up to the climax, when I stood and grasped the vase from the piano top, holding it out for all to admire the lovely flowers.

"Just as our Heavenly bodies will resemble these beautiful daffodils, so our earthy bodies are alike the dirty, ugly, dried-up bulbs they spring from," and I triumphantly reached into my pocket for the aforesaid bulb. Tears filled many eyes, and I was proudly thinking that the Lord had obviously put me here just for this moment. I stood there, holding the vase in one hand, the bulb in my other extended palm, as the class cried and marveled at my God-given teaching skills. What a perfect time it would have been for Gabriel to blow his horn and rapture us all.

But it wasn't Gabe who blew the mood. It was Susan, who stood and pointed out in a loud voice, "Ahem. . . that's a GLADIOLA bulb, dummy!"

It seems like the class awarded her the first Yard-Of-The-Week Award.

We gave a good many awards over the years in that class. Only a few weeks after that, another good-looking young lady was involved in an award as a result of her teacher's visual aiding. We had switched to a study of the Old Testament; that particular literature used to trade back and forth quarterly between Old and New Testaments. One Sunday I came prepared to show the class something on the map, and another teacher had apparently snagged the free-standing set of maps that usually stayed in the room. The same teacher had obviously gotten the chalk from our blackboard -- possibly an unreformed Episcopalian? Undaunted, I turned to Donna, sitting next to me, and asked her to stand.

Careful to keep my geographic perspective, I used her to give the class an idea of the distance covered by whomever we happened to be talking about that day. She blushed, but held still as required while I pointed out that if the River Jordan flowed down her right arm, then the Amorites would be here, the Ammonites there, and the Philistines over yonder. I have tried to give one an idea of how on-the-ball this class was: quick to catch on. It was Beau who asked the first geographical question, and there were many that morning: "Uncle Bob, could you show us the mountains that the Hebrew Children hollered back and forth from, please?"

The Donna Memorial Map Award was presented the next Sunday, and attendance was high for a while, in anticipation of more geography lessons.

Said attendance could be counted on to lag somewhat at certain times of the year. The Delta is farming country, and many men would be absent during both planting and harvest seasons. The standard reply, "The ox is in the ditch," would usually be the answer when a wife would be asked where her husband was that day. When Xan missed about three Sundays in a row, claiming ox-in-the-ditch, Cameron suggested that such consistence from an ox deserved an award. Sure enough, the next week, after it had rained and the fields were wet enough to anticipate his return, the Alexander Memorial Ox-In-The-Ditch Award was presented, with appropriate fanfare. He got his revenge, however, for the very next week Cameron's ox had gotten in the same ditch. That award was passed around a good bit over the years.

There was even a special off-premises presentation of the Ox-In-The-Ditch Award. Tommy had picked up some acreage right outside of town, and was planting soybeans one Sunday morning, as revealed unto the class by his wife. After church, a cavalcade of cars from the Couples Class drove from church to the field, and we all got out and pantomimed praying for our absent buddy. He parked the tractor on the far end of the rows, refusing to come close enough for a proper presentation of his Award. He was in church the following

Sabbath to receive it, however.

We also passed around the Yard-Of-The-Week Award a good bit, for those town dwellers who had been seen by classmates on their way to Sunday School. One man's absence was explained so much by solicitous neighbor David as, "I saw him mowin' the yard when I drove by," that it was renamed in his honor.

The other times that low attendance could be depended on were during deer and turkey season. They even got the teacher sometimes on that. Tommy and Janice repaid me for that earlier on-farm end-of-turnrow class visit with a cap complete with turkey head on the front and turkey fan behind, presented with appropriate platitudes.

It wasn't the first time I had been cited for absence during turkey season. A few years before I had been threatened with a fine by another Sunday School class, and I had retained legal counsel. The Honorable E. Barnett Loudon, Jr., consented to argue my case before the class, entering a plea of insanity. "It should be apparent to everyone that Uncle Bob must be crazy to admit publicly to missing as many wild turkeys as he does," was his plea. Oh, he was eloquent in my defense.

So eloquent, in fact, that the class doubled my fine from two dollars to four dollars, and then fined E. Barnett ten bucks for defending a crazy person in Sunday School!

We organized a church softball league in town, then formed a Couples Class team as an outreach tool. There was a lot of talent in class, and we had a heckuva team, so attracted several other good players to the field. If they were unchurched, or better yet, non-attending husbands of Baptist wives, we'd invite them to play with us. That bunch had so much fun in practice and games, that within two weeks, new teammates would be addicted to the team. It would be at that point when we would casually inform them that the rule was, if one missed three Sunday School classes in a row, he couldn't

56

play in the games. Once they came and saw that the class had just as much fun, they'd be hooked.

Please don't get the idea that we didn't learn anything Biblical; we just enjoyed doing it. One discussion lasted more than three weeks: the assigning of fault in the David and Bathsheba affair. One of our young ladies was particularly hard on King David, and went from there to the attitude of modern men concerning sexual matters. I was quick to point out that one version clearly stated that Bathsheba had lit the lamp, instead of bathing modestly in the dark. Since the Bible also indicated that David made a habit of walking the palace roof, it seemed obvious to the men in the class that had Bathsheba bathed in the dark, or even with the curtain closed, Uriah might have lived to a ripe old age. That discussion precipitated the Wilma Memorial Light My Lamp Award, and she's still known in some circles as Bathsheba.

King David's actions also instigated another award that went around several times. The assigned lesson for Sunday concerned the defeat of King Hadadezer of Zobah, and the "houghing" (or, hamstringing) of his chariot horses. On Saturday, our first baseman pulled a hamstring himself, trying to stretch a single into a double. It was another Sign from Above, obviously, and Ricky was presented with his own Memorial Houghing Award in class the next day. We did win the ball game, by the way.

One of the most memorable lessons in that Couples Class came about not because of Little David's giant Goliath, but because of other giants, observed by Joshua, Caleb, and the lesser scouts whom Moses sent into Canaan. I was using this as an illustration that many times nowadays the Lord will open a door He wants us to walk through, but we often are guilty of refusing to enter because of the obstacles we perceive, never giving God credit for being able to conquer those giants on our behalf, if we'll just enter the land on faith in Him.

Caught up in the moment, I arose, stomped to the door,

flung it open, stepped into the hall, bellowed, "There's GIANTS OUT HERE!!!", and retreated into the room, slamming the door behind me. It was a wonderful demonstration to our class.

However, half a dozen other classrooms also opened into that same hall. After my horrifying pronouncement and slamming door, they all sat transfixed. Not even the teachers spoke, for fear that the aforementioned giants would hear and invade their own classrooms, after they finished consuming the Couples Class. Up in the sanctuary, the pianist and choir director ceased their practice and made their escape out the seldom-used front doors. My shout echoed into the ladies' lounge, where someone called the office in a panic, wanting to know had the nursery been evacuated. The acoustics were great in that church.

A few minutes later, there was a tentative knock on our classroom door, and the preacher stuck his head in, rather timidly, I thought. "Y'all okay in here?" James asked.

Right. We got moved again, to a room with those accordion-like dividers. No doors to go through, or to slam.

One could never predict the spinoff benefits of a class that so enjoyed their fellowship and Bible study. We averaged one fellowship supper every five weeks during those years, most at our home at Brownspur. There was one party scheduled that happened to fall on a young member's birthday, and his wife came to ask me if it would be all right for her to bake a birthday cake for him. Of course it was, but I went one step further, contacting the other members and asking them to bring gag gifts for a surprise party. It was a total surprise.

Some folks put a lot of time and effort into their presents, and presented them with much pomp and circumstance, for this guy was one of the favorite class agitators, and had dished out a lot of gags himself. We had a lot of laughs at his party, put on a spiritual skit or something afterward, ate cake and ice cream, and went home.

Sunday he was not in class.

But he sent a note. It said, paraphrased, that he had grown up in not the best of family situations, and had even been raised to some extent in foster homes. He had not enjoyed some of the things many of us take for granted in childhood.

It was the first birthday party anyone had ever given for him. Even though the gifts were mostly gag (we had gotten something nice from the class fund), they had been given in such a loving, laughing spirit, that it had touched his heart. He had sent the note because he didn't think he'd be able to say it out loud, but he was there from then on.

There was another time that I felt moved to "chase a rabbit," as the preacher put it. We had studied the Apostle Paul's views on women and marriage, and it seemed that the discussion had ended on a little bit of a sour note. As a matter of fact, even I considered that Paul had missed some of the benefits of a happy, loving relationship with a wife and family. So the next week, I made up a lesson on love and marriage, going through the Bible for every good thing that the Good Book says on the subject. It ended up on a high note, and for some strange reason, we were all couples that Sabbath. Usually some husbands are absent and their wives attend, or vice versa; I can't recall another time, to be honest, when the same combination of all pairs occurred.

Again, I claim Divine Inspiration. I ended the lesson by having all the couples turn to each other, and then led them in restating the marriage vows. It was another case of few dry eyes when we broke up for church and choir.

That next week, one of the men came out to Brownspur and looked me up in the field. Seems like we were beginning to harvest milo, and I was walking behind the combine, checking for wasted grain. The man hailed me and walked across the field. I met him halfway.

"Like to invite you to a wedding this weekend," he offered, shaking hands.

This guy had only been in town for a few months, and I

didn't know his family. I hedged, because I had planned to hunt that weekend, and we live in the country. "Well, I think we're gonna be outa town Saturday."

"Okay; no sweat. Just wanted you to know," he replied.

"Who's gettin' married?" I asked, relieved.

"Me and Pauline," he answered, naming his wife.

"Y'all are re-doin' your vows?" I was confused.

He was just a little sheepish about it. "Well, not exactly. See, we've been just livin' together for the past couple years before we moved here last spring. Never had tied the knot. But after that lesson Sunday. . . well, we just figured we ought to do it right. Love for you to come, but we weren't gonna tell anyone else. You don't mind keepin' this under your hat, do you?"

I changed the names, so I still ain't told anybody.

This same type discussion on marriage led to the most embarrassing introduction any speaker ever had, I betcha.

When I was growing up, I heard Big Robert hold forth many a time with "A woman, a dog, and a walnut tree: the more you beat 'em, the better they be!" which the literary-minded will possibly recognize as a quote from a Civil War novel. That quotation came up many times over the years, but I tried to always follow it with what Daddy told me right before I got married myself: "Son, I know what you've heard me say all these years, but now you're fixin' to get married yourself, so I wanta tell you the truth: The way to handle a woman is to find out what she wants to do -- and then make her do it!" Now, that ought to be in the Bible somewhere, but I don't know chapter and verse. It works, though.

Jackie and Wynn attended our class for several years, and then moved away. A couple of years later, I received an invitation from the Baptist church in their town to preach on Baptist Men's Day, when laymen generally fill the pulpit and preachers go fishing. To my pleasant surprise, the minister had asked Jackie to introduce me to the congregation. He did.

He stood in the pulpit and announced, "Uncle Bob taught our Sunday School Couples Class, and we all really enjoyed it. I'll never forget the one lesson I've gotten the most out of: 'A woman, a dog, and a walnut tree: the more you beat 'em, the better they be!' Here's Bob Neill, folks." And he sat down.

You try preaching after that!

Jackie's team won first place in the First Annual Brownspur Olympics that our Sunday School class ever held. I'll never forget that, because he was a big, muscular man, and the prize tee shirt had been bought for a medium or small person. Jackie got it on, but as the song says, he was "bustin' out all over!" His lady co-captain Nancy was a very small girl, however, and her shirt hid her from shoulders to the ground. They had switched.

We inaugurated the Brownspur Olympics as a fun and outreach tool one summer after softball season was over. The games were held on a Saturday, and we invited not only Couples Class members and potential members, but also couples of about the same age who were serving in other capacities in the church. Participants were divided into four teams of about a dozen each, and contests included everything from water bucket relays and egg tosses to spontaneous parable skits and personal testimonies. Ed and Jane volunteered to babysit, and took the children roller skating, a chore for which they deserved canonization, but it left the parents free to join in the fun and fellowship.

You want spiritual fun? Try assigning parable skits. The antics of Beau, as a 135-pound alcoholic bum, being snubbed by debutant Debbie and then tenderly rescued from the gutter by the 250-pound Ronnie as the Good Samaritan, were tear-jerking in both emotional directions. Jackie on his knees fighting with the hogs David and Ricky for scraps had witnesses rolling with laughter, but the message hit hard when Dean then welcomed his Prodigal Son home. The Brownspur Olympics

61

went for several years and through more than one church, and worked with both adults and youth.

A teacher must be careful with the illustrations that he uses to make the points he wants to, and once I thought I had crossed the line. We had gone to watch our son Adam pitch in a baseball tournament one Saturday, and it was hot as the proverbial hinges, to stay in a Biblical context. I had a seat by the aisle, and all day long this one kid kept climbing by me, back and forth, up and down the steps. He had on a tee shirt which proclaimed, "Faster horses, older whiskey, younger women, more money!" He might have been five or six years old.

That next morning, teaching from Hebrews, where Paul is trying to make the point that Christians just flat-out have it better than other folks, that slogan popped into my mind, and I used it. While most of the class took it in stride, one young lady in particular took offense, and I ended up backing down and apologizing. Sadly, the church suffered a split within a year or so, and that class was scattered to the winds. No, the split was not caused by that slogan, thank you. See the discussion on differing viewpoints some pages back.

But maybe five years later, I ran into one of the men who had been in class that day, and who had not been attending church anywhere since the split. "By the way," he interjected as we conversed on other matters, "I thought about that old Couples Class we used to have yesterday. There was a guy at the cafe whose belt buckle had that saying on it. You remember: 'Faster horses, older whiskey, younger women, more money!' Made me think of the good times we used to have together, and I went home and told my wife that we had to find some place to go back to Sunday School and church."

Truth is where you find it. We do have it better.

The Brownspur Children In The Fiery Furnace

The kids were gone, I was printing out the last couple of chapters on a new fall book over in the office, Betsy had put the grease on for french fries, and I had started a fire in the patio grill for hamburgers. It looked like a fine evening.

Then we heard a soft "WWHHHOOOMMPP!" from across the patio, and I glanced through the window to see our kitchen in flames! Yelling, "Betsy, we got a fire!" I charged from the office, forgetting about the computer still printing away.

The new-type cooking oil for the french fries had vaporized, and then ignited almost like gasoline fumes. There was no midpoint. One moment there was no fire, and the next, half the kitchen was burning, all the way to the twelve-foot ceiling. The cabinets were aflame; the vent-a-hood was roaring; glasses in the cabinets over the stove were bursting from the heat; the formica was giving off an oily black smoke as it burned and curled; and the skillet of grease itself sent tongues of fire leaping six feet up the walls and out into the middle of the room. The smoke was a solid dense cloud from four feet on up to the ceiling, and the air was filled with the crackling, popping noise that any good bonfire makes. We charged into the kitchen fearfully; what to do?

"Don't put water on a grease fire!" my spouse ordered in a scream, as I reached for the cabinet under the sink. Actually, I wasn't going for the water, as she thought; though I'd lived in this house over twenty years, at that particular time, I was under the impression that she kept the skillet lids under the sink. Of course, in non-emergencies one has time to look through all the cabinets if one needs to, as I later pointed out. But while the kitchen burned, every time I reached toward the sink, she jerked me away from the faucets, yelling, "No water!"

She found a cast-iron lid and pitched it frisbee-like onto the flaming pot, a feat she couldn't repeat in a hundred non-emergency tries. While it didn't completely smother the flames, it did calm them enough for me to get an oven mitt on and grab the handle to move the pot outside. One mitt wasn't enough; I had to set it down on the floor for a second hold when it got too hot. Grease sloshed onto my arm, and my hand was burned through the glove. Still, I made it to the porch door and pitched skillet and all into the yard.

The roaring of the kitchen bonfire was increasing to an inferno, as I re-entered the porch and turned to run down its length to the garage, where fifty feet of inch-and-a-half fire hose waited, for just such an emergency. I was halfway down the porch, when the telephone by the chaise lounge rang.

Can you believe I stopped and ANSWERED the blame thing?!!

(And left the skin of three fingertips on the receiver, for us to find post-fire!)

Some guy says, "I'd like to order a book. . ." and I interrupted with, "We're having a house fire right now; could you call back later?" And he did!

The big fire hose got the job done, and the hundred-gallon-a-minute rate had the fire out within a minute after I introduced the hose to the kitchen. The first time. I had taken the hose back outside ("don't get anything in the dining room wet!" Betsy had warned me) when the plastic stuff inside the cabinets re-ignited, and I had to give it a second dose. Though the volunteer fire department was on the scene (from seven miles away!) within fifteen minutes, they didn't even need to unravel a hose. They set up fans to suck the smoke out, and checked to be sure everything was okay. One of the firemen did note that the dog had just eaten our hamburgers.

There are still places in this great land where doctors will treat after-hours injuries, just as firemen will make out-of-town calls. An hour later, my burns had been treated, and I was on my way home. As I passed the Sonic, I remembered that we were still supperless, so I wheeled in to pick up some hamburgers.

I'll let you guess what I told the waitress when she asked the standard question: "You want some french fries with that?" My reply wasn't particularly Christian.

But my neighbors were: Jim and Trey Nichols, my brother Beau, and the Giesbrecht family were all at the house cleaning up when I returned from the doctor. Jim was the unlucky one who learned that the fire had burned through and shorted the kitchen circuits, when he grabbed the refrigerator door and almost couldn't turn it loose. The neighbors had most of the immediate mess cleaned up by the time I got home from the doctor's office.

Then two months later, we had another fire! Apparently some old model airplane paint and glue upstairs ignited, perhaps from the surge of heat up there as a result of the kitchen fire. We learned an awful lot about ourselves, our neighbors, and our fellow church members during these trials by fire.

Take kids, for instance.

It's all too easy nowadays to read or hear bad tidings about our nation's youth in the media. Gangs are running rampant in not only the big cities, it seems, but in small towns too. Drugs in the schools are a problem everywhere, and the statistics on youthful drunk drivers and teenage pregnancies are alarming. The music is too loud, too profane, and Elvis is probably turning over in his grave, assuming he's really in there. What are we going to do to correct this image of youngsters going to hell in a handbasket?

Well, one could have a fire and have a bunch of good kids invited over for -- literally -- hot dogs and marshmallows.

We did that; it was unplanned -- spontaneous, so to speak -- and I wouldn't want to do it again, nor wish it on anyone else. But it sure gave some kids a chance to give a good account of themselves. We'd have lost the house and/or a lot of possessions without them.

The June kitchen fire was minor league, compared to the one that gutted the upstairs. When discovered, it was an evil, roaring, ink-black and flame-orange thing; crackling and snapping twelve feet up and twenty feet out as it greedily consumed everything upstairs, charring what it didn't burn. The air wasn't just foul up there; there was no air, except within two inches of the floor. The firemen later said it probably was a thousand degrees next to the roof, and light bulbs were exploding fifty feet away while the plastic shower curtain hooks melted almost seventy feet from the flames through the closed bathroom door.

Into this inferno charged son Adam with a fire hose, bellowing instructions to those behind. Both Beau and I had fire fighting training in the Navy, but the kid was leading the way. Of course, as he later pointed out, it was his room that was afire; his britches that were burning. But as an aside here, I was worried about my own britches, strangely.

Used to be, britches went through a standard cycle: brand new jeans were suitable for Sunday wear, though a boy also had a Sunday suit in the closet for state occasions; after being washed maybe a dozen times, new jeans became school jeans, though there were two standards for these: those pairs with patches on the knees, and those without. Once a knee gave out, that pair became play jeans, and Momma would put patches on both knees for the sake of the match; when holes appeared elsewhere, the jeans were relegated to the back of the closet for work and hunting; the final stage was for cutoffs, when the britches legs gave out entirely. Jeans were expected to last years back then, and woe betide the kid who got too big for his britches before they reached the hunting stage.

On Sundays, a kid could participate in the quick football game between Sunday school and church only if he had on Sunday jeans; a grass stain on a pair of suit pants was grounds for a chewing out at the least, and a hide-tanning at the most. It was unthinkable for a youngster to undertake any activity that would endanger his Sunday britches. Most suits had either been passed down likeunto family heirlooms, or if bought new, were expected to pass down through three more generations. Almost like the Family Bible.

Now, consider that I had just returned from Mrs. Maisenhelder's funeral, in which I was a pallbearer, and the blaze was discovered almost upon my entering the house. I was taking my coat and tie off in the kitchen when Adam screamed that the upstairs was aflame. Reaction took over as we ran for the hose, and my next really conscious thought was several minutes later when he and I were crawling into the smoke-filled room where the heat from the raging red monster approached a thousand degrees.

Halfway into the room, holding the bucking hose, I remember thinking, "Dadgummit! I've got my Sunday pants on!"

And would you believe that, while Adam and Beau manned the hose upstairs, I actually descended the ladder, ran into the bedroom -- right below the fire, water pouring through the ceiling -- and changed into a pair of cut-offs, folding the suit pants neatly on the bed, with my billfold still in the back pocket? After the emergency was over, however, I couldn't recall exactly when I did that.

Old church habits are hard to break!

Adrenalin is a wonderful thing in times like these; Deadeye hauled off and chunked a full inch-and-a-half fire hose complete with nozzle twenty feet up to me on the roof. We later figured that must have weighed nearly a hundred pounds, and he declined to try it again under less stressful conditions. When Adam yelled for someone to open the front gable windows, young Mac sprinted barefooted up and across the roof; which doesn't seem remarkable unless you've seen this roof -- it's a steep thirty-foot rise at about an eighty-degree pitch. It can't be walked up, yet I saw Bryon stand straight up and run over it -- though he was flapping his hands as he ran. Maybe that helped. Of course, the roof was so hot he ended up with second-degree burns on his feet!

At one point, when we mistook the snapping and crackling of a box of .22 cartridges in the smoke-filled room cooking off for the snapping and crackling of additional flames we could neither see nor reach from our prone hose position just inside the balcony, we thought we'd lost the battle. Beau yelled to me, "Better go down and tell them to get everything out." I left the fight to him and the three college-age boys.

Everyone has their own priorities. I headed down the ladder again and ran straight to the gun cabinet. As I exited the den with an armload of my precious guns, I met Betsy racing from the bedroom -- with her sable stole over her arm!

Downstairs, Betsy, B.C., and the neighbors had been joined by several youngsters who had come early for B.C.'s cast party. Our youngest had played a Wicked Witch in the summer youth musical, "The Wizard of Oz," and we were hosting the cast party. Almost two dozen kids, including Munchkins, had showed up for -- a bonfire and weenie roast! Just as so many had done for church youth group outings in the past out here.

Now, the Scarecrow and the Good Witch were taking pictures off the walls and moving furniture out, along with several others I couldn't count. Five kids in the ten-to-twelve bracket were as calm as at a Sunday School picnic, and Tin Man cracked a joke as he handed one something. It frightened me that there were so many youngsters downstairs, saving our possessions in hurried but composed manner, when I fully expected the roof to begin caving in at any moment. I yelled at

Beverly to get her kids out and make a head count, but they all ignored me until the job was done. In about fifteen minutes, all our stuff was sitting in the front yard, except for what was too heavy downstairs or afire upstairs. And when I sprinted back through on my return to the fire, there were B.C., the Scarecrow, and the Good Witch busily mopping the dining room floor as hot water poured through the ceilings around them. We did manage to save the house, and not a board of the hardwood floors downstairs buckled despite maybe three thousand gallons of water on them.

You expect level-headedness in a crisis from adults. But without those youngsters, we'd have lost our home and most of our possessions. Those kids dumped their ice chests and washtubs in the front yard and charged into the burning house without even a thought of their own safety, apparently. After they got our possessions outside, they returned with the large containers to place them under the worst water streams (they said later that the water coming through the ceilings was hotter than you like your shower, but not hot enough to scald them), then found brooms, mops, and towels to get the water off of the floors once it appeared that our upstairs fire-fighting efforts were going to save the structure. Their roll of garbage bags for cast party clean-up was used to cover beds, wardrobes, bookcases, and large pieces of furniture from the upstairs water pouring through. Then after Betsy & I returned from the doctor (again!) that evening, the kids met us with supper: they had gone ahead with plans for the cast party, and set up tents out at the Swimming Hole in the pasture. They even had pitched a tent for us!

Kids ain't all bad.

And then here came the church folks, for the Sealing Party.

"A Sealing Party? What are we gonna seal?" asked Gene, my bass companion.

I've heard foreigners declare that English is one of the

toughest languages to learn, because so many similar-sounding words have different meanings. It works the same way over the telephone sometimes, even when you're talking to an Alabaman.

"Not a Sealing Party. . . a ceiling party," I corrected. "You know, the part of your house us Navy boys call the overhead. As in where ceiling fans hang from."

"Oh," he said, still a little at sea, "sure, count me in."

In saving the house, I figured we had used close to five thousand gallons of water this time -- all upstairs. And while a lot of that water literally went up in steam, a lot of it also came downstairs, removing most of the first floor ceilings in the process. That's not so remarkable, when you think about it; we're not talking about a trickle here -- that much water weighs twelve tons!

It's depressing to rebuild from one fire, then have another eighteen hours after the two-month remodeling job is finished. It's depressing to have to stay in a home permeated by that sicky-sweet smoke smell. But it's worse to have no ceilings in the part still habitable -- you feel like something's always fixing to fall on you at any minute. Tough as she is, Betsy even cried a little.

People reacted almost at once. A choir member who had lost her own home -- and husband -- to fire showed up the next morning with broom, dust pan, garbage bags, and rubber gloves. "I know what to do, just move out of the way," Nancy said, and went to work. Perrin parked his lowboy trailer next to the house, saying, "Call when it's loaded and I'll pick it up to take to the dump." And he did that when I called, then brought it back for more.

Two van loads of Mennonite ladies – I'd sold several house sites to members of that denomination, and with Lawrence and Beverly's four boys growing up next door in my parents' old home, our pasture Swimming Hole had introduced us to many of that wonderful congregation over the past several years – showed up unannounced on Tuesday and trooped

70

upstairs with cleaning equipment, working all day each day. By Friday, I asked Betsy what she had agreed to pay them, so I could run to the bank for cash. "I thought YOU had hired them!" she exclaimed. When she asked one of the ladies what we owed, it was clear that she had almost insulted them: "You're neighbors, and you needed our help," one told her gently.

Ladies not only brought meals, but diminutive redhead Nancy (the co-captain on that first Brownspur Olympics winning team) forced us to stop working long enough to sit down and eat ham sandwiches she sliced from her gift, accompanied by (of all things!) hot tamales that Margaret showed up with, saying, "I'm so sorry y'all have to go through this!" Sally Baker brought a lemon meringue pie that became chocolate -- Betsy's favorite -- when we cut into it. I mean, when she handed it to me, she assured me it was a lemon pie -- my own preference. Even she was surprised when I called and told her about the Changing-Lemon-to-Chocolate Miracle. The Lord works in mysterious ways!

And that next Saturday, around fifteen church folks showed up for a Sealin. . .ceiling party. Mark and Tommy brought tall sturdy ladders and Joe brought a short study one. Janice volunteered to hold my tall unsturdy ladder, even though I wasn't much use, still bandaged from my burns. Tommy brought a dump truck to haul the trash away. The ladies brought brooms and mops and buckets and dustpans, some of which we still haven't gotten sorted out. Gene and Nancy cut tile; Mark, Beau, and Tommy manned the ladders most of the afternoon; Robbie even cleaned things that were dirty pre-fire; Marion was intent on finishing the Seal. . .ceiling party and starting a wallpaper party; Jody was there with a broom at a critical point when a grid threatened to come down -- friends were all over the house doing what needed doing.

And in four hours, they had the Seal. . .ceilings back in the whole downstairs!

As the men finished Sealing a room, the ladies would sweep up, mop, and wax the floor; then move the furniture back inside -- they'd all been in our home enough to know where everything went -- into place and polish it.

Nor were they satisfied with that. Nancy wouldn't let me say grace over the best ribs Betsy or anyone else ever grilled until the dining room silver was polished, and proper place settings were in place on the table.

It changed from a burnt, gutted, stinking structure back into a home, when all the downstairs Sealings. . .ceilings were intact and the furniture not only replaced from where most of it sat in the front yard, but dusted and waxed. Betsy sent the menfolks out to the Swimming Hole to clean up, then Jody organized a pick-up baseball game while supper was being served in a dining room that had been a total wreck four hours before. Most of the food had been brought by the ladies, and most of it was consumed forthwith. Sealing parties make you hungry. By nine, Betsy and I were once again all alone in our newly ceiled. . .Sealed home.

During the next week, word got around about the second fire, and friends in the publishing industry called from Dallas, Atlanta, Orlando, New York, Memphis, Nashville, Birmingham, and other cities. To a person, they were amazed at the news of our Sealing Party. "That kind of thing wouldn't happen around here," was the universal sentiment, delivered in wistful, admiring tones.

Maybe small-town rural living doesn't have all the social and cultural advantages of the bright lights; maybe it's tough to make a living out here in the sticks; maybe a rural state is last in a lot of categories, even in church membership.

But just try having a Sealing Party somewhere else!

That's a chapter in our lives that's hopefully over and done with: in sixteen months, we had a tornado that got the roof, two fires, and eight hospitalizations or surgeries. But Brownspur is rebuilt (although my standard advice now is, "if your house catches fire, get the picture albums and guns, and run. The reason you get the guns out is so, if someone tries to put it out before it's burnt to the ground, you can kill him!" It ain't worth the hassle with the banks and insurance companies), and guess what was asked us in Sunday School one week? "When are we gonna have another Brownspur Olympics?"

So when the kids were home over Easter Holidays, I advised them that we had been considering -- nay, had even been urged -- to re-inaugurate the Brownspur Olympics, which were so popular during the years before they had gone off to college. There have been few dinners when we've all laughed so hard, planning these New Brownspur Olympics. It was great to see that no one had lost their sense of humor through our trials by fire.

In light of the string of tragedies, Adam and B.C. began to suggest even more events to add to the competitions, which were pretty stiff anyway. Some of these new events might be:

1) The cast-iron skillet-lid frisbee throw -- contestants must stand ten feet away from a flaming skillet of grease and attempt to flip the lid onto the burning pot. The lid must land on top of the skillet and smother at least half the flames, to qualify. Current record holder: Betsy Neill.

2) The ring-around-the-house with the ladder contest -- entrants must hold a twenty-foot extension ladder across their chests and sprint around the house three times to find a place not burning or endangered by electrical wires to place the ladder, extend it, and run up it. Electrocution disqualifies. Current record holder: Bob Neill

3) The roof run -- competitors must race barefooted up an eighty-degree-pitched roof, which has been heated to 650 degrees on the outside (roofer's estimate) by a fire on the inside. Flapping of the arms is allowed. Current record holder: Bryon McIntire.

4) The fire hose toss -- contestants must throw a fully-charged inch-and-a-half fire hose, complete with brass nozzle, to a

partner twenty feet up on the roof. Current record holder: Deadeye Borgognoni.

5) The closet-cleaning contest -- entrants must run through a burning home, complete with collapsing ceilings, and gather the entire contents of a woman's closet, in which exactly fifty percent of the coat hangers are turned the wrong way, into their arms and sprint back outside. Current record holder: B.C. Neill.

6) The suit-changing race -- contestants must crawl into a burning upstairs, fully clothed in a three-piece suit, then back out, descend a ladder, enter a bedroom in which water pours through the ceiling, remove the suit, fold it neatly on a bed in the burning room (wallet in pocket), pull on cut-off jeans, and race back upstairs. Current record holder: Bob Neill.

7) The decanter sprint -- athletes must race through a burning home while balancing a full crystal decanter of cognac (VSOP) and six crystal glasses on a silver tray. Breakage of more than one glass or consumption of cognac during the race disqualifies. Current record holder: John Hinkle.

8) Picture clearing contest -- entrants must take every picture off the walls of a large burning home in less than ten minutes. Current record co-holders: Scott Edwards & Monica Louwerens.

9) Short refrigerator hold -- competitors must stand in a puddle of water and grasp the metal door handle of an electrically-shorted refrigerator until sparks can be seen between their teeth. Current record holder: Jim Nichols.

10) Celebrity scramble -- entrants must scramble through a pile of burnt mattresses, carpeting, clothes, bedding, and other waterlogged materials to find an assortment of autographs by Nolan Ryan, Mike Tyson, Boo Ferris, Ronald Reagan, Kirk Douglas, Charlie Daniels, and other celebrities. Current record holder: Trey Nichols.

11) Exit under live fire race -- contestants must race through a smoke-filled room after a full box of .22 rifle cartridges has been heated to the point of ignition within that same room.

Bullet holes in mortal places disqualify. Current record co-holders: Adam & Beau Neill.

We'll need to notify the appropriate authorities for judging the new Brownspur Olympics. The Leland Volunteer Fire Department has served as judges during the last few competitions, and they know the fastest way out here to Brownspur, though few of them are Baptist. But then, we haven't been particularly denominational-minded, as noted in earlier chapters.

We had pre-fire considered moving closer to a major airport, for business and health reasons. But if we just had to burn, I cannot imagine a better place than Brownspur, where the church folks can Seal your home, and heal your heart. If it had to happen, I'm glad it was here, around these folks.

In Sickness Or In Health

Well, every book ought to touch on a little controversy, just for the fun of it, right? Since we've just touched on some Sealing, let's look at the healing. During my pilgrimage to this point, I had run up on a couple of instances that baffled me, even though I was the main player in one of them. Most mainline Protestant preachers are somewhat cautious on the subject of Divine Healing. It used to happen, but now we have doctors, is a common refrain. The problem seems to be that we can't understand how come some folks get healed, apparently, while some don't. Were the healed just more worthy than the unhealed, who must have been closet sinners?

Have we, as practicing Christians, somehow gone beyond the ability to say, "I don't know?" Even Saint Paul said, "Now we see as through a glass darkly." Just because we can't quite figure it out doesn't necessarily mean it ain't so!

During the latter stages of my aforementioned problems with dizzy spells, there was one night when I just slap could not go to prayer meeting and choir practice; I wasn't up to it, and admitted it, flat out. Betsy went without me.

She answered the questions as to my whereabouts and condition truthfully: I was home, feeling bad, and not one of the several doctors I had consulted had been able to suggest a solution, or worse yet, a diagnosis, in over two years.

Prayer meeting was generally held after choir at that time of year. But that night, when practice was over, most of the choir members apparently skipped prayer meeting in the chapel, to stay in the choir room and pray -- for me!

That was Wednesday night. No one bothered to inform me that I was being prayed for, either. On Sunday morning, I was reading the paper, and ran across an article about some lady in Texas whose symptoms sounded almost exactly like mine. Seems that she had gotten some relief by going to a chiropractor. What could I lose? Monday morning, I hied me off to Dr. Mitchell, an osteopath, who had helped me recover from a ruptured hip joint years before when I'd been clipped going down on a punt, playing football at Ole Miss.

He examined me, took a couple of x-rays, and determined that a hard lick on the head a while back had compacted my skull against my top vertebrae. Took him three treatments to relieve most of the pressure, and I was singing again in another week. It was a month before I learned of the special prayer meeting.

Coincidence?

Maybe so. You believe what you want. I think that God heard the prayers of Ed and Jane, George and Nancy, Dianne, Gene, Roy and Ricki, and several others that night. I think He arranged for me to read a section of the Sunday paper that I hardly ever look at, and arranged for that article to be there. I think He had arranged the cancellation on Dr. Mitchell's books that next day, and guided the doctor's manipulations to help me.

I am certain of this, in retrospect: had those Christian friends not prayed especially for Neill, I never would have seen that article, and never would have considered going to Dr. Mitchell. I believe that with all my heart.

Turned out it was a double problem. An old teammate of mine moved back here from the service, having become one of the top hematologists in the country. I went to him for some tests not long after Dr. Mitchell's work had me feeling some better. That appointment was arranged, not by a doctor, but by two nurses who were also members of the church, and who had

77

raised me from childhood -- and one of whose husbands sang tenor in the choir.

I had swung by Dr. Nichols' office to pay a bill, and Nurse Ruby looked closely at my eyes. "What's wrong with you, boy?" she demanded.

Bear in mind that I felt better than I had in a couple of years, and said so. "Nurse Ann, come up here and look at this boy," she insisted. Her companion came from the back of the clinic and looked closely at me.

"My goodness, son!" she exclaimed. "Come sit down and let me get some blood from you." Protesting, I was led down the hall and pricked, when all I had come to do was pay a bill!

I was severely anemic. They sent me to Dr. Bob Bowman, who took it as a personal vendetta to solve what turned out to be a very rare problem: Babesiosis, a companion disease to Lyme Disease, which I was diagnosed with several years later by a Lyme specialist. My red-blood cells were passing off before they were full grown, and if I had cut myself shaving, I might have gone into shock, he ventured. Within a year, I was fine as frog hair, but thirty years later, I still catch Nurse Ruby around town and get her to inspect me visually.

Coincidence? To you, maybe. But I was the one hurting. To me, it all goes back to that choir prayer meeting, praying for Neill to be healed. If that's coincidence, so be it.

A few years before that, I had been a witness to what I considered an even more graphic healing. Several couples of us had gone off to a religious retreat, driving most of the day to get to where the three-day meeting was being held. We had rented houses to stay in, and ours was on a high cliff overlooking the swiftly-flowing river, a beautiful location.

One young lady in our company had left home somewhat reluctantly, having hurt her arm in a tennis accident the day before, though she didn't realize that it was serious at the time. She just didn't feel good when we left, but was in real pain by the time the seven-hour journey ended. She didn't even want to go to the opening ceremony that evening, but the other girls encouraged her, and we arrived on time.

The speaker spoke on the subject of healing.

"Jenny's" arm was hurting so much by the middle of the service that a couple of the girls led her out to the auditorium lounge, and one of them asked me to locate a doctor. I did so, having to use the microphone during a break in the program. He accompanied me back to examine Jenny, and sent me to get his bag. He didn't feel that the arm was broken, but advised her not to use it, and gave her some painkiller pills. By the time he finished, the healing-subject speaker was just finishing up, and announced that he would be holding a private healing service in a small back room, if anyone was interested in attending.

Our girls grabbed Jenny, who was rather groggy by this time, and were the first in the room. I slipped in to observe, as did the doctor, I noticed.

Having never attended a healing service, I'm not sure what I expected: yelling and jumping up and down, I suppose. Certainly not a quiet, sympathetic approach, with a gentle laying on of hands. Yet that's what transpired. Several people came forward, both to whisper encouragement -- or prayer, or something -- to Jenny and some others who professed to being under the weather. Our friend had not volunteered of her own free will; she was out of it from the painkillers, and had been shoved forward by her companions.

We took her home and put her to bed, under the effects of the painkillers, which the doctor had told me would knock her out for a while. The rest of us stayed up and prayed for her, among other things.

I was as usual the first up that next morning, and was making coffee when Jenny came into the kitchen, smiling. She greeted me sleepily and opened the refrigerator door. We exchanged the customary good mornings and weather observations as she took out a full half gallon jug of orange juice, carried it to the counter, and poured glasses for me, herself, and her husband, still in bed. She put the jug back in the fridge and picked up their glasses, promising to return when I finished up the coffee.

She had used her injured hand, and not only had never winced once, she hadn't even been conscious of using it.

By the time she came back, I had briefed the rest of the group, and not a soul broached the subject of the hurt arm. She never said a word about it, and used it completely normally for the rest of the trip. It was as if it had never happened.

I made it a point to ask the doctor who had treated her that first night for his opinion, and was pleasantly surprised by his reply. "Son, I've seen people healed by my own ministrations, and I've seen the Lord obviously guiding my hands in healing through operations that I knew I didn't have the ability to perform. I know that He can heal without me, and I know that He can use me to heal through me. It doesn't bother me either way. I'm here if He wants to use me."

Yet the biggest healing that weekend involved a birthday, on another night. Betsy and Dale had learned that one of their friend's birthday fell during our stay, and they somehow managed to get together the makings for a cake, sent a couple of us menfolks out for ice cream, and alerted the rest of our group that a surprise party was in the offing after the nightly services.

It was a total surprise! I've seen that once or twice, and this was a good one. No one spent money for a gift, but there were some doozies, that had obviously been prepared with a lot of care and love, though on short notice. The best was the pet rock, from the police chief.

Chief McMaster made his presentation on bended knee, describing how he had hunted the rock down, cut it daringly from the herd, and cornered it high atop the cliff. Instead of giving up, the rock had gone over the cliff, and Chief told how he had climbed down at the risk of his own life to capture this one particular rock for the fair lady. After clambering back up with his prize, he had bathed it gently, perfumed it (shaving lotion), housebroken it, and taught it to sit for her before wrapping it in aluminum foil for this gift presentation. Everyone was in hysterics by the time Chief finished, but the tears in the honoree's eyes weren't strictly from laughter. These people cared for her. And at that particular time in her life, she needed to know that, for reasons best left unsaid here.

Healing can be in spirit, too.

You don't believe in healing, you say?

Fine. That's your little red wagon, and you can pull it like you want to. But the next time you get sick, do you want your name put on the prayer list?

You do? How come?

Oh. That's called "hedging your bets," in some circles.

At one time in our church, the deacons were assigned a certain number of church families to look after. Well, that's not the right term, I guess; sounds like meddling, doesn't it? And we all know that's the preacher's job. Vernon, one of our Sunday School class members, defined the difference between "sermon" and "message" from the pulpit: "A sermon is when he gets to meddling!"

The deacon was just to be there for his families; to be part of a church family in every sense of the word. And if we deacons would do our jobs better, it would take a lot of pressure off of the preacher, who can't be everywhere all the time.

One year, a name on my list was unfamiliar: a Mrs. Connie McCain. I dropped by the house to make her acquaintance, and invite her to be a little more regular in her attendance, so that her deacon could get to know her better. To my surprise, the door was opened by a lady whom I did know very well from church: "Mrs. Boyd! Oh, I was given this address for Mrs. Connie McCain."

Mrs. Boyd smiled and said, "Sure. Come on in and I'll go get her." A few minutes later, she came into the living room pushing a wheelchair.

Connie McCain had probably the biggest, most beautiful, green-grey eyes I had ever seen, and an eager smile. I fell in love with her immediately.

She was also a long-time stroke victim. On good days, she could dress and get into her wheelchair. Her sister lived with her and took care of her. My brief call turned into many pleasant, long visits, and there were always cookies for my kids when I took them along.

Connie McCain was confined to bed and wheelchair, but she had a ministry of her own, which she felt she had been called unto. Every week, when the church newsletter came out, she would send cards to the hospital patients, and those under the weather at home who were listed for prayers. Mrs. Boyd bought the cards, and mailed them. How many folks over the years had been cheered up by a card from this lady?

Sure made me mind my deacon job better, when families on my list were sick or hurt!

Possibly the most traumatic hospital visitation I ever undertook was when Billy was operated on for a pinched nerve in his neck. The doctor went in from the front instead of the back, but the operation was a complete success. I arrived during the surgery and kept Martha company in the hospital room. The doctor brought us the good news and said that Billy would be coming in from Recovery soon. Everything was fine.

Sure enough, an orderly came in, wheeling Billy on a gurney, followed by a nurse. I helped transfer the patient to the bed, and the orderly left with the gurney. The nurse had a pitcher of ice water that she set on the table, and instructed us that he would have to be kept still and quiet for a while. "I'll bring you his hospital kit," she said as she closed the door. Billy groaned and opened his eyes as Martha and I leaned over to tell him that the operation had been proclaimed a success.

Suddenly the door burst open, and a nurse shouted, "DO NOT GO OUT INTO THE HALL!!!" and slammed the door.

"CODE RED! CODE RED!" called the loudspeaker system. "Security to the fourth floor STAT!" Martha and I looked at each other, wide-eyed.

Turned out that a police informant had fingered a dope dealer, and the gang had hunted him down for revenge. He had been left for dead, but someone had gotten him to the hospital in time, and my old hunting buddy Dr. Brooks had saved his life. The informant was two doors down from Billy's room. And two members of the gang had just been seen entering the hospital, presumably to finish the man off. Hospital authorities had sealed off the building and cleared the halls until police could arrive and the outlaws could be arrested.

Leaving Martha and me with a now-recovering major surgery patient!

"Ohhh, Bob! I feel bad!" Billy moaned, clutching my hand and trying to sit up.

I tried to hold him down gently. "Be still, buddy," I urged, wondering when the nurse would be back in to tell us a little more about what to do.

"Ohhhh, Baby! I feel bad!" our patient groaned to his wife, who was almost in tears. Then the after-effects of the anesthetic began to hit, and he tried feebly to retch. "Ohhh, Bob! I feel bad!" he insisted.

I had a roommate for one semester in college who was well on his way to becoming an alcoholic, and I could recall him urping while lying on his back, resulting in a near drowning -- not that I would have particularly minded, at that point, for Johnny used to come in bombed and wake me up well after midnight.

At any rate, I knew that we could not allow Billy to vomit while lying on his back, but the nurse had not told us whether we could lift him; would that undo the good the surgery had done? I tried the telephone, but got no answer at the nurses' station. Apparently Security had shut down the floor. Billy grasped the rail and pulled himself off the bed, making that retching sound again as Martha fought to hold him down. "Help, Bob!"

I pushed my friend back flat as he rolled his eyes at me. "Ohhh, Bob! I feel bad!" Martha was praying at the foot of the bed. Billy tried to lean sideways to upchuck.

"Find me a bowl, Martha!" I interrupted her beseeching. "Hurry!" She went through the cabinets to no avail as her husband continued the dry retching sounds. There was absolutely nothing in the cabinet. "Pull the drawer out!" I commanded. But the bedside table wasn't made that way; the drawer wouldn't detach. There wasn't even a wastebasket. Martha peeked out the door, but slammed it quickly.

"There's men with guns out there!" she whispered fearfully.

"Come help hold him, then!" When she grabbed her struggling mate, I leapt to the window ledge, where sat a brand new box of chocolates someone had brought for Billy. With my pocketknife, I slit the wrapping and removed the top of the box, which had been hinged. Billy had fought to a position where he could lean over the side of the bed. I arrived with the box top just in time.

"Ohhhh, Bob! I feel bad!" my hurting comrade exclaimed afterward.

There wasn't even a glass to give him a sip of water. However, a rubber glove lay on the floor, dropped from the gurney. We filled it with ice, and used it to cool Billy's head, while Martha handfed him crushed ice. Now and then he would lean over to retch again, lying back with his now-familiar refrain: "Ohhh, Bob! I feel bad!"

I got him back, though, a couple of years later.

Their son had suffered a concussion in a football practice, and neither Billy nor Martha was home; they could not be located. Someone called me, since he farmed out our way. Though I was on crutches from a recent knee reconstruction, I got in the pickup and drove down to Billy's place, but he wasn't in the fields. I headed over to the hospital myself to see about the boy, for I was still his Duty Deacon.

They had taken the kid to the emergency room, which had a limited access, for security reasons. Most visitors had to go through the lobby and get passes. However, when I parked in a handicapped space by the emergency room doors and crutched up to the door, both guards rushed to open them for me. I heard a call, and looked back to see Martha just arriving, so I held the door for her, and we made our way to the examining room together, where the doctor assured her that the boy was fine; just somewhat woozy. I leaned against the wall as she went with the doctor to see her son. Screeching tires attracted my attention back to the doors.

Billy's truck was stopped in the middle of the drive as he ran toward the doors, which would not open from the outside. He pounded on the glass, but the guard shook his head and pointed toward the front lobby, half a block away. Billy's mouth worked angrily, but fortunately, no one could hear a word through the door. The guard shook his head again and pointed. The frustrated father shook his fist and gestured. Then he saw me, leaning against the back wall. He frantically pounded and motioned for me to come open the door.

Grinning, I shook my head and pointed with my crutch toward the lobby.

In retrospect, it's a good thing Billy didn't then have a weak heart, for I believe that might have touched off a fatal attack.

He later berated me, "Some deacon you are! 'Behold, I stand at the door and knock' but you wouldn't let me in!" he quoted.

Actually, Billy did suffer a serious heart attack a few years later, and, as one of his sons related, "We thought he was gone until we got him to the emergency room and they gave him one of those Beta Buster shots!" This attack came at a crucial time in the family's life, for his oldest son was being married in a town 75 miles away that next week. But Martha refused to leave his side for long enough to go to the ceremony, since ICU visits were every two hours, even though several of us volunteered to make that visit for her.

But her Duty Deacon was on the job! Our son-in-law John is a pilot, and his roommate at Delta State in the Commercial Aviation program was Matt Morgan, who had come to college from California with his own small two-seater airplane. I cornered Matt and we worked out this scenario: he would be on the runway, engine running, when the 12:20 ICU visit ended, and I would whisk Martha out to the airport as she changed into her wedding duds in the back seat. This was a small airport, so I could pull right up next to Matt's plane, so she could be inside and belted in within moments, then Matt would take off for the short flight. I contacted Johnny Keesee, a Rural Crisis Committee member and turkey hunting buddy, and he agreed to meet Martha at the small Clarksdale airport, then whisk her to the church in time for the 1:00 wedding. He would wait outside until the ceremony was over, then zip her back to Matt's waiting plane, so he could quickly fly her back to me, still waiting at the Greenville airport. She could change back to her hospital clothes as we sped to the hospital, and be there well before time for the 2:00 ICU visit. That's known as Deacon Coordination!

Only problem was, Martha had never flown before, and wasn't enthusiastic about her first flight being a high-speed low-level race over the Mississippi Delta with a student pilot. "Besides, what will Matt charge me for that?" she worried. The tall blonde kid shook his head. "Miss Martha, you don't even have to buy the gas for me. The only thing that you'll have to bring – and I'm sure Uncle Bob could pick this up for you – is a case of cold beer!"

The Groom's Mother immediately changed her image of a high-speed low-level race over the Delta with a student pilot, to include a beer-guzzling student pilot, and emphatically shook her head to decline the invitation. "I don't believe in people drinking beer and driving, so I sure won't agree to someone piloting an airplane while drinking," she exclaimed righteously.

"Oh, no, Ma'am," Matt corrected her. "The beer isn't for me, it's for you! You said you had never flown before, so I figured that would settle you down while we flew up there!"

No, she refused our efforts, but if there was a Duty Deacon Award, I'm sure the Neill Wedding Flight Plan would have been nominated for it!

Duty Deacons need to identify themselves as such when they make hospital visits, I once learned. One of my families was blessed with a baby, which they decided would be their last. When I heard news of the birth, I went over to the hospital early the next morning to offer my congratulations. Naturally, I first stopped at the big nursery window to mirate over the children therein, before strolling down the hall to her room. No one answered my knock, but a nurse came by and said, "Just go on in, Sir. She'll be back in a minute."

I did so, and was sitting there reading the paper a few minutes later when she was wheeled in. "Hi! Just had my tubes tied," she announced, clearly still high from the effects of the anesthesia. The nurse and orderly moved her onto the bed, in the meantime blocking my exit. When the orderly turned and left with the gurney, the nurse began to affix a drip bottle to the stand by the bed, and the patient immediately passed out. I headed for the door too, as the nurse left just in front of me.

But then I glanced back to notice that the clear plastic tube from bottle to arm was filling with blood. "Hey!" I called to the nurse, pointing back into the room. "It's going backwards!"

"Oh, my goodness!" she exclaimed as she ran back in. "Give me a hand!" She handed me the drip bottle to hold as she made some adjustments, then pulled the needle from the vein, spraying blood across the bed. She reinserted the needle, taped it down, noted that the stuff in the bottle was running like it should, then relieved me of the bottle, hanging it on the stand in the corner. I couldn't get past the nurse to leave as she bent over the bed once more.

And removed the blood-spotted hospital gown from her patient!

I shoved her aside and ran from the room. Turned out that the nurse had just assumed that I was the husband, and would not be shocked at her changing the lady to a clean gown in my presence. Now I identify myself right off the bat as the family's deacon!

Being a Duty Deacon, or a caring preacher, can be a bloody business at times, not trying to be indelicate. Once the mother of my next-door neighbor was visiting, not knowing that she was suffering from a bleeding ulcer. Just before supper one night, the poor lady threw up blood and collapsed. The family rushed her to the hospital, while I called the preacher, who lived on my block. He came by the house to pick me up and we went to the hospital together to be with the family as a successful operation was performed. Once the mother was pronounced out of danger, the minister beckoned to me. We hugged the family, assured them that we'd be back the next day, and left the hospital.

As my house was next door to the family's home, my companion parked out front and got out of the car. "Where are you headed?" I asked.

James nodded toward the house knowingly. "Thought I'd check the house," he said. "You go ahead on home." I did.

A few minutes later, I noticed that his car was still there. Thinking that maybe something was wrong, I put my shoes back on and walked next door. The preacher was upstairs, in the hall where the elderly lady had collapsed. He was on his knees, sleeves rolled up, a stack of towels and basin of water at his side. Blood was everywhere.

As I stared in horror, he calmly picked up a towel and dipped it into the water. As he began scrubbing, he remarked,

"I was scared of this."

Turned out that he had been a service chaplain. That experience, combined with over twenty years of ministry, had prepared him for being of practical as well as spiritual help. He had suspected that the home would need some cleaning, and had quietly gone to do that himself. I sighed and rolled up my sleeves, too.

We scrubbed for two hours. I've been in combat, but have never seen that much blood from one person -- especially who lived!

It was a real sermon, to a young deacon from a longtime minister. He could have blessed the family and left, or even called a cleaning service to be there bright and early the next morning. He could at least have asked a deacon or so to help him, or called a deacons meeting, even. Instead, he rolled up his sleeves and showed his love in the most basic way. We finished close to two in the morning, before the family came home. I gathered up the red towels to take to my house and wash them.

"Remember, don't wash them in hot water," he warned. "That will set the bloodstains. 'Though your sins be as scarlet, they shall be as wool' -- washed in cold water," he grinned.

He was right on that, too.

Wandering In The Wilderness:
Turtle Baptist Church

There was a period of time when we just flat quit going to church. Without going into all the gruesome details, I think I can claim without flinching, having so far survived five different church splits in three denominations, that I've seen how the Devil can infect church folks and get more bad things done in the name of religion, than non-church folks would believe possible. Of course, not everyone in church was involved in the agitation, and I'm sure everyone agitating was convinced that their viewpoint was the one that God was blessing. Howsomever, I finally tired of seeing my friends and family hurt -- on both sides (or neither!) of whatever issue -- and told Betsy that I was for calling it quits.

I think my exact words were, "If we want to watch folks hurt one another, let's go watch Saturday Night Wrestling; let's don't go to church and watch it on Sunday morning!"

She kept going for a while without me, and friends like Joe and Susan tried to minister to me, but my heart was hardened worse than old Pharaoh's ever was. At the time, we were going through a hard period financially, my parents had died and the estate was in a wrangle, and farming was tough. I was mad at the world in general and the church in particular. I mean, the church should be where a guy can get a little relief, surely? A respite from the wars? Where was God's love when I needed it?

Mark these words, if nothing else in this book is worth remembering: there is no denominational cause that can possibly be worth arousing bile in the individual churches and splitting up local congregations.

Period. Exclamation Point!

Sometimes the movers and shakers who play denominational politics forget about the folks in the trenches. God is love, and if we can agree to disagree in love, fine. But when love leaves a church, there is nothing left but the building -- which must then begin building again from scratch. Whatever we were arguing about back then -- and I wasn't one of them at the time -- it wasn't worth my being unable to worship any longer with Joe and Susan, Beau and Marion, Ed and Jane, Mike and Frances, Ted and Sally, George and Nancy, Gene and Malinda -- or any of the others, all of whom I loved (though I guess I never told them that at the time -- nor since, more's the pity).

That Couples Class we talked about in an earlier chapter? It had gone from nine on the roll to sixty-two plus a good many in-service (teaching mostly) spouses, in three years. I found my old teacher's family info book on it the other day (it survived the fire) and sat down to list where they all go to church now. Near as I could find out, they are scattered amongst fifteen different denominations and churches, but the real tragedy is that at least nine of the couples have split, and another dozen don't even attend church any more, as far as I could learn. About twenty are still on the roll at that church, but only half a dozen attend Sunday School regularly.

Having been there, I can testify that "Once burnt, twice shy," is a true proverb, and many others apparently feel the same. Though we once again attend church, sing in the choir, and teach Sunday School, I'm ashamed to say that it is with some reservations. When you've been hurt in a situation where there was a lot of love, even if the folks you loved weren't the ones responsible for the hurting, it makes you less willing to

love again. You're no longer willing to stick your neck out.
Heck, I don't even like for folks to hug me any more, even the
good- looking ladies, simply because there was a period of time
there when before I'd let some of the church folks hug me, I'd
frisk them to be sure they weren't going to stick a knife in my
back while their arms were around me!

Ed and I used to joke during those troubled times about
forming the "Turtle Baptist Church" out here in the old
Brownspur commissary store. We'd put a steeple on it, we'd be
really hard-shelled about everything, and we wouldn't stick our
necks out any more; instead, we'd just pull our heads in and
watch the world go by. What a great Christian ethic!

But that's essentially what I did, personally, for several
years. I quit. And I dragged Betsy and the kids down with me,
to some extent. Of course, they were all big enough by then to
make their own decisions: Christie and Adam were in college
and B.C. was fixing to be. Their foundations were okay; matter
of fact, Adam went to a college that required religion courses,
but had a liberal outlook. He was the main one to stand up to
the professor on theological questions (until the mid-term
grades came out, that is!) and take the conservative side.

Coincidently, it was during this time -- life-changing in
many aspects -- when my writing began being published, and it
appeared that a literary and speaking career had opened up just
as the farm career was shutting down. Some of my first
speaking opportunities were due to church groups involved in
trying to help their members cope with the worsening Rural
Crisis in America. The Episcopal and Southern Baptist
denominations (strange bedfellows indeed!) even funded Rural
Crisis Committees in farm states across the nation, complete
with a Farm Suicide Hotline, on which I served as an unpaid
volunteer for a few years. I became a real (as in, paid!)
storyteller, my presentations geared to helping others
understand what was happening in rural America, and how to
help cope with it. The Southern Baptist Home Mission Board

got involved in sponsoring me for appearances, and even had me come to Atlanta to cut a video for distribution to their churches, for which I was later honored with their Volunteer Missionary to Rural America Award. Dr. Jim Baugh and I, companions of that RCC & Suicide Hotline, co-authored a little book that was nominated for the Pulitzer Prize, entitled tongue-in-cheek, *HOW TO LOSE YOUR FARM IN TEN EASY LESSONS AND COPE WITH IT.*

Admittedly, it was a catharsis for me personally. Yet it also seemed to help others. At one of my first presentations, an anonymous note was passed to me: "I am the reason God brought you here today." After one presentation in a midwestern state, on the way to another, Betsy asked me thoughtfully, "You know, you turned your stories from funny to serious after five funny ones today, but yesterday you used seven funny stories, and the day before only three. What's the difference?"

"I don't know, I hadn't noticed that I was doing that," I admitted.

"Well, you are," my spouse declared. "Start noticing why."

So I did, and finally figured out that, at these presentations there was always one guy who came in late. He still had mud on his boots, grease on his hands, and would not take his coat or cap off. It was obvious that someone – his wife, preacher, banker, counselor – had made him come, and as soon as that Mississippi idiot would shut up and sit down, he'd be gone again. I realized that I was targeting on that guy, and that when I could make him laugh and sit back in his chair, then I could turn the stories to the serious kind and make my point.

At another RCC program, I think in Kansas, a lady strode up to me before we started, and proclaimed in a peeved manner, "I've read your farm book, and if you'd written that damn thing two years ago, I'd still be married!"

I stuttered, backing away, "Lady, I'm sorry! I wasn't

even writing two years ago! I wish I'd written you a letter, or. .
. ."

"I didn't understand him then, and I didn't understand why he couldn't tell me what was wrong with him!" She was really laying a guilt trip on this li'l ole Mississippi farm boy! "Excuse my language, but I was really a bitch then, and I don't blame him for leaving me."

But then she reached into her purse and pulled out a plane ticket to show me. "But I want you to know that I'm flying to Denver tomorrow – that's where he lives now – and I'm going to ask him to take me back." Her voice began to break: "Because I still love him – and now I understand him, after your book." She and I both were weeping as she turned away.

"Lady," I touched her arm, "If they call on me before I get back inside, tell 'em I'll be right back." I headed for the car to get an extra bandana handkerchief.

I could see that, even in my semi-estranged state from His house, God was using me to help others.

Right from the beginning, I had tried to incorporate into my programs that, "God isn't mad at you." I'd been through the praying for rain, but seeing my crops dry up, then making a good crop and seeing it drown in the mud and water of record fall rains, even though I was praying for dry weather to let me pick cotton and combine beans. I'm not really sure I believed it myself, but it seemed important to convince others, as if by convincing them, I'd also come under conviction. My Bible was dogeared in the book of Job (still is!), and I have learned that, while we may not understand why God lets Christians go through tough times, He can be the only Way we can get past them.

There is actually a progression, but one doesn't realize it at the time. As the financial burdens become harder to bear, the man (and I'm not being sexist here; it's just that most of them were men) tries to protect his family by keeping the news from them, until suddenly it seems that the roof falls in without warning. I liken it to the caveman philosophy: the man doesn't want to disturb the wife and babies with the news that a dragon is at the mouth of the cave, so he fights it alone; yet when the dragon whips the man and gets into the cave, it's too late to tell the family then! It's all too obvious.

It's also easy to fall into the trap of believing that God is personally mad at us, when things go bad. One could fill a library with volumes written to explain why bad things happen to good people, so I won't attempt to do that here. There is a notecard in my Bible from John Lundy, Senator Trent Lott's Chief of Staff, who is an old friend from neighboring Tribbett, and his parents had told him about our house fire. The note simply says, "Remember: God won't put on us more than we can stand." That maybe seems trite sometimes, but that doesn't make it any less true. John concluded simply, "If I can help you from here in D.C., just call me." He was Being There for us!

All this came back three years ago, when I had a phone call one night from a guy who identified himself as a resident of a south Mississippi town where my newspaper column runs. For twenty-five years, I have written a weekly newspaper column which has been in over one hundred papers nationally before that syndicate went bust. I picked up a few dozen of my oldest Southern papers to self-syndicate, all smaller dailies and weeklies. This man then declared, "You talked to me from one until four in the morning about fifteen years ago."

I couldn't connect him up, so went to my standard excuse: "Well, I've had Lyme Disease so I've got a medical excuse for forgetting things. What, were we on deer camp or duck camp together once?"

"No, it was when I called that Farm Suicide Hotline," he confessed. "I never connected the Bob Neill I talked to that night with the Robert Hitt Neill whose columns have been in our local paper down here for years, but today in your column you mentioned that you had once worked on a Farm Suicide

Hotline, and I told my wife that it had to be the same guy. Then I got to wondering: how many folks ever called y'all back?"

"Well, Mister, as far as I know, you're the only one who has," I answered.

"So I'm calling you back, to say thanks for talking to me that night. I didn't do it. I did lose my farm, but I kept my family and my faith, which you said were the most important things. I got a job, and my wife did too, and we saved the house, got the kids through school, and we're making it okay now. I thought I'd just call back and tell you thanks."

"Okay, since it's your nickel: why didn't you do it?" I asked. "What made the difference?"

He cogitated for a moment before replying, "You made me laugh. You told a story that, on the face of it, was somewhat tragic, but you put a spin on it that made it funny. When I finally hung up that night, I put the pistol back in the drawer, thinking I'd do it tomorrow. I went through eighteen months of tomorrows before I unloaded that pistol, but every time I'd get it out, I'd picture that big black foreman of yours, Bumpy, throwing that toolbox down the turnrow, and all the tools scattering out across the cotton field – and I'd laugh. You know," he mused pensively, "You can't hardly shoot yourself when you're laughing!"

"Cap'n, I don't know how many other people's days you've made, but you sure made mine. Thank you for calling me back," I exclaimed.

Never heard from him again, but during the next few days I tried to relate that callback to the other half-dozen men who manned that Mississippi Farm Suicide Hotline: Johnny, Philo, Joe G, Denny, and Jim. More than we six had originally volunteered to go through the counseling sessions required (not even compensated for gas money!) to man that hotline, but after the first two weeks of calls, several dropped out, saying it was too hard. I agree: it was the toughest thing I've ever done, including combat. In combat, there's a rush, but there was not even that on the FSH. Sometimes you lost them right on the phone.

During that time – the late 1980s – farm-related suicides went up nationally over 20%, and farm-related "accidental" deaths (my quotes) went up about 30%. Double indemnity life insurance took care of the farmer's family better.

I had to build a mental box to lock those memories in, just like I had earlier built to cope with combat stuff, as well as a Pain Box after the broken back. Yet several years after that Rural Crisis Committee's duties were taken over, thankfully, by the state Ag Department, I was working as a news and advertising consultant at a local television station when the receptionist called me to the lobby: "Uncle Bob, there's a deputy sheriff here to see you."

There was. He introduced himself to me and asked if I had time to accompany him on a "rescue mission." When I was in the car, he explained, "You worked on that Farm Suicide Hotline several years ago, remember?" I nodded, wondering if I was being arrested now for fielding those calls. "My son called you one day, and he made it through those days because of that call. This morning, there's a farmer locked in his pickup on the levee here. He got his production loan for the farm yesterday and went to the casino last night to try to make it bigger, but he lost it all, and now he's holding a gun to his head in the truck. I'm sure he knows you because of your books and columns, and you've got the experience needed to talk yourself into the pickup and to help us talk him out of it."

It wasn't easy, but as far as I know, that man is still alive today.

I don't ever want to do that again, but in hard times, the key is to not let a friend or family member isolate himself or herself when things go bad. "Being there," is a popular saying these days, and there's a lot to that. Just Be There, and let God use you as He will to help tote the load.

I was extremely fortunate that God had blessed me with

some ability to write and speak, and my writings began being published about the time the farming was going to the dogs for a whole generation, nationally. There is a card over my desk depicting a small knight in shining armor holding a sword which looks too large for him to swing, and facing a huge, fire-breathing dragon. The caption underneath says, "No Guts, No Glory!" Dave Bradham sent it to me when I left farming and went to writing books. Dave was one of my closest childhood friends and high school classmates, and he was also Being There for me!

In all of my writings and speakings, I make a conscious effort to work in a witness, though my main thrust is entertaining stories. It seemed to work. It wasn't until I got convicted that staying away from church wasn't the right thing to do and rejoined the fellowship, that I realized that maybe God had used me in spite of myself. That is nothing to be the least bit proud of, atall.

Neither was mine and Ed's "Turtle Baptist Church." Withdrawing from your friends and from Christian fellowship is never the answer to whatever ails you, I found that out.

To be willing to love someone is to take a risk. Granted, it may backfire, because you may get hurt. But to go through life being unwilling to love, and thereby unwilling to let others love you, is worse than anything else. Bless Betsy's heart, she hung in there with me while I attempted to limit my list of folks whom I was willing to love to her and the kids, my old circle of long-time hunting buddies, and a select group of church friends (selected by me, of course). Joe and Susan seemed to take it as a challenge to love me in spite of myself, and they beat the walls down on a regular basis, though I'd rebuild them after they left.

Others kept after me, Beau in particular. Mike and Frances moved away, but wrote and called regularly to say they were praying for me whether I liked it or not. I wasn't much fun to be around, I know that now. It would have been a lot easier for those folks to just forget about Mullygrub Neill. But they kept loving me and praying for me.

Finally, Beau and Mark Kurtz hemmed me up to go on a weekend retreat known around here as an "Emmaus Walk." I just flat ran out of excuses, and had to go, or else get another brother, and I had spent forty years breaking this one in right. But I made it plain that I didn't want to, and made up my mind that I was NOT going to have a good time!

I didn't.

First thing out of the box was, this guy who said he loved my books wanted to hug me. Then several men who didn't even know I wrote wanted to hug me. If I'd been able, I'd have gone home then, but Beau and Mark had brought me over to the place, and then left me without a vehicle. When I went to bed that night, the mattress and springs were far too soft -- I have a broken back, so need to sleep on a hard bed. That next morning, I was hurting physically as well as mentally, and didn't care who knew it. It was a bad day, simply because I made up my mind that it was going to be thataway early on.

But that night, when I went to bed, I found that the same guy who had first tried to hug me had gone upstairs and taken a dormitory door off its hinges to slide under my mattress. Allen Shaffer wanted to be sure that I slept well the second night. I did.

I finished the retreat still in a huff, but that one act of love broke through to me. After I got back home, I was convicted of what a knothead I had been, and within a week, I sat down and wrote a letter of apology to every member of the Team, and every Pilgrim. That was in 1990. I led the music on an Emmaus Walk for Rob Burnham last September (2009) and two of the Team members made occasion to sidle up to me and confide, "You know, I still have that letter you wrote nearly twenty years ago!"

Within the month after my Emmaus experience, I returned to church after an absence of almost three years. My choir chair was still there, I found, and Gene leaned over to whisper at the first practice, "I still don't eat onions on Wednesday nights!"

Took me another year or so to get back to going to the old Couples Class, and when I did, Ed was teaching out of the book of Nehemiah, along about where the Hebrew Children were rebuilding the wall of Jerusalem. Suddenly it hit me: like the Israelites, I had been in exile; but when I returned from my captivity, there was no need for me to go to the trouble of rebuilding my walls. They were still just fine. I was carrying them around with me, had them on wheels so to speak, still keeping folks at a distance, even though I was back in church. They're still there, at times, but He's let me know that they ain't His walls, either.

He's Everywhere, He's Everywhere!

Too often, I believe, we tend to put God in a box: a local box, too. Congregations get used to doing things certain ways, and before long, you're hearing those Seven Last Words Of The Church again: "We never did it that way before!"

Our family has been blessed, in one sense, by having the previously-explained interdenominational outlook: My Daddy was Presbyterian, Momma was Episcopalian; Betsy's Daddy was Catholic, her Momma was Methodist. At least we have used that experience to allow others to express their beliefs without stomping all over them. Then, if they're wrong, we can always straighten them out later, right?

One summer I was laid up with an operation and subsequent infection that almost cost me my foot. Doctor Sandifer said someone must have sneezed in the operating room. At any rate, I was condemned to crutching between the bedroom, bathroom, and den, with my foot propped up at all times possible for three months.

We were having some soil testing done on the farm that year, and since I was unable to shoulder my part of the field work, it fell to me to coordinate with the guy who was doing the testing. James would drop by my house almost every day for an hour or so discussion of what the Bumpy Cut or the Pea Hole or the Thirty-Two Acre Piece needed: lime, potash, whatever. We became friends quickly.

James was a Mormon.

I was a Baptist.

I'm not sure there has ever been a period in my life when I learned as much theology -- especially in self-defense. James and I took it as a challenge, in gentle fun, of course, to convert the other to his faith. I say he started it; he says I did. The discussions got so regular -- he had a true captive audience -- that he even brought his jar of Postum to leave in our kitchen. Mormons, at that time anyway, were forbidden to drink coffee, cokes, or any caffeinated beverages. So he brought his Postum to join me in the cup of Slung Coffee I always offered him, pretending to be hurt when he wouldn't accept my black brew.

Let me inject here that I make the best coffee in the world: it's the old-style boiled coffee with the grounds in the bottom of the pot, and one doesn't drink the last swallow in the cup. If I'm making it outside over a campfire, using the pot with the bail handle, I settle the grounds when it's at the right stage by centrifugal force, by swinging it around my head about three times. Same motion you'd use to pop the head off of a cottonmouth. Betsy won't let me do that anymore inside, since I repainted the kitchen ceiling. Anyway, the smell is hard to resist for even a Mormon.

When we burnt the house nearly fifteen years later, we found his Postum still in the back of one of the top kitchen cabinets.

We had at each other all summer, until the testing was finished and my foot had healed, but neither of us converted. However, I did learn what Mormons believed, at that time, and still have the publications he gave me; they didn't burn. And he learned not only what Baptists believe, but got a pretty good dose of Presbyterian and Episcopalian theology, as well.

He gave me the ultimate compliment a year or so later, for he continued to come around on occasion, and a couple of times even brought pairs of young missionaries around to make their presentations. After the second time, I asked him privately what the idea was: if he hadn't been able to sway me, he knew those youngsters sure couldn't.

His reply was that, if the young missionaries could survive my theology and my coffee, he knew they were ready to tackle the rest of the world! I still treasure that time of friendship.

Our closest neighbors are Mennonites, and our last secretary, Sandy, is Mennonite, so we feel close to that denomination. Matter of fact, after attending Sandy's wedding that spring, I considered joining the Mennonite church, but my beard is snow white, which just doesn't go with still-blonde hair. Although Lord knows that's rapidly changing, too! It also seems to be a lot simpler and less expensive to marry off a daughter in that denomination.

When we first bought this house in 1970, it needed a lot of work. While we did a lot of it ourselves, I am not a competent carpenter: if it doesn't fit after the first cut, then my idea is to get a bigger hammer. We therefore needed lots of carpentry help, and many of our Mennonite friends around town were wonderful carpenters. We asked Virgil Kohen and Robert Ratzloff to do the hard part.

The house had no heat, and it was the middle of a pretty hard winter, for our part of the country. There was a stove in the kitchen, so I brought over my big coffeepot and made Slung Coffee twice a day, Mennonites not being coffeeshy like Mormons.

This is a real tribute to a denomination which actively demands that its members live like Christians during the week as well as Sunday: whenever Virgil and Robert could be coaxed into a coffee break, they looked at their watches when they sat down, and looked again when they stood up. Their employer was not billed for their time spent drinking coffee. Of course, my coffee is so good, that may have been just as great a compliment to my brewing ability.

It was over these coffee cups that Robert and I engaged in hours of theological discussion during that winter, and I learned a great deal about his faith. I can only hope he learned as much about mine. Between James and Robert, and mine and Betsy's denominational backgrounds, I do know that when the church needed a Doctrinal Training teacher for a course called "Beliefs of Other Kinds," I was eminently qualified to volunteer.

When we moved our home to the country in 1978, the move went fine, but the subsequent total remodeling dragged for several months, then came to a complete stop. The out-of-town company we had hired to remove the roof, then put it back on, ended up in jail. We had a leaky empty house that was rapidly deteriorating. Virgil, Robert, and all the other carpenters we knew to call were already on jobs. We tried to cope ourselves, but the job was just too much for us. Other things we needed to be spending time on were neglected as we worked desperately on what seemed to be rapidly becoming a salvage operation instead of a big old home remodeling. Among the things neglected was our planning for the church youth program, which we were still nominally in charge of.

Finally, in frustration, we sat down and prayed about it, which seems to be a pattern in my life. Mike Bedford once told a parable about the little boy with the fishing pole whose line looped once over the rod tip. His father asked if he needed help to straighten it out. Stubbornly, the kid refused, and began to swing his rod from side to side, to flip the line back over. The problem, predictably, worsened. The father reached to take the rod tip, but the boy angrily declared that he could do it himself, and continued to flail away. Finally, the son had a snarled ball attached to the end of his pole. At that point, he turned to his father and asked, "Daddy, can you straighten this out for me?"

We'd messed it up good, and as usual, had to ask our Father to straighten out a really tough snarl instead of a simple loop.

Betsy and I prayed, then tackled the youth schedule for the next year. You wouldn't believe how things fell into place;

well, maybe you would, come to think of it. Anyhow, the speakers and places were all available on the dates we needed them. A year's worth of planning was done, essentially, in one day, when we had put it off for maybe six weeks.

And late that afternoon, a strange pickup drove up in the driveway. An older man got out, introduced himself as Allen Collins, and said he understood we needed a crew of carpenters, and he had a crew that had just finished a job. We made a couple of calls to check his references, and hired him on the spot, though he said he'd work with any others we might have hired. He left, and within an hour, another pickup pulled up with two bearded Mennonites who looked familiar.

We had met Mervin Boehs and his wife Carrie on a Sunday School visitation. He and his brother Emory were carpenters, and had just finished a job. They had heard that we might need a crew. Yes, they'd work with the Collins crew.

That next morning after we had finished the youth schedule, eight carpenters showed up for work. Before noon, the plumber and electrician both arrived, and by that evening, someone was under the house assembling the heating ductwork. We moved back into the house in July, a year's work having been finished in six months. After we had finally asked our Father to help!

Guess where we held that month's Youth Fellowship?

It was at a similar youth meeting out here (we averaged at least one either youth or Sunday School fellowship at Brownspur every five weeks for a period of several years) when we were miraculously spared by a tornado. The weather was threatening when we picked the kids and other chaperones up at the church, but that's normal for more than half the year in the Mississippi Delta, source of the world's most powerful and treacherous thunderstorms.

We were playing some type parlor games in our guesthouse, the remodeled old plantation commissary store which we still call "The Store," with the kids -- adults pitching right in too -- when my ears popped. I have a low pressure sensitivity that causes such a reaction when storms are near. It's even awakened me in the middle of the night. I slid open the patio door, and the rain was going around IN CIRCLES HORIZONTALLY!

Our youngest and a friend were in the house across the patio, watching television. B.C. and Tina were only seven at the time, and I knew I had to get them to safety, as well as the older youth. I yelled at the chaperones, "Get the kids into the bathrooms! Now!" and dashed out of The Store. The bathrooms were the only windowless rooms, of course. As I ran out the door headed to the house, I heard Xan yell behind me, "The bathrooms? What kinda game are we gonna play now, Uncle Bob?"

I sprinted into the house, veered into the library with the storm roaring in my ears, grabbed B.C. and Tina by their shoulders, and jerked them into yet another bathroom for cover. As I did so, I glanced at the barometer on the den wall.

I stuck the frightened girls into the bathtub, told them to put their heads between their legs and be still, and sprinted back to The Store to make sure that the church youth had followed my bellowed instructions. As I passed the barometer, I glanced at it again. It had fallen over a whole point in less than a minute!

But that meant the system was here. The tornado roared over the house, touched back down before it got out of the yard, and blew away the house across the road from us. It had bounced completely over our home, without harming anything!

Of course, all this happened in seconds, and when the scare was over, we had a lot of fun kidding Xan about mistaking my shouted warning as signaling another parlor game.

A similar shout in the dark that startled me almost had tragic results once. Our pastor was finishing up his last semester at seminary, a three-hour drive from here. Several of us deacons were drafted to chauffeur Mike back and forth after his weekends, while Frances and the boys were staying in The Store and house hunting during the week. At the time, I owned a big Chevrolet custom van, and it had a bed in back. Mike preferred to ride with me, since we had to leave by 3:00 a.m. to get him to class before 7:30, and he could sleep during the drive. And he needed the rest, to be ready for classes.

Usually, there would be two deacons as escorts, to keep each other company on the six-hour round trip. However, on one particular morning, my partner backed out, so I was driving alone. Mike politely stayed awake for about twenty miles, then excused himself for the couch in back, and went to sleep.

Soon thereafter, I ran into a heavy fog. But at 4:00 a.m. on Monday, there isn't much traffic, so I didn't reduce my speed at all. Matter of fact, since there was no one to talk to, I gradually increased the pace. After all, how could a Highway Patrolman catch me if he couldn't see me? (Can I classify that as "confessing my sins"?) At any rate, I must have been doing almost ninety on a dark and foggy but familiarly flat straight highway at 5:00 a.m., when suddenly a voice cried out, "Good Lord! Do you know how fast you're going where you can't see?!"

I'd never heard Mike shout before, and I almost ran off the road in surprise. He later said that when he awoke and looked out, he assumed we had crashed and were on the Express Bus to Heaven, speeding through the Clouds of Glory!

In our travels these past few years since I began speaking and publishing, we've met many wonderful people across America who have enriched our lives. One such couple we encountered on a spring visit to South Louisiana.

Betsy and I had an extra day between speaking engagements in Louisiana and Texas, and detoured down to Holly Beach, which advertises itself as "The Cajun Riviera." Of course, this was the off season, you have to realize that; but we're talking only a couple of telephones in the whole town during the winter. We stayed in a room with -- praise the Lord!

-- no television; just the roaring of the surf singing us a lullaby as we walked along the deserted Gulf beach in the twilight. The bedroom was less than fifty yards from the water, so we were lulled to sleep by the muffled crash and swish of the waves.

That next morning, our hostess brought us a pot of coffee in bed, and passed the time of day for awhile, sharing a cup of the rich Louisiana brew. Jewell said that she and her husband had stopped there years ago enroute to his new job in Florida, and had just never left. It's that kind of place.

We ventured down the beach aways once the sun had warmed things up, and ran into a couple who were doing a little work on their beachside home. Turned out that Ron was an artist: a seashell artist. He proudly showed us some of his creations, including a real, sho'nuff "Boobee Bird." This couple had also been a "we just never left" case. Now they're planning the rest of their career in The Cajun Riviera; and Ron dates the change in his life to Easter week several years ago.

He had suffered a disabling injury, and had come South to try to recover his health. Walking on the beach was part of his therapy, and he began to pick up interesting shells, driftwood, and other flotsam he noticed. His art form -- fitting those objects together to make interesting sculptures -- began simply as a diversion, and grew into a business.

But his life still lacked purpose, it seemed. Then one spring day he found the skull of a "crucifix fish" -- don't ask me for scientific terms here, but the bleached bone on the inside forms a cross, with the vaguest hint of a figure hanging on it. If one looks at it closely, there seem to be holes in the hands, feet, and the chest. I'm looking at one right now, that Ron gave me. He sells them, framed upright in a plastic box. But mine is not like the special one he has framed on his mantle, which he found on a beach walk that day.

They aren't uncommon, but when he picked his up, there seemed to be something special about it. True, it was larger than usual, but then he noticed that the figure on the cross had been pierced though the side by a small sharp object, which was still imbedded in the bone.

It was then that he remembered the date: Good Friday! The very day that Christ's side was pierced by the Roman spear as He hung on the Cross at Golgotha -- the place of the skull.

He said that standing on the beach holding that crucifix fish skull in his hand, he suddenly realized that this day, that figure was pierced for him! And this skull was his own personal reminder of that fact -- placed on the beach only for him. Ron says his physical and mental and spiritual healing began that Good Friday.

Of course, we're all grownups; we know that coincidences happen, and one shouldn't read too much into them. The scientists later told Ron that the sharp object was a sea urchin spine, which is not nearly hard enough to penetrate solid bone, much less to stick all the way through that figure on the cross. Some special circumstance must have softened a spot on the skull, and that particular spine must have been unusually stiff. Maybe the sea urchin tapped a baby crucifix fish, which grew bone around the spine, then died. Maybe it was just a soft-headed fish, or a tough urchin. Maybe. . . .

Ron had no maybes. He knew that he needed some sign that his life was worth something more than just limping up and down a beach, feeling sorry for himself. He sells sculptures now, and skulls in boxes, though there's one large crucifix fish skull on his mantle that he'll never sell. He doesn't have to; the price has been paid.

And not just for Ron; for all of us.

So I can't help but think of Ron, and Jesus, every time I look at the crucifix fish skull he gave to me.

It's strange how sometimes a gift is given with one supposed meaning -- say, humor -- and then it turns out to be something entirely different.

At an outdoor writers' convention, we had an auction to benefit the organization's scholarship fund, among other things, and a writer from North Carolina had donated some very unusual items: shooting range pop-up targets, used for training U.S. Special Forces. The nearly-life-size silhouettes are made of hard plastic, and had been well used, that was obvious from all the bullet holes and bayonet slashes. Each figure was painted to resemble a Russian soldier, complete with the red star on his helmet, and the donating writer, who was an ex-Green Beret himself, told us the history of the targets.

Seems the new administration, what with the change in the status of the Soviet Union from Number One foe to being a possible friend, had decreed that the Russian-resembling targets must now be replaced with something more politically correct. Tom made us know that these figures he had donated were true collector's items. As the organization's President, I began the bidding and bought one for son Adam's Christmas present.

The auction ended close to midnight, and as I stood in line to pay for my prize, I noticed the lady behind me had also won one of the targets. "A real fine hang-on-the-wall collector's item, right, Pris?" I enthused.

She shook her head and spoke softly. "No. I'm going to set this in the yard and use it for daily target practice. And every time that I hit it will bring me immense pleasure."

I frowned, puzzled. "You'll put more holes in it? Why?"

Priscilla answered quietly, in a voice that I now noticed her accent in more, for some reason. "I was born in Hungary; my father was a doctor, treating World War II refugees in the castle at Budapest, and the Russians took him outside and executed him. They killed two of my brothers, executing one in the town square with a tank flamethrower. We were of the royal Hapsburg family, you see. The rest of us fled, trying to reach Austria, but we were caught by the Russians less than three kilometers from the border, just days before the war ended. Only about 75 of us survived the march back, though more than 300 began it. I was six years old, and spent the next seven years in prison camps. My mother died in one."

I was not the only one now listening to her story, told almost without emotion. The line to pay passed us by. Mary Ann borrowed my hanky. David Hawkins touched my target reverently. Priscilla continued, "I escaped seven times, but was caught six. When my sister and I finally got away, it was by jumping from a cattle car bound for Siberia. The railway was littered with bodies thrown from the trains anyway, so we played dead as the soldiers checking the tracks kicked us, knowing that to flinch or groan would bring a bullet. We lay still in the snow until night, then crawled away and finally made it to the border."

Mary Ann reached to touch the red star on my target. It seemed different now to all of us. "Good Lord," Hawk breathed.

Pris nodded agreement. "It was my faith in the Good Lord that brought me through; that, and an ability to see His beauty in the world. Even when we only had a crate for a dinner table, I'd still manage to find a flower or two to stick in a tin can for beauty."

Her husband Cliff nodded, "Even today, she has flowers all over the yard and the house, and thanks the Lord for their beauty."

Merry Christmas, Adam. That target is a true collector's item, all right. But Tom had no idea of the real meaning of his donation that night. Like the old violin in "The Touch Of The Master's Hand" poem, the price of those Red Star targets would have been more had we all known Priscilla's story beforehand.

Soon after that, there were two special occasions to get outside and observe the stars and heavenly sights. Late that fall, there was a meteor shower which extended through three nights, one of which Betsy and I spent out on the balcony until well after midnight. I'll bet I saw fifty falling stars, and one went over so close that I was rather surprised to see neighbor Cameron Dean at church the next Sunday, for I figured the meteor had to have landed smack-dab on his house, a couple of miles down the old Black Dog dummy line from Brownspur. Lying there on the balcony, I tried to pick out constellations and stars I had taken sextant shots on to navigate back during my Navy days. It's amazing how much I've forgotten.

Then we were treated to a total eclipse of a full moon just a couple of weeks later, on one of the clearest nights I've ever seen. Somehow I was under the impression that it was in the Bible that eclipses only occur when it's cloudy, but this one broke the rule. We screwed the rifle scope up to full power and watched in fascination as the shadow crept across the face of the full moon. Once the moon was blotted out, it was truly amazing how much starlight illuminated the Earth below. The stars shone brightly enough to guide one's journey, just as that Star led the Three Kings of Orey and Tar nearly two thousand years ago.

Out here at Brownspur, it used to be a rule that a house couldn't have a nightlight. What with the crime problem nowadays, a couple of families have resorted to putting up a light, and I understand that: safety first, of course. But too many lights spoil the view, and I didn't realize that fully until my New York daughter came home for Christmas one year.

Christie's plane was coming into Memphis after dark that night, so I made the three-hour drive to meet her at the airport. By the time we got her luggage and a bite to eat, we were nine o'clock coming out of the city down Highway 61. It was therefore after midnight when we turned off of 61 onto the Tribbett Road, headed toward Brownspur six miles further. We lapsed into silence as we drove through familiar territory which she had not seen for over two years.

It was a beautiful clear night, I now noticed, away from the homes or businesses with nightlights and the small towns with streetlights that line the length of Highway 61. We were halfway between Hollyknowe and the Brownspur turnoff when Chris suddenly cried, "Daddy, stop the van!"

I protested, "Hey, we're only a couple miles from the house. Surely you can wait that long!"

"No!" she declared. "Stop the van, now!"

"Well, when you gotta go, you gotta go," I figured, and slammed on the brakes. I didn't even pull to the side of the road, since both of us knew the chance of another vehicle coming along at this hour was nil.

"Cut off the headlights," she ordered.

I did so, understanding the need for privacy. My New York City daughter then stepped from the van, walked around and stood in the middle of the road, gazing upward reverently. Puzzled, I, too, looked up through the windshield, but I didn't see anything out of the ordinary. I rolled down my window and leaned out, looking at the night sky: there was no moon atall, just billions of stars against the velvet black sky. No airplanes, no narc helicopters, no satellites, no UFOs – nothing that I could see for her to be looking at. Finally, I got out and stood next to her, trying to see what she was seeing. "What are we lookin' at?" I asked.

"You can see the stars!" Christie breathed.

We stood there in the middle of the dark road until I got a crick in my neck. Finally, Chris shook her head in admiration of the Heavens over Brownspur. "Gosh, I'd almost forgotten!" she said reverently. "Y'all can still see the stars down here." Of course, one cannot see the stars in most towns and cities, because of the city lights. We drove on home in silence.

But I had to wonder, after I took her back to the airport a few days later: maybe that's part of what's wrong with the world today. Maybe the folks who really run this country all live in the big cities; and maybe it's been so long since they've seen the stars that they've all forgotten about the Heavens -- and the One who made them. Maybe they've gone so long with nothing to look up for, that they've forgotten how to look up, or why they even need to. Can metropolitan residents imagine the Power of the Christmas Star, much less look to it for their own guidance?

113

Would modern-day Wise Men have a chance to find the Stable of the Christ Child, if it were located in New York City?

Step outside the next clear night and look Heavenward. Don't take the stars -- or The Star -- for granted. Then thank the God who made this world, the heavens over it, and us.

The Holy Ghost Has A Funny Bone!

On the wall of our kitchen is a charcoal sketch of Jesus. But it's different than most other pictures of the Lord. He's laughing!

Maybe this is sacrilegious, and all of our food will spoil or something. Nonetheless, I think it's great that the Bible teaches "A Merry Heart doeth good, like medicine," and similar scriptures. We all know that Christ has been described as a "Man of sorrows," and rightly so: He took upon Himself the sins of the world in general and mine in particular. Yet He taught that love is the greatest Christian virtue; that's how others will know we're His disciples. Joy is one of the Gifts of the Spirit. Granted that I have an especially finite human mind, but I still can't think of love and joy without extrapolating happiness and laughter from those Gifts. Excuse me, if I'm wrong.

The Easter after our fires had to be one of the most joyous holidays we've had as a family, though we were in the middle of healing and rebuilding, and deeply in debt as a result -- it would eventually result in a bankruptcy. All of us had been hurt and lost prized possessions and dreams. We joked about the old saying, "If it weren't for bad luck, I'd have no luck atall!" Our three neighbors, who had troubles of their own as well, began to speak of a curse on Brownspur, seriously. There seemed to be a cloud over all of us.

With all the horrors we had gone through, and knowing more were still to be endured, our kids could have covered themselves with sackcloth and ashes. Yet within half an hour, we were all rolling on the floor in laughter, as Adam and B.C., mostly, recalled not the bad stuff, but the funny things that happened during the fires.

We'd already discussed how, in the first one, my hand was badly burnt getting the grease pot outside, and when I chunked out the flaming skillet, part of my skin went with it. Yet in running from the back door to the garage, where the fire hose was, the porch telephone rang. And I stopped and answered it, leaving more skin on the phone!

Deadeye was close enough to the same telephone during the second fire to hear B.C. call 911. He swore the conversation he heard went something like this: "A fire! At Bob Neill's house! East of Leland, south of highway 82. . . . Bob Neill's house is on fire!. . . . Just off the Tribbett Road. . . . It's on Geneill Road!. . . . Geneill Road!!. . . . G-E-N-E. . . . I AM SPELLING IT, YOU STUPID ILLITERATE DUMMY!!"

Adam claims that I took the extension ladder and had lapped the house three times before he tackled me and made me put it up against the roof. Then the upstairs balcony door was locked, and neither of us had a key. His shouted conversation down to B.C. to instruct her to throw up his car key ring would have stunned car manufacturers the world over, who probably have no inkling of the number of terms for the little secret compartment right under the car radio, where he kept the keys. When he finally unlocked the balcony door, he for some reason turned and threw the car keys across the yard. Took us a day to find them, and then it was by accident.

Deadeye threw a fully charged fire hose -- had to have weighed nearly a hundred pounds -- twenty feet up to me on the roof, on his first try. I didn't even have to bend over! Then as we were crawling into the inferno, Beau suddenly turned to Adam and said, "I want to know just two things: where do you keep the fireworks, and where do you keep the shotgun shells or rifle cartridges, up here?"

The kids told these and other stories that Easter night until we all had tears of laughter in our eyes, and suddenly I realized I needed to go somewhere and thank God for children who were able to take adversity and find a lighter side to it. I did so, and have many times since.

When my first book, *THE FLAMING TURKEY*, came out, the wife of my high school superintendent called to say that her husband had had a heart attack, but now she knew that he was going to survive, thanks to the book, which someone had sent him in the hospital. "He was reading a copy, started laughing, and FELL OUT OF BED!" she exclaimed. "If that didn't kill him, and he can laugh like that, he'll make it!" They did put the rails up after that, though.

A lady from Georgia really got to me about the same book. Her son, a college student, had been diagnosed with a brain tumor just before Christmas, and the doctors had prepared them for the worst. "Take him home and have a good Christmas," they instructed, clearly implying that it might be the boy's last one. "Bring him back after New Years, and we'll operate, but it doesn't look good at all."

His mother called to relate this in early January. Seems that a cousin had given the kid a copy of *FLAMING TURKEY*, and he had read it immediately, laughing all the way through. Then he read it again, the same way, before New Years, coming into his parents' room to read passages for them to laugh at with him. When the day finally came, they checked into the hospital, and he was wheeled off for pre-op X-rays.

An hour later, they notified his folks that the hospital's X-ray machine was busted, and they were going to transport him to another hospital for X-rays. That one didn't work either.

Maybe you're ahead of me here. The mother said they simply could not find the large tumor that had threatened her son's life a couple of weeks before. She quoted the Proverb to me about a Merry Heart, and when I demurred, she said softly, "I know. There was a Southwide prayer chain lifting him up, and our church was deep in prayer, and some of the doctors were Christians, and our family was praying. . .but I'm just covering all the bases. It did make all of us happy for part of what was a sad time, just watching him reading your book. And who knows? He definitely had a Merry Heart during the holidays. Thanks."

Please don't get the wrong idea. I'm just telling it like she did, and it brought tears to my eyes. Like you, I know it was the prayers that healed him. That was in January 1987; this past spring of 2010 this young man's cousin called to ask for prayers for Landy once again. He's married and got a couple of kids, and had a seizure: the doctors had found another tumor and are treating him for it, 23 years after the first one was healed.

A judicial insertion of humor can often defuse tempers, which sometimes surface even in church. There was one deacons' meeting I recall back when the Presbyterian denomination was undergoing a schism. People on both sides of the issue were understandably upset, and we deacons were divided as well. I don't recall what the particular issue that night was that had gotten everybody at loggerheads, but the church treasurer finally made the remark that we'd better get something settled soon, or else we could just close the doors, because all the church collections were steadily going down, down, down. "Pretty soon, we're going to have to cut the lights out," Jimmy opined.

Just as seriously and straight-faced as I could, I proposed, "Why don't we try taking up the offerings BEFORE the sermon, instead of AFTER?"

The preacher almost bit his pipe stem in two, but the remark was greeted with howls of laughter by my fellow deacons. Others began to propose similar light-hearted solutions, and we left the meeting in good humor again (except maybe the preacher was a little miffed; he still wasn't sure I was kidding), though without finding a way to keep the church together.

Incidentally, it was a church collecting the Sunday offering which convinced me that the Baptists were worth looking at when or if my church split. There had been a rare earthquake in the Mississippi Delta one Sunday morning, in the middle of the service. Our pastor calmly said, as the exposed beams rocked crazily, "Please stand and exit out the front doors, quickly, but without panic. Stay calm." We did so.

Outside, the quaking had subsided, but we could see that other churches had vacated, too. Across the street from us stood the Baptist congregation, in similar awe at such an earth-shaking occurrence. Yet the Baptist deacons had not been deterred from the purpose they had obviously been performing when the quake hit. They were calmly still passing the offering plates through the crowd in the street! Now, that was serious Christianity, I thought!

Our Baptist youth group recently took a look at how other folks live, while practicing some pretty serious Christianity themselves. Accompanied by half a dozen chaperones, they set out for Fort Worth, Texas, for a week to help with a Habitat For Humanity building project. Everyone pitched in, sheetrocking a home which another group had framed up, and an older local man wandered up to observe while Nancy, the little redhead who had helped us with the Sealing Party a couple of years before, was operating an electric saw, cutting sheetrock. As she paused, he tried to make conversation.

"So, you're a real sheetrocker, huh, lady?" he asked.

Nancy had just been operating the saw, plus she has a chronic hearing loss anyway. Witnesses said she jerked upright and shrieked in indignation.

"A STREETWALKER?!" she yelled. "Mister, let me tell you..."

They got her quieted down, and really, considering the

neighborhood, it might have been a natural conclusion had she actually heard what she thought she heard. But the elderly man departed; he was mature enough to know better than to stand before the wrath of a redheaded woman, be she streetwalker or good-looking sheetrocker!

We've already discussed to some extent how sex, or the rumors thereof, often rears its not-so-ugly head in church, and that isn't just limited to elderly men, or even adults. Not long after we returned home from the service, I hydroplaned and wrecked my pickup truck, breaking four vertebrae and crushing my chest. The hospital stay was over a month, and my recuperation lasted most of the next two years. I had to farm with a walking cane in the pickup gunrack.

During that time, when I had to confine myself to mostly non-physical exercises, two of my buddies were serving tours in Viet Nam, and their wives, both hometown girls my age, were left alone with their infants in apartments in town. Betsy and I struck up a several-night-a-week bridge quartet with Jody and Rachel, both of whom had been high school friends.

Rachel was also a Presbyterian, and since we often played bridge on Saturday nights, Betsy and I often offered to pick her and the baby up for church the next morning. One Sabbath, our daughter Christie woke up with the croup, so Betsy sent me to church alone, except that I stopped to pick up Rachel on the way, as previously arranged. We came walking in together right before services started, and of course, sat together.

Larkin Tucker later told me that his own young daughter Michelle, who was maybe four at the time, leaned over to him and whispered suspiciously, "That's Twistie's daddy. But that ain't Twistie's momma!"

No telling what the older folks thought!

Back during the time when my leading the church music had led to rumors of my messing around with not one, not two, but maybe all three of the church piano players, who were

120

having to help me learn the melody on Baptist hymns, another deacon and I took a load of clothes to a man whose trailer had burned. He thanked us and offered a cup of coffee, and in the course of the conversation screwed up his courage and asked me point-blank, "Listen: I heard Betsy had caught you messing around with another woman in the church and kicked you out. Is that true?"

I had already heard the rumors, so simply shrugged and grinned, "Well, she hadn't when I left home a few minutes ago, but if my stuff's in the driveway when I get back, can I spend the night with you here?" Of course, I then went on to explain the misunderstandings, and the reasons thereunto. We all had a good laugh, and said our good-byes.

When I returned home, my stuff wasn't in the driveway, but the car of one of the piano players was. Her husband was gone to National Guard camp, and Betsy had invited her out for supper. I couldn't wait to spring the news: "Hey, guess what the latest rumor is!" I exclaimed, proceeding to relate the conversation.

"Wonder who the woman is?" Betsy speculated, grinning. "I bet it's you, Susan."

Susan considered seriously before replying, "No, I bet they're thinking about Vickie. You remember when. . . ."

Betsy interrupted, "No, I bet it's Frances! Remember when Bob was wiping the lipstick off her tooth and. . . ."

About that time, the phone rang. It was another deacon, with some furniture for the burned-out guy, and he wanted my help finding the man's new trailer, and unloading the stuff there. I agreed, and he said he'd be out in a few minutes. When I told the girls what he wanted, they apparently had the same thought at exactly the same moment. Agitators!

Betsy ran out and drove our van around to the side of the house, while Susan pulled her car into the garage next to my truck. Not five minutes later, the doorbell rang, and Betsy grabbed me. "Just let Susan answer it," she giggled.

121

Susan did. We heard the deacon stutter, "Er. . um. . .is, well, er. . . Hello. Is. . .is Bob here?" One could tell he had heard the rumors already.

And Susan called back down the hall, honey dripping from her voice, "Bob, dear? Can you come to the door? Charley's here." But her composure broke then, and she burst out laughing, joined by Betsy, to the confused, open-mouthed stare of my fellow deacon. They then proceeded to upbraid him for listening to the rumors. He shook his head as I finally followed him to his truck, with peals of laughter echoing behind us.

"Boy, you've sure got some weird women in your life!" he muttered sourly. I had to agree, but mentioned that they were fun weird, at least.

Okay, I know that they maybe were wrong for giving a bad impression, even in fun. Yet they were not only still giggling when I got back, but they had called half the women in the church to share the dumb rumors, and to tell about the great joke they had played on a deacon who probably had heard and believed the worst without seeking the truth from his fellow Christians. How much better would we all be, if when those type situations occur, we went straight to the horse's mouth, so to speak, and got the truth to begin with, rather than talking it around town?

And if the same rumor gets started about your deacon, I hope you can burst into laughter, and say, "What a stupid thing to say!"

I'll never forget the night after a deacons' meeting when Guy Pearson, Joe Simcox, and I were closing up the church, and a tramp walked in, asking for a handout. "Boys, I ain't had a good meal in a month. Reckon y'all could spare me ten bucks?"

He was an older man who looked vaguely familiar to me, but I couldn't place him. His clothes were rumpled, and bits of cotton lint stuck to them, as well as to his stubbly beard. As he talked, I suddenly recalled where I had seen him. At the time, I was operating our family cotton gin north of town. Just that morning, I had seen a fellow climbing down from one of the trailers loaded with cotton on the gin yard, and when we had pulled that trailer up to gin off, the sucker boy had thrown down a couple of empty whiskey bottles. Same guy! He'd spent the night in the warm cotton, just out of town.

And he did smell of whiskey, we noted. But if the man wanted a good meal, he had come to the right church, for we had enjoyed a fellowship supper before deacons' meeting, and the leftovers were in the refrigerator. Guy and Joe began to get out roast, rice and gravy, green beans, milk, and lemon pie. "Hey, we'll heat this up in a jiffy and sit with you," Joe enthused. "I might even have me some seconds on the pie. How about it, Bob?"

"Oh, no," the fellow protested, "Don't go to all that trouble! Just let me have ten bucks and I'll be on my way."

Guy was heating up a plate in the microwave. "Aw, it's no trouble, mister. Shoot, Jesus fed five thousand when they got hungry, and all He had were five loaves and two fishes. We've got a whole refrigerator full of food. Why don't we fix you something for the road, too?"

Again, the man protested, "Look, all I want is ten dollars to get me a little something, and I'll be out of your hair."

Joe was cutting pie for all of us now. "You aren't in our hair. This is church, man. Are you a Christian?"

The tramp bridled. "Christian! You all call yourselves Christians, and you won't even give a fellow down on his luck ten bucks? Some Christians you are!"

Guy tried to settle him down. "C'mon and eat, and then if you need some money for a room or something, we'll go down to the motel with you and pay for it. Here, have a seat." He placed the plates and glass on the table while I got out silverware.

The tramp flew into a rage. "Listen! I don't want your damned food! If you church folks ain't gonna gimme ten bucks, then to hell with you!" And he stormed out, slamming the door behind him.

Guy looked at us sorrowfully. "He'd have gone straight to the liquor store if we'd given him money. He didn't want food, he wanted drink!" We nodded, and ate our pie.

Isn't it sad that when God spreads a feast before us, we sometimes want to cling to a stale crust of bread and cheap whiskey?

Holy and Unholy Ghosts

Okay, here comes a little more controversy, at which some readers will snort, "This Neill guy is either lying, or off his rocker!"

I ain't lying, but won't argue about being off my rocker. After all, I just got out of prison.

Back in my speaking days, before the broke back came back to haunt me, I had contracted with the folks in Natchez who put on the annual Magnolia Storytelling Festival, to be one of the headliners of that event. After we had shaken hands on all the details, though, they had one last request, being Mississippi home folks, so to speak: "We know that you travel all over speaking, so do us this favor – if you are going to be coming back through here anytimes, give us a call and we'll set you up to speak before civic clubs, just to build interest in the Festival during these next few months."

I thought that was reasonable, and agreed. A couple months later I had an engagement in New Orleans, so notified them that I'd be coming back up Highway 61 afterward. They booked me to speak to some group at the King's Tavern, supposedly the oldest building in the state, which they gave me directions to get to. When I arrived late that morning, I had on shorts and tee shirt, so I got my sport coat, slacks, and tie out of the van and walked into the old wooden building. A waitress on the first floor, a restaurant, directed me to the second floor, where some ladies were setting up for the luncheon I was to speak for. Upstairs, I asked if there was a room where I could change into other clothes, and a lady pointed. "There's a small bedroom and bath on the third floor, right up those stairs. No one's in there, so make yourself at home." I went up.

I had changed, and was sitting down tying my shoes, when suddenly a puddle of water began appearing on the floor just in front of me, about three feet away. I finished my knot and looked up to see water running from a rafter – the room had exposed rafters – and forming a good-sized puddle on the hardwood floor. I went to the bathroom for a towel, placed it over the puddle to catch more water, and pulled a chair over to stand on and see where the water was coming from. There were no air conditioning ducts up there – it was a hot summer day – nor any water lines. I glanced out the window, and it was still a bright sunshiny day – no clouds.

Reaching up, I ran my hand along the topside of the rafter – it came away dusty, but the water immediately stopped running. I could feel nothing up there where it might have come from. I got off the chair and walked to small balcony to look up on the roof. It was a simple old shake shingle roof, and there were no air conditioning units, no water lines, no big birds – nothing there from which the water might have emanated. Shaking my head, I went back in, wiped up the dampness with the towel, spread that on the side of the bathtub, gathered up my clothes, and went downstairs.

I approached the lady and informed her, "Listen, I didn't do it, but you have a leak up there that I couldn't find, but it's stopped for right now, seems like." I told her what had happened. She listened, then laughed.

"Oh, that's just Madelyn!" she exclaimed.

"Er. . . I was the only one up there, Lady."

"You don't know about Madelyn?"

"Lady, I've never been here in my life, and have no idea who you're talking about."

She explained, "There's a legend here that the innkeeper

126

back in the 1800s was having an affair with a young woman named Madelyn, and one dark stormy night the lovers met, but his wife caught them in the act, and stabbed Madelyn to death. Then she made her husband help her place the body inside one of the brick fireplaces up here, and they bricked up the front of it, to hide the deed. Years ago, this place was remodeled, and that fireplace was unbricked, revealing a woman's skeleton, with a knife still embedded in the breastbone. Ever since then, there have been these type appearances, always seeming to be associated with water. Sometimes a couple will be sleeping up in that bedroom, and hear the door open, then footsteps squishing across the floor. When they cut the light on, there will be wet footprints leading to a puddle forming in front of the fireplace, like water dripping from a wet coat. Sometimes water faucets come on all by themselves. Sometimes puddles appear, like you saw, with no water fixtures anywhere near. We just attribute it to the ghost of Madelyn. She's never hurt anyone."

Okay, you're going to say you don't believe in ghosts, even though the Bible does mention ghosts (besides the Holy Ghost). I didn't either before that day.

But your Uncle Bob wiped up the water, and there was no other explanation for it.

Do-dee-do-dee, do-dee-do-dee.

I'm just going back to I Corinthians on this subject: "Now we see as through a glass darkly, but then we'll see as face to face." When I get up there, I'm gonna ask, and He's gonna tell me, and I'll bet we'll have a good laugh over it.

Ain't no such thing as UFOs either, but Brer Beau and I saw a large greenish-yellow light descend into the north newground pasture one night when we were frog-gigging right across the Little Canal. We cut the Jeep off, and watched as it silently settled just below the treetops on the ditchbank. We figured it had to be an airplane going down, or a parachute, so we climbed the ditchbank and yelled, but no one answered, though we could see the glow through the trees. We went back to the Jeep and drove back to the blacktop road, crossed the Canal on the bridge, then took the turnrow up to the newground pasture. Using our gigging spotlight we searched for whatever we'd seen, but there was no sign, nor answer to our calls. We gave up and went back to the house to wake up Big Robert, who called the airport 25 miles away to report a possible crash, but they had no reports of such, nor planes missing. The next morning, Daddy took a half-dozen tractor drivers and us up there, and we walked the pasture and woods, without finding a trace of anything that might have made that silent glowing descent. Nothing. UFO? I dunno.

On Woodstock Island late one afternoon I was sitting against a big sycamore tree calling occasionally for wild turkeys, but hadn't seen or heard anything all evening, and it was getting dusk. There was a white log out in front of me about forty yards, my range marker, in case a turkey got within shotgun range. I had settled into a routine of cutting my eyes far right, searching for movement, then barely turning my head so that I could cut my eyes far left, covering about a 200-degree arc with hardly any movement at all, for turkeys are very wary birds. So I had been scanning that big white log for a couple of hours.

They teach you in combat training to never look closely at an enemy soldier approaching your ambush position, for a good soldier develops that "Sixth Sense" of being able to feel the presence of someone or something watching you. Now I began to feel thataway: was a turkey gobbler responding silently to my calls? I eased my thumb to the shotgun safety and swung my eyes from left to right once more.

There was the head and shoulders of a man behind that white log, looking dead at me. He was covered with long reddish hair, and for a moment, I thought it might be a bear, but no, he did not have a bear's ears or snout. He was more flat-nosed, and we locked eyes for what seemed like five minutes before I suddenly wondered, "What if there are TWO of these suckers!" I cut my eyes right, barely moving my head, but clicking the gun safety to off, for a shot in defense, if need be. I didn't see anything else, and when I looked at the white log again, whatever it was, was gone. Yeti? Sasquatch? Bigfoot? I dunno.

But I guarantee that I grabbed my cushion and water bottle, and made a beeline for the Jeep!

Back in 1970, after the arrival of our second kid, we bought a big old home on Deer Creek in Leland, remodeled it to some extent, and lived in it for seven years, all the while saving up so that we could build on the farm, but in the '70s, every time we saved a thousand bucks, building costs went up two thousand bucks! Then Betsy saw an article about moving older homes, contacted Hayes Brothers Moving in Clarksdale, and I walked in one evening to hear her proclaim that we were moving to the country – and taking our house!

One of the best decisions we ever made, even though we've burnt it a couple of times, had three tornadoes bounce over us, and gone through three ice storms. This old house was started in 1898, finished in 1902, moved in 1978, burnt in 1991, and still survives today. Yet something in the moving of it apparently discombobulated the spirits within.

Our oldest daughter, Christie, got the front bedroom after the move and remodeling, while Adam had the whole upstairs to himself (and the group of boys known as "The Jakes") and B.C. had a bedroom across the hall from ours at the back of the house. One thing about older houses: they seldom have much closet space, but Betsy's mother had been an antique dealer and collector, so we inherited several huge antique wardrobes, which work fine to supplement small closets. There is a beautiful carved wardrobe in the front bedroom.

But Christie started mentioning at breakfast every so often, "I heard something growl in my room last night." Well, her windows open onto the front porch, so I figured it was a cat or dog or possum or coon, and said so. "I don't know," she'd respond doubtfully, "it sounds like it's in the room with me."

That kept on for a month or so, with Chris getting obviously a little more upset about it, so Adam, three years younger but a hunter scared of nothing, volunteered to sleep up there for a few nights. Sure enough, he came to the kitchen one morning saying that he had heard a menacing growl during the night. "Daddy, I got up and tiptoed to the front door, jerked it open and flipped on the porch lights, but there was nothing out there atall. Not in the bushes either. It does seem like it's in the room, like Chris says."

I still figured it was an animal of some kind, maybe even a rat inside the house, as country homes often have for unwanted guests. Christie graduated from high school and went off to college at Tulane, in New Orleans, so B.C. inherited the front bedroom. Soon she too started reporting on the growling sounds during the night. I stayed up there a few nights, but never heard a thing. Adam once again spent a night or two in that room, and again reported hearing the growls, reiterating that he thought it was in the room, too.

Then B.C. came to breakfast one morning obviously shaken. "I heard the growl again last night, about two o'clock, and woke up looking around. There was a soft light coming from within the wardrobe, although the doors were closed, but the light was seeping out between, under, and over them. It was yellowish, not blinking, and I watched it for a few minutes, thinking that it must be some battery-powered toy or flashlight that had come on in there. So I got up and opened the doors.

"Then the light went out! I cut on the bedside light and could see nothing in the wardrobe, so I started unloading it. There was nothing in there but sheets, blankets, towels, and clothes. No flashlights, no toys, nothing that had a light or battery. Daddy, I'm scared!"

Okay, I had not seen the light, had not heard the growls, but three of my kids had seen or heard something strange and unexplainable up there, and it had frightened them. Remember

130

when I said that I had sense enough to know that just 'cause I don't see or hear something doesn't mean that someone else hasn't seen or heard something? We had a problem that needed solving.

That's what preachers are for; that's why we pay them the Big Bucks, right?

I told B.C. that I'd take care of it, and she went on to school. Later that morning I went to the church and sat myself down with Mike Bedford, my preacher. I told him all of the above and informed him that he was going to come out to Brownspur that afternoon and perform an exorcism in that front bedroom.

He sat there for a moment, then declared, "Baptists don't do exorcisms. You need to go see a Catholic priest."

I corrected him. "No, Mike. I am a Baptist, and I am your music minister and my kids have been frightened by something strange and unexplainable in our front bedroom. *YOU* may need to see a Catholic priest, but I'm expecting you to be at the house when B.C. gets home from school, and to take your Bible and go rebuke whatever is scaring my kids in that room."

By golly, he was there when the kids got home, armed with the Sword: God's Word. We all trooped up to the front bedroom. This was sunny warm day, but the central A/C unit was not on, nor was the ceiling fan. As we watched from the foyer, Mike opened his Bible and began reading, rebuking evil spirits, praying – whatever, as we watched wide-eyed. I'm not sure what we expected, because we as a family do not watch horror movies, but we had faith that God could handle the problem, through Mike, if needed.

He told us later that he had advanced to the middle of the room, then suddenly he felt very cold, "like someone had opened the door of the freezer." But he kept right on praying and reading scripture. "Then all of a sudden there was this 'swoosh' sound, and it was normal temperatured again – but I felt that dread lifted off of me, that I had felt when I entered the room." Mike prayed some more, prayed with us as a family, then sat with B.C. as she went through her stereo collection: "This is okay, this is okay. . . oh, this is devil music! This is okay, this is okay. . . ." They went through her collection, then took the questionable stuff outside, where I built a little fire of sticks in the parking bay, and she fed the devil music tapes into the flames one by one. Mike then produced several Christian music tapes and asked her to play them continuously for the next week, even at night – "just cut the volume off." She did that.

No one has ever complained of hearing growls or seeing strange lights in the front bedroom since then. Perfectly normal room.

Was there a ghost? Demon? Evil Spirit? All of those are Biblical.

I dunno. But I do know that God took care of the problem.

You may be saying at this point that you don't believe a word of this chapter. I don't care. It's all the truth, but I ain't gonna fight about it.

"Now we see as through a glass darkly, but then we'll see as face to face."

I'm going ask Him one day, and like I say, I bet we have a laugh over it together.

Kid Stuff

At one point in my life I was an active member and officer of the local area Arts Council, since I was a geen-you-wine author of books in the art of writing. I was driving somewhere one day when a cell phone call came in from our Arts Council Director, who had come upon an innovative program that she thought just might work in our territory. It was a Creative Writing Anti-Violence Program, she explained, targeted for reform schools, or local "Alternative Schools" to which kids who had discipline problems were assigned as a last resort, before they were actually consigned to a reform school, or worse. Since I was already involved in the Kairos Prison Ministry, since I had once been a Baptist Church Youth Minister, and since I was a Creative Writer, the lady gushed that I was a natural choice to pilot such a program locally.

"You could take your lunch hour from the TV station twice a week, for an hour-and-a-half Tuesdays and Thursdays," Amy enthused. "We might even be able to find some funds to pay you from somewhere."

I turned her down flat. The Alternative School was twenty miles from my house, in the high crime section of a nearby city. I was white. Nearly 100 % of the students were black. "There ain't no way I'd be interested in doing that," I answered, and hung up.

Not one minute later I almost slammed on the brakes, in traffic. "Dummy!" I grated out between my teeth. "You just spent four days in Parchman Prison working with people in striped britches, convicted murderers, robbers, drug dealers, and at least two serial rapists, almost all of whom are black. Wouldn't it make sense to try to catch them before they get to prison?"

I hit Redial. The lady seemed surprised when I said that I had reconsidered, and that I would volunteer to teach such a course. Duuhhh, Neill!

There was a notebook of lessons, piloted by an Arts organization in Alabama. Much of it involved getting the students to write poetry, to try to express their feelings. Didn't sound like much of a chance to me, but like I said, "Why not try to change them before they're wearing striped britches?" As I read through the lesson plans, though, I realized that there would probably be a hitch, from the school's standpoint: the lessons worked up to mentioning God toward the latter part of the course, and even involved the kids writing their impressions of God, then ending up writing a letter to God. This was in a public school, remember. I scheduled a preliminary meeting with the principal to explain the course, then asked if the mention of God would cause any problems for him.

Abe Hudson, Sr. grinned and stuck out his hand. "Son, if you'd like to be here at seven o'clock every morning, you can accompany me on my rounds: see, I walk into every classroom before the kids or teachers get here each day, and I pray for God to bless them all. We ain't got a problem for you to be mentioning God in this school!"

We started out the course with the basic goal being to get the kids to write the bad stuff out of their heads and to get it on paper. From there they could save it in a notebook, wad it up in the trashcan, burn it, shred it, or even – publish it! Really, this course included the publication of a chapbook of their writings at the end of each school year.

That first year both the students and I were learning. Many were reluctant to participate, but some got the hang of it, and one kid in particular finally caught on. He was a very angry youngster, who had been burned on the face in a house fire – that was what finally connected us. I read to them an account of our house fire, showed the scars, and he changed in his attitude toward me overnight! His first writings were about suicide, but by the semester's end he was telling of his nature observations, of seeing God in a rain shower, then a poem about getting to Heaven, and his concept of that. By the year's end, he was the star of the class, and showed some real talent for getting his thoughts down on paper. Many of his poems and stories were included in that first chapbook the class produced.

But when the books arrived that last week of school, he was not in class. All the rest of the kids signed copies of the books for parents and teachers at a reception, but Johnny wasn't there. When I asked where he might be, one of the other boys chuckled: "You wanta see Johnny, you gotta go to the courthouse 'cause his hearing is today," he reported.

"What happened? I thought he was doing good?" I asked.

"Oh, he has been doing good. This is for something he got into nearly a year ago, but just now coming up for sentencing," I was told. Thing was, I did have to drive right by the courthouse on my way home, so I got all the other kids to sign a couple of books for Johnny, and took them upstairs to the Youth Court Judge's Office, as directed.

When I walked in, a familiar voice exclaimed, "Uncle Bob! What are you doing here?" Markita had also worked part-time at the TV station, but now she was the Judge's secretary. Then she looked at the books in my hand, and suddenly made a connection. "Hey, Judge!" she called toward the back office. "Come out here. I think I just found Johnny's Uncle Bob."

The Judge came out, a black lady, and looked askance at me, then Markita. "Are you Johnny's Uncle Bob?" she asked doubtfully.

135

"Yes, Ma'am, I am," I admitted. "Why?"

Markita laughed: "He's everybody's Uncle Bob, Judge."

The Judge nodded across the hall: "I've got Johnny and a dozen other kids over there for sentencing, for some shenanigans they pulled last fall, but when I had each of them come up before me, I told Johnny that he seemed like he had changed more than the others, and asked him if that was so, why?

"He told me, 'Yes, Judge, my Uncle Bob has been teaching me to write that bad stuff out of my head and get it onto paper, where I can deal with it, and Judge – I ain't mad no more!' So I recessed Court, came over here and asked Markita to call his momma and find out how I could talk to his Uncle Bob to see what's going on. But his momma just told me, 'He ain't got no Uncle Bob!' So, what's going on, Uncle Bob?" she asked.

I described the Creative Writing Anti-Violence Course to her, and showed her some of Johnny's poems in the books I held, pointing out his progression. "I brought a couple of books for him, plus I wanted him to sign one for me while I'm here, if that's okay. He was my best student this year," I bragged.

A smile came over her face. "Come on, Uncle Bob. We're gonna make an impression with this book signing," she grinned mischievously. We entered the courtroom and she took her place up on the bench while I settled into a pew behind a dozen young men in yellow jumpsuits who wore chains on their ankles, wrists, and waists, all connected together.

"Boys!" she rapped for attention and quiet. "Uncle Bob would like to make a presentation." There was a wide railing between the pews and the bench, and she beckoned me forward with my books. "Johnny, your Uncle Bob wants you to sign one of your books to him, and wants to give you the books that all your classmates have signed for you. He says you were his best student, and he's proud of you. Come on forward, Son."

For Johnny to come to the railing, every kid in the

yellow, chained line had to rise and shuffle forward with him. He could not raise his hands high enough to hug me, which I could tell he wanted to do. I held open a book for him to sign to me, then he held the two I'd brought him open for me to sign to him. "Thank you for coming, Uncle Bob," he murmured, and I shook his hand. Then the kids all shuffled backwards to sit down again. I gathered up my book, thanked the Judge, and gave Johnny a thumbs-up as I left the courtroom. He was sent to juvenile detention for the summer, where I visited him a couple of times.

The next year we resumed the CWAVP in the same school, same principal, and it was even better, but about the middle of the first semester, Johnny showed up again. I asked Mr. Hudson: "What's with Johnny coming back? I thought he was doing a lot better?" See, the goal of an Alternative School is to motivate their kids into improving their behavior and returning in good grace to their home school again.

The principal smiled. "He is doing better. But they didn't have a writing course at his school, so he asked them to let him come back here again, so he could learn from his Uncle Bob."

A year later, I was crossing the street when someone hailed me. It was Markita, and she wanted to tell me that she'd heard from Johnny the week before. He was out west, in the Job Corps, and had asked for writing materials for Christmas. "He said if I see Uncle Bob, to tell him that I'm still writing the bad stuff out of my head.'" she grinned.

The third year was the best for that course. Mrs. Ada Daniels was teacher of a class of 13 and 14 year-olds, and she never raised her voice, but those kids were the most polite, quietest kids I've ever seen, and they wrote some wonderful stuff for the chapbook that year. Matter of fact, that was eight years ago, and just last month, as I was buying a paper at the Kroger after church Sunday morning, a hand tapped me on the shoulder. I turned, and a well-built black guy was grinning at me from under a black cap which proclaimed, "Police" over the bill.

"You remember me, Uncle Bob?" he asked. I pleaded Lyme Disease.

"I'm John. Remember Mrs. Daniels' class?"

I did. "So, are you a policeman now?" I asked, shaking hands.

"No, Sir, not yet. But I graduate from the Police Academy in two weeks. You know, I still sit down and write the bad stuff out every now and then," he grinned.

When that particular class graduated that spring, the chapbooks were late coming in, so I went to Mr. Hudson for a solution to getting the class back together. "Could you come up with a school bus, driver, and a couple of chaperones?" I challenged. He said he could, but for what? "I'm gonna host an end-of-school party out at the Swimming Hole, in the pasture next to my house," I declared. "You get the kids out there, I'm gonna feed 'em and host 'em."

Mrs. Daniels herded her class off the school bus at the Swimming Hole that next week, and the first girl to get off almost stepped on a green grass snake. These were town kids, so one can imagine all the squealing and hollering. But I caught the snake, then got her to touch it, pet it, then hold it, then pass it around to the others. The snake got tired of that a lot quicker than the 28 kids did. That same girl volunteered to take the snake across the pasture to turn it aloose on the Mammy Grudge ditchbank.

Betsy baked a cake, made ice cream, and I grilled hamburgers and hot dogs while the kids enjoyed the Swimming Hole and admired the books, while signing for each other. Then after lunch I drove my old 1991 Ford pickup out to the pasture and asked, "Okay, who's going to be the first to turn 15 this year?" That's when a kid could get a driver's permit!

One girl stepped out, hand raised, and I pitched her the truck keys. "Don't run over my neighbor's fence, don't drive it into the Swimming Hole, and don't run over Miss Betsy's flower beds," I instructed. Those kids took turns driving in circles in the pasture for two hours, and if we had scheduled an election for that afternoon, I could have been elected King of the World!

The stat is that most prison inmates have less than eight grades of school, so their educational level (we ain't talking Sunday School, either!) is like unto a 13 or 14 year-old kid, and granted, there are 13 and 14 year-olds in prison, too. I was going over some papers from that very special class of kids that age, and wanted share some images of God they wrote about, from that age's viewpoint. Some comments are funny; some will make you cry.

"I think God is old, black, and has long gray hair. I think He is drug-free."

"I see God as a woman, light-skinned, with green eyes and long hair."

"God is a Man of Power; He can do the unthinkable and make things happen!"

"God is mighty, powerful, grateful, and very tall."

(*Grateful? That's never occurred to me, but do you reckon He does feel akin to that when we do the right things instead of the wrong things? Maybe even proud of us?*)

"God is not a man, but a Spirit filled with such pride and joy. God do not use drugs."

"God is powerful, strange-looking, untouchable, pure in heart."

"My God is my strong Hero. He makes the wind good and smelly."

"God is the supreme and almighty Reality; He can show Himself in many ways."

"He's something like a cloud, but no one really knows what He looks like."

"I can't see God, but I know He is right here by me."

"When it rains, that is God crying because people aren't doing what He tells us to do. You shouldn't make God mad at you. I believe in God, and He believes in me!"

(That's strong! And if a 13-14 year-old could ask God for one thing, what might it be?) "There are a lot of guns and drugs on the streets killing people. HIV is really bad. It needs to be a lot of programs for kids. Drugs shouldn't be made or grown."

"I would want violence to stop, and everyone to get along with each other. I'd want the gang bangers to leave me alone and just let me be me."

"If I could ask you one question, it would be: why do we have to die?"

"Crime and drugs is everywhere; people get killed or kidnapped. Could You fix everything so my kids won't have to see this stuff? I don't want my kid to get killed."

"I wish You could stop people from doing drugs. God, sometimes I think some people don't believe in You, and that's why they do the things they do." *(AMEN!)*

"Dear God: I just want to thank you for every little thing you've done in my life."

"I pray every time I need You, but I know I need to pray every night, not just when I need You. I wish we didn't have to worry about being killed outside our door."

"Why do I have to go through the things I do? Why does it have to be me? Couldn't something good happen to me some days? Can I be a good child for a minute or two? Please help with my ups and downs! Thanks for what you've done for me."

"I need your help to make the world a better place: people are doing drugs and killing people over dumb things. I try to help, but they don't want to hear your name."

"It has been a long time since I asked for your forgiveness. There's a lot I need to talk to you about. I got back with old friends and I wonder if that wasn't a mistake."

"There's something going on in my mind: I just get mad. I try to control it, but it just doesn't work. Can you help me, please?" *(And me, too, when you got time, God!)*

"Help me change my attitude; I need to be a better person and do the right thing."

"Help me to help You make this world a better place. You always been there for me, You always seen me in my good and bad. I know You know what I want."

I know college-educated upper crust folks who couldn't have said it better, just in more and longer words. The Good Book says, "Unless you become like a Little Child."

That Creative Writing Anti-Violence Program went on for over five years in that Alternative School, but the administration changed, and discipline within the classroom went to pot. Mrs. Daniels retired, as did Mr. Hudson. The last spring I taught, there was one older kid who would not quiet down, would disturb the class for most of the hour, then in five minutes turn in a better paper than anyone else. He had talent, but no discipline. One day, in exasperation, I just burst out, "Paulie, if you don't get some discipline and respect in your life, either you are going to wind up in prison, or you're gonna be dead!"

Ten days later, that boy was shot to death in a drug deal gone bad.

When I walked into the classroom the next time, there was total silence. But it was too late in the year to regain what we had lost, and the Arts Council did not renew the program for the next year.

At about the same time the Anti-Violence Writing was going on, the Department of Humanities started a Family Reading Bonds Program, a six-weeks program of children's book reading for younger kids, with a storyteller "reading" the books assigned for each week. The idea was to encourage parents to take time to read with their kids, to build enthusiasm for education in the early years. It worked, too, and that Team: Aza, Jauretta, Libby, David, and Uncle Bob, even won a state-wide Award for our efforts.

The best stories were those in which I could get the kids enthusiastic and participating in, including singing "Amazing Grace," calling the dogs, hooting like owls, enunciating the catch-phrases of different books – oh, we had a good time, and most weeks one of us would find a way to work in a little witness in one way or another.

They gave us our Award at a statewide Banquet, with 600 dressed-up folks in attendance. Yet at one point in the program, Uncle Bob had them enthusiastically Calling the Dogs, then divided them into beagles, redbones, Plott hounds, and blueticks, with coaching for each distinctive voice, then the whole pack charging forth at full voice to drive away The Hairy Man, who had the boy Wiley on his menu!

Also during those years I was storytelling for some annual Summer Arts Camps at the nearby Bologna Performing Arts Center at week-long sessions, and I made a tradition of ending the week with ghost stories, doing some ghostly poems, as well as the strange stories I have related in an earlier chapter, which had happened to me personally. At each class we had dimmed the lights, and the kids were suitably spooked, so to speak, quiet and entranced by these adventures into the unknown. To end the sessions, I would then step to the closed door, blocking it, and cut out the lights entirely, to announce, "And I want you to know that there really is a ghost in this room with us – right now!" Then I'd flip the lights back on and explain briefly The Holy Ghost, and how one can receive that good Ghost, then use that Power for rest of one's life. It was not meant to be an "invitation" nor a sermon, but I did intend for the kids to go home and ask Daddy and Momma for further information. As far as I know, no one ever protested that I'd gone beyond a line, but I had many parents over the years who called or met me to thank me for stirring their kid's interest in a subject that's often hard to broach to a kid. Often we leave that for the preacher to do, right? That's why we pay them the Big Bucks.

A greater reward than the thanks of a parent was when some kid would burst out that he or she had already received that Holy Ghost, and then tell that story themselves to Uncle Bob. Twice, I had kids contact me weeks later to say that they had accepted Christ, which was an unexpected bonus.

Then one fall I was at a meeting of that Summer Arts Camps Board, and as the meeting ended, the lady next to me asked, "Aren't you Uncle Bob?" I had to admit that I was.

She smiled, "You know, the kids really do love your stories. My six-year-old granddaughter could recite them for me by heart every evening during the week." Then she leaned closer and lowered her voice: "You know, don't you, that many of those kids take your stories literally?"

I nodded. "Yessum, that's why I'm always careful to tell only true stories that have happened to me. That way, I'm not passing along anything I don't know is absolutely true."

She leaned closer: "I mean, they actually believe even those Ghost Stories you always tell the last day."

"Yessum, I hope they do, because except for those few poems, like 'The Cremation of Sam McGee' and 'Little Orphant Annie,' those are true stories just like the rest of my stories, and they really have happened to me."

Now there was a gleam in her eye: "Well, I don't believe in ghosts, myself!"

I nodded, "I didn't either till I met Madelyn at the King's Tavern in Natchez."

"That really happened?"

"I mopped up the water myownself, and there was no other explanation, Ma'am."

"And the Ghost in your wardrobe? She told me that one too."

"Happened just like I told it, Ma'am. Can't help it if you don't believe it." I was about ready to end the interview. I dislike theological discussions in which folks have differing viewpoints and tend to get "het-up" about them, as I thought she was fixing to do.

Then the lady smiled, "But listen: after I had given this six-year-old girl a thorough talking-to about believing in ghosts, she came over and got in my lap and asked, 'so you don't believe in ghosts, Granny?' I told her that I certainly did not. Then she repeated, 'you don't believe in ANY ghosts, Granny?' I was firm in my denial. One more time the child asked, 'NO ghosts?' 'No ghosts!' I declared, figuring to settle the matter once and for all."

She started laughing: "Then this six-year-old girl, with a smile like the cat who ate the canary, demanded, 'well, what about the Holy Ghost?'"

I held my breath. Finishing off the Ghost Story sessions with a simple explanation of the Holy Ghost, announcing first to the darkened room that, "Ghosts are real, and there's a real one in this room right now!" -- had that gone awry, after all these years?

The lady picked up a tissue to dab at her eyes, laughing. "She had me exactly where she wanted me! She had baited the trap and waited until I was all the way into it before she sprung it! No preacher in the world could have done a better job of setting that up. Then she gave me the clearest, simplest picture of how to experience that particular Ghost. All I could do was hug her and take her for some cookies and milk, so I could get out of her hearing and laugh as hard as I wanted to, without her thinking that I was laughing at her. What a gift you gave to my granddaughter, to be able to pass that gift along to me in her own words!"

Now I could chuckle along with her and uncross my fingers: I did so.

But as we were leaving the reception a little while later, the lady caught me and twinkled, "But I still don't believe in any other kinds of ghosts!"

I grinned, "No'm, I used to not either."

There's a moral to be repeated here: just because I don't

see something, doesn't mean that somebody else may not have seen it, whether one believes in it or not. The Bible makes the point several times that we aren't equipped to fully understand all the things of this world, and that often those who think they do, get "puffed up."

But some things are easy to understand, like, "Love one another," or, "People will know that you are My disciples, because you love one another."

And how to experience the Holy Ghost can even be taught by a six-year-old, to a grandmother!

Selah.

The Cross Story

When I was just a shirttail boy, we went to the Leland Presbyterian Church, because Big Robert was one. Momma, however, was Episcopalian, and several local Episcopalians got together and formed a mission, that eventually grew large enough to be a real church. They started raising money to build, operating on a shoestring, trading for used pews, altars, hymnbooks, and such churchly accouterments. Big Robert, who was going to go where Miz Janice went, finally declared, "By golly, y'all are going to have one thing that's new and yours!"

My father was a hobby woodcarver, and a good one. He ordered a piece of red mahogany from South America, and designed a Celtic Cross over two feet high and a foot wide, decorated with smaller crosses of different styles carved into its front. It must have taken him two years to carve it and to put a hand-rubbed oil finish on it. He presented it to the new church, for the altar.

Then I went to Ole Miss, married Betsy after graduation, and went into the Navy. We moved back home two years later, but a broken back prevented me from going anywhere for a while, then we became Baptists. When I finally visited the little Episcopal church again, it had been over a decade, and the mahogany Cross was nowhere to be seen. Instead, a large beautiful shiny brass Cross hung over the altar, and no one seemed to know what had become of the old wooden Cross.

146

A couple of decades later, I became involved in the Kairos International Prison Ministry. On my first Kairos weekend, at Parchman Prison, two brothers who were in that Leland Episcopal church were unloading their truck. I offered to help, and the younger McGee brother handed me a Cross to take inside. I was flabbergasted!

"Where'd you get this?!" I stammered. I had not seen it in 30 years.

Ump looked at me like I was retarded. "Well, your Daddy carved it."

"I know that! But how did YOU know that?" I replied.

Again the insulting look: "He signed it, on the back." Ralph McGee leaned over and pointed. I had never known that Big Robert had engraved a dedication on it.

Humphreys cautioned me, "I found that Cross in a cupboard in the back of the church. We've been sneaking it out for Kairos, and for Cursillo. Don't tell anybody."

During that Kairos, when I made my talk, I first thanked the residents for the opportunity to not only worship before my father's Cross, but to speak from behind it. That story has been told on numerous Kairoses since then, and that Cross has been used on many Kairoses, and other weekends in the free world that are similar, like Emmaus Walks, Chrysalis, and Cursillo.

Over the years, the Cross has had its share of accidents, of course. On CMCF Men's Kairos # 2 in the spring of 2000, when Humphreys McGee led the music and I was a table clergy, Ump had of course snuk the Cross out again. After Closing, he picked it up to pack it (two pieces of cardboard duct-taped together) to go home, and dropped it! The front "IHS" piece came off, just as I turned at the clatter. Ump thought I was going to kill him, which of course I felt obligated to do, but team member Mickey Plunkett stepped between us. "Wait! Don't kill Ump! I can fix this. I'm a woodworker, and I'm good. Let me keep it for a couple of weeks. The glue has just gotten old. It's not broken."

Sure enough, Mickey gave it back, good as new, at the Instructional weekend two weeks later, and Ump snuk it back into the church cupboard.

In September of 2001, (ten days after 9/11) I was Rector of a Kairos, a once-in-a-lifetime thrill. However, a Rector doesn't really do the work – the Coordinator actually makes the weekend go. Of course, what really makes it go right is all the prayers by volunteers in and out of prison. We had plenty of that, and CMCF Men's Kairos # 5 was the best ever – not that I'm prejudiced atall!

Mickey Plunkett, as my Coordinator, did such a great job that I told Betsy on the way home Monday, "Honey, I dreamed I was Rector of a Kairos – and I never had to DO anything!" I was like a sailing ship before the wind – of the Holy Ghost!

As usual, I had gotten the Big Robert Cross from the Leland church for Kairos. Thursday afternoon, we set it up on the prison chapel altar. Yet when we left the prison and returned to the church at Pearl for the team supper, I noticed someone had brought it back and set it on the head table. Friday morning, I arrived early at the church for breakfast, and Mickey got there early, too. "Why don't we step into the chapel and pray this weekend up, while the ladies finish getting breakfast ready?" I suggested. We went into the little chapel the team ladies had set up, and knelt to pray together, and I saw that the Cross had been moved in there when they'd cleaned up from last night's supper.

When we finished praying, Mickey said softly, "By the way, that's your Cross."

"I know," I said, "And we need to be sure it goes back to prison with us today."

"You don't understand, Uncle Bob," he replied, "This is Your Cross!"

I tried to be patient: "Mickey, I know that. But I'd rather have it in the prison chapel than back here at the church with the kitchen team, so let's not forget to take it on the bus. And by the way, let's don't chance another accident by taking it back and forth each day, okay?"

"Listen to me," my Coordinator enunciated: "There IS a Cross in the prison, on the altar in the chapel. THIS Cross is YOURS!"

Mickey is a really good hobby woodworker, like Big Robert was. Two years before, when Mickey had Big Robert's Cross to repair, he had made measurements, traced it, even Xeroxed it! He then spent over a year carving an exact replica of Daddy's Cross, and GAVE it to ME on Kairos # 5, which I Rectored!

I was stunned, and of course teared up. My friend enthused, "No one could tell the difference, unless they look at the back. You can take this Cross back to that church in Leland, and then keep your Daddy's Cross for yourself. No one will ever know!"

I shook my head. "No, Mick. Daddy carved his Cross because he loved my mother, and knew how much she loved that little church. But this Cross was carved for me by a man who loves me, and this Kairos Ministry that we work together in. This is a no-brainer. Big Robert's Cross goes back to the church. This Cross goes home with me, but it comes back to prison for every Kairos!"

The Mississippi Kairos Cross has made several Kairoses a year since then, at Parchman Prison, and at the Central Mississippi Correctional Facility in Pearl, both Men's and Women's Prisons. It was there for Unit 32 # 1 Kairos, South MS Correctional Facility # 1, Kairos Outside #1 thru 4, and Kairos Torch # 1 (ministry to juvenile offenders) at Walnut Grove YCF, as well as Yazoo City Federal Prison # 1 thru 3. Plus, it has made several Cursillos, Emmaus Walks, and a boy's Chrysalis.

And since that Cross has to travel so much, it needed better packaging than two large pieces of cardboard duct-taped

149

together with string loops to carry it by, right? Here comes Mickey Plunkett to the rescue again, folks!

Mickey had agreed to be my Coordinator on Kairos # 5, if in return I would lead the music when he was Rector of Kairos # 9 two years later, which I was glad to do. What a joyous weekend that was, but when it was over, after the Closing Ceremony with the Karo Cross there in front of the podium, our Rector just flat disappeared! The Coordinator took over instructing everyone in the rapid clean-up, and Mickey reappeared in time for the final fast Team meeting and prayer huddle, then everyone hugged and headed for home.

Betsy had come down early for the Closing, and had done some shopping while in the big city, so when we got home to Brownspur at nearly midnight, she suggested that we leave almost everything in the car until the next morning, which I was glad to agree to. We slept late Monday, then after a few cups of coffee, I bestirred myself to unload the car of both shopping goods and Kairos gear, including both Crosses – obviously, Mickey's Kairos deserved having both present. I had settled down for a final cup of coffee when Betsy stuck her head into the den: "Did you get everything out of the car?" she asked.

"Yes, Ma'am," I nodded.

"What about those two green cases in the trunk?"

I had noticed them, figuring she'd bought some junior-sized foot lockers with brass fittings for the kids, or something. "They're in the sewing room, by the back door." I was trying to catch up on four days of papers I had missed while in prison.

"Did you look at them?" I shook my head: her business. "Not even the brass plates by the handles you carried them in by?" She shook her head now: "I think you'd better go check them out, Bob."

Oh, boy! She must have done some shopping for me, too. Maybe a matched set of pistols? No, the cases were a little large for pistols, but too small for a shotgun or rifle. What else would need an elegant presentation case like these, now that I

150

was looking at them? I set one up on its side to check out the brass plate by the handle: it read "Uncle Bob's Cross." The other said: "Big Robert's Cross."

Plunkett! Seeing the jury-rigged cardboard carrying case we'd been wagging the Karo Crosses back and forth in, he had spent the last two years hand-making these beautiful brass-bound junior-sized foot lockers, padded and felt-covered on the insides, with cut-outs in the foam for the Cross and its three-tiered base, and each case labeled. Then he had called before the Kairos weekend to be sure Betsy was coming to Closing, clued her in on the conspiracy, then slipped out after his own Closing Ceremony, to meet her in the prison parking lot and transfer the cases into our car trunk in secret! Sneaky!

But if you ever need to see beautiful examples of God's Agape Love, give your Uncle Bob a holler and come to Brownspur!

One of the most memorable chapters in the Cross Story came on Mississippi Kairos Outside # 2, which Betsy led, in March 2005 at Camp Henry Jacobs in Utica.

The weekend began with a powerful confirmation. The team meeting was held at 3:00 p.m. in the Camp Jacobs Chapel, which also serves as a Jewish museum. Behind the podium was a massive carved dark wood replica of the Temple, with the stone tablets bearing the Ten Commandments between the columns, carved from ivory. After the Spiritual Directors set the chapel up for the KO weekend, the Cross was placed on the podium (with permission of the Camp Director), with small statuettes of Jesus on the steps beneath it. The Team Commitment Service was held, then KO # 2 Leader Betsy Neill stepped to the podium to give final instructions for the weekend.

At that exact moment, the sun shone through the west windows high up on the wall facing the sanctuary – and the beams focused directly on the Cross! It absolutely glowed! It was breathtaking, the glowing Cross standing before the massive Old Testament images. Betsy stopped speaking as the whole Team was awe-struck; then she pointed out that the Cross was the fulfillment of the Old Covenant, represented on the darker wall behind her. What a confirmation for being there at that exact time!

Big Robert's Cross, and now Uncle Bob's Cross: The Karo Cross Story just keeps on going here in Mississippi!

But that Cross is also a Family Cross for the Neill family, and that is hopefully a never-ending story, as well. Several years after I got involved in Kairos and thereby got re-acquainted with Big Robert's Cross, son Adam was sponsored on an Emmaus Walk – think of that retreat as a free-world Kairos weekend, if you like – by my old college roommate and hunting buddy Ronny James. Unlike his sire, Adam had a wonderful time on the weekend.

Before the weekend started, I had been serving on another Kairos, and happened to have the Cross in my possession, so as to sneak it back into the Leland Episcopal church cupboard. But on impulse, I called Ronny, who was scheduled to be an Assistant Lay Director on Adam's Walk, to ask if it would be possible to use Big Robert's Cross for Emmaus, it having been carved by Adam's late granddaddy. Ronny was enthusiastic: "What a great idea! I'll drive up there to get it." I met him and delivered the Cross, to be used in the Prayer Room, where each Pilgrim's Cross on a neckchain would be hung during the weekend.

At the conclusion of the weekend, after each Pilgrim had been presented with his Cross, the Team's Spiritual Director, Rev. Willie Varnado, an old Kairos friend and teammate, asked if he could tell a short little story to the assembled Team and Pilgrims. He had heard me tell the Big Robert Cross story in prison several times, and could deliver that tale from memory, and did so, but without using names or towns for identification. When he finished the part about the man getting to meet his father's-carved Cross in prison, there was hardly a dry eye in the chapel.

Then Willie delivered the clincher: "Here is that Cross; and Pilgrims, those Crosses which you have around your necks now have been hanging on this Cross all weekend, for the Team and your sponsors to pray over. But there's an extra blessing on this Emmaus Walk: one of you Pilgrims is the grandson of the man who carved this Cross," and Willie picked it up to display it better, "nearly a half-century ago." He paused for effect, then announced: "Adam Neill, would you like to come up here and hold your Granddaddy's Cross?"

Certainly not a dry eye in the chapel, after that!!

When daughter B.C. (Betsy Claire) married John Irwin ("The Flying Jake") they wanted the original Big Robert Cross on the altar at the First Baptist Church, where the ceremony was to take place. I cleared it with the Episcopalians, Humphreys snagged it from the dusty cupboard, and we polished it up and placed it on the altar, which was head-high at the back of the stage, right in front of the baptismal. Before and after we all posed for pictures in front of it, but the best part was to come from the ceremony itself, unbeknownst to us.

The wedding was on November 1st, which meant that the rehearsal dinner, for almost 100 people, was on Halloween night. B. C., always the Thespian, clapped her hands and declared, "Great! We'll have a costume party!" She came as a bobby-soxer, John was a knight in chain-mail armor, the groom's parents were the king and queen, various bridesmaids were Mrs. Nerd, Cat Woman, Miss Mississippi (Top Ten Miss America) came as Mr. Potato Head, Mr. Spock from Star Trek was there, The Cat in the Hat, a Camo Ranger, a Roman Senator – you name it. I had drafted a young TV weatherman (I was a news & ad consultant at the TV station back then) named Robert Thornton, a newcomer to the Delta from Texas, to film the rehearsal celebration on a borrowed video camera. Then after seeing his handiwork the next morning, B.C. suddenly decided that she DID want the wedding ceremony to be filmed, as well. She had earlier decided against that, but now changed her mind, a bride's prerogative. I called Robert's apartment, got no answer, but left a message that, if he could come and bring the camera, his Uncle Bob would appreciate it. He arrived maybe ten minutes before the ceremony began, and I barely had time to get him upstairs into the balcony, advising, "Don't move around, or distract the preacher," and headed back down to escort my daughter down the aisle.

Robert knew absolutely nothing about the family history, nor the Cross, okay?

When we watched the video the next day, Robert started off the camera with a close-up shot of the Cross, then expanded and backed it off to include the whole auditorium, filmed the entire ceremony, then after the last attendant had exited the stage area, he closed the video production with a close-up of the Big Robert Cross!

What a coincidence!

Right.

Several years later, I got a call from a younger friend who had helped me publish my book *THE BAREFOOT DODGERS,* and Mark was asking me to lead the music on an Emmaus Walk which he had been scheduled to be Lay Director of. I agreed, immediately contacting fellow Kairos musician Jesse Heath to get him to accompany me on his guitar. When I packed the car to drive down to Gallman for the weekend, on an impulse I snagged that Cross from the church, now in Mickey's Case, and took both it and the Uncle Bob Cross with me. Once at Camp Wesley Pines for the retreat, I asked Mark to come out to the car with me, and opened up the Case to show him the Cross.

"I should have asked you before now, but I was wondering if you might be able to use this Cross this weekend, in the chapel or prayer room maybe. Lemme tell you why I brought it: see, my Daddy. . . ."

Mark stopped me by reaching out to grasp the Cross in

154

awe. "I know the history. This was the Cross that was used on my Emmaus Walk years ago. I was a pilgrim on that same weekend as Adam was!"

We used both those Crosses, one in the prayer room, one in the chapel, for a wonderful, joyous, spiritual Emmaus Walk weekend!

What a coincidence!!

Right.

Kaaa-Roooooo!

Okay, so I flunked my Emmaus Walk experience. But it did open the door for a ministry that I've seen God do more in than I would have thought possible, except for having seen Him work so well through the youth ministry those many years before.

It is called Kairos, which is a Greek word meaning "God's Special Time." The Kairos International Prison Ministry dates back to the seventies, and is presently operating in about 32 states and ten foreign countries to date. It's sort of like the free-world weekends of Emmaus Walk or Cursillo or Tres Dias or FaithWalk – there are many similar experiences, where the object is to get away from the world for just a few days, and say, "Okay, I'm here, and God is over there: now, what can I do to get us closer together?"

Kairos is just done in prisons.

Now, I'm not a Bleeding Heart. I believe that people who commit crimes should pay the penalty, and I ain't much on the need for extra lawyers and judges to delay matters and muddy the waters. Civil rights are fine, but folks who do wrong belong to be disciplined, and fairly quickly, as far as I'm concerned. I'm skeptical of Jailhouse Conversions. I not only believe in the Death Penalty, I believe that it's a crime that we don't use it more often than we do.

I've already clued you in on our house fire, and the subsequent rebuilding of the charred ruin, which with all the hassle from insurance and banks and lawyers had to be the most frustrating time of my life, and eventually led to a bankruptcy, all of that having come upon us during a time of extreme financial stress from farming and my parents' estates. Not a happy time, except for the folks who ministered to us in so many ways during those bad days.

One of those was a plumber from nearby Indianola, who almost became my brother-in-law, but made a better deal. Tommy had helped me plumb the house when we moved it from town a dozen years before, and he returned to help us get it back into livable shape after the fire.

Tommy had just been on a Kairos # 1 weekend at Unit 29 in the Parchman Prison, the unit that at the time was known as "The Throwaway Unit" by the inmates. He had served on a spring team, and once a prison begins building a Kairos community therein, an agreement is signed to insure that another four-day weekend is scheduled every six months thereafter. The volunteers who make up the 50-person team also agree to return on a monthly basis to the prison to meet with those inmates who go through Kairos; in Mississippi that's on the Second Saturday of each month. They also commit to make a weekly team meeting for two months before going into the prison for the weekend, as a team-bonding measure. It's not a light commitment.

Tommy had not only taken his Kairos commitment seriously, he was on a mission to recruit others, including me, for the next team. He talked about it constantly when we were together, and finally time came for volunteers to sign on the dotted line to go to prison voluntarily. Tommy showed up with the document to join Rob Burnham's team # 2/U29. Tommy had not yet billed me for his work. I was near'bout broke and hadn't had much luck working out financing with the insurance company or bank. Maybe I could get a break on plumbing expenses? I signed up for Kairos, despite misgivings.

I was not prepared for the blessings, and that's an

understatement.

Not only were Tommy and Rosemary on the team, so I could ride with them three hours a week to and from team meetings, but so was Mark Kurtz, plus the McGee brothers, Ralph and Humphreys, whom I had known from childhood. Several others whom I knew were there, including Green Baggett and his wife Sandra; I had worked with Green on a Rural Crisis Committee award-winning film documentary several years before. Onliest thing was, I learned quickly that these people were huggers, the which Tommy had not informed me. I quickly found a corner and defended myself. This became a game for some of the women, especially, once they found out that Uncle Bob did not care about hugging. This was going to be a test of my endurance and good will, I could tell.

In another chapter I've told the story of my reunion with the Big Robert Cross, so I won't go into detail here, but that was a pretty powerful confirmation that I was supposed to be there. Yet the most powerful confirmation came about on the last day of the weekend. Sunday after lunch, Joey Donnell was making a talk, and since I was the Table Assistant, I was trying to do a good job of taking notes during the entire weekend, in case some of the 42 inmates were not really literate, and needed me to leave my notes for them. It was also an example to the six inmates at my table, with the three volunteers: me and Pat McNease and Earle Burkley. I was right with Joey, leaning on my elbows with my notebook open in front of me, taking notes until he started to tell a story – no notes needed here. After a moment, I leaned back in my folding chair, left my pencil on the table, and clasped my hands behind my head, rocking backwards in my chair as I often do.

We were in one end of the Unit 29 gymnasium, and ours was an outside table, so no one was behind me. The rest of the men at the table were still leaning forward with arms on the table as Joey talked. The rule is that no one can be walking around during a talk, so no one was moving about.

After a moment, I felt something in my hair, which ain't thick atall, nor is it long, and I had washed it that morning.

Let me say here that, at every team meeting leading up to the weekend, then at every table and team discussion during the weekend, whenever our needs were inquired unto, my need was always "Financial." I realize now that everyone must have been sick of hearing how Neill was going bust with a capital B, but I was a broken record then (in this CD age!).

I wiggled my fingers around and got the object in my hair between two fingers, and brought it around to look at it.

It was just a penny. Wasn't even new. Just a common ordinary penny that could not possibly have been caught up in my short fine hair for the whole day. I glanced around. No one was near me from behind. No one was looking at me. No one had been moving around back there. I looked back at the penny, closely.

In tiny letters, it proclaimed, "In God we trust."

Okay, I know what you're going to say here: but my hands had not gone into my pockets, just straight from the table to the back of my head. No one else had opportunity to put it there.

I realized that God had placed that penny in my hair, as a sign to me that He was going to take care of me financially, if I'd just trust Him. Though we still had some hard times to go through, the publishing and writing business bloomed, and the speakings got more and higher paid for a while.

And, to this day, two decades later, I'm still finding pennies: walking across the street, in parking lots, at the gas pumps, just laying around on the floors or ground wherever I go. I think God is still letting me know that He will take care of me; I ain't ever going to be rich, I know that, but if I just trust Him, we'll make it through!

You don't believe that? Fine. Just don't bother me with your explanation!

This past dozen years, I have written the monthly Mississippi Kairos newsletter, KaroTales (Rosemary asked, "Why did he give it a Mexican name, I wonder?") and that's been a huge Blessing, because so many Kairos volunteers or inmates call or write Uncle Bob to share their own Blessings with me. This chapter of this book, and a couple of other chapters, will be reproduced in whole or part for a companion book that I am publishing of Kairos stories: mine and others, throughout the years of Mississippi Kairos. It is being done as a fund-raiser, and I won't make anything atall off of that book, so you may go to the kairos-mississippi.org website and order copies from there, secure in knowing that all the money from that book will go towards the Kairos Prison Ministry, whereas the bucks for this book gravitate to your Uncle Bob! But if you get both books, you may get to enjoy some of these stories twice. Maybe more than that, because some of these ran in my weekly syndicated newspaper column; such as:

THE DAY WE BROKE INTO THE PRISON

Most folks who go to prison don't have to break into the joint – their main priority is perhaps breaking OUT of the place. However, I was with a gang of guys who actually broke into prison once – and got away with it!

See, I work in the Kairos Prison Ministry (a Greek word meaning "God's Special Time") and have to spend a couple dozen days a year behind bars. Oh, it's a volunteer organization – no one gets paid for going to prison with Kairos. Matter of fact, it can cost each volunteer as much as a hundred fifty bucks to get locked up!

We do a strange thing, that I have told you about in the past: we take as many as 15,000 dozen cookies into prison with us (or we used to before the threat of frivolous lawsuits stopped that). The cookies are examples of God's unconditional love, and are prayed over as they are baked by men, women, and children in communities all over the map.

The recidivism rate for graduates who stay faithful to the

160

Kairos program is only 15%, as opposed to around 80% nationally. At over $25,000 to keep someone in prison for a year, that's a considerable tax savings for the rest of you, for a few dozen cookies!

We'd take cookies in by the van load, and one time the van driver, a former resident in the prison himself who now works in Kairos, literally broke into prison, in his enthusiasm.

When you visit a prison, which I'm going to assume few readers have, you go through a series of locked doors and gates. They check you in at the prison front gate, you drive to the Unit and park, they check you in at the first gate of the Unit, open that gate, and you walk through it. It closes behind you. Then they open the second gate, and you walk through it. It closes behind you also. Then you walk through a heavy door into the lobby and deposit your car keys, etc., not to include a pocketknife! When that's done, they open the heavy steel door toward the gym, where Kairos meets, and you walk through. That door is locked behind you. They then open the second steel door, and you walk into the gym, and that door is closed and locked behind you. And then they let the inmates in to eat your cookies!

It was between the first and second gates of the Unit, that our hero broke into prison.

While most Team members had parked and walked to the first gate, the cookie van pulled up to the first gate, and the guard walked out to check for contraband. Finding only cookies, he went back to the gatehouse and hit the switch to slide the huge gate back – this gate is probably 20 feet wide by 15 feet tall, steel and heavy wire, topped with barbed and razor wire. As it rolled open enough to allow the van to drive through, our Hero pulled into the enclosure and stopped before the second gate, along with a dozen or so Team members on foot. The first gate closed behind them.

The second gate, identical to the first, began to roll open. Again, just as it was wide enough to allow the van through, our

Hero put it in gear and accelerated. Problem was, he had to turn to the right as he entered the Unit grounds, which he did.

The guard, seeing the van was going through, stopped the gate, then started it to closing.

The combination of a right turn, throwing the rear van bumper closer to the gate, as the gate itself started toward the van again, closing, was our undoing. You guessed it: the bumper hooked the gate, on the side away from the sight of both driver and guard.

Our hero, feeling the van start to lose acceleration for some reason, put the pedal to the metal. It became obvious to the running, dodging Team members afoot (of whom I was one) that the Department Of Corrections had never actually field-tested their gates, at least not against the horsepower of modern cookie vans. That gate never stood a chance, with the van's added traction of all those chocolate chips. The van surged into the compound, dragging the whole gate across the yard, until our shouts attracted the attention of the driver. The foremost thought in all our minds was, "Will they let us out again?"

Our hero, however, had a different premonition: "Oh, Lord! I'm the only Team member who has actually been incarcerated at one time in this prison, and now they've caught me red-handed, trying to break INTO the prison again! Lord, I need your help right now, please, Sir!"

THE DAY WE BLEW UP THE PRISON

Not long after I got involved in Kairos, I was in the speaking and book-signing business and used to travel all over the eastern half of the United States selling my books. Well, that's what I thought I was doing, until a lady corrected me. I had learned early on that a book-signing in a town works a lot better if it is connected with one or more speaking engagements in that town, the freebie kind, to the garden club, Rotary, Lions, library club, schools, whatever. I was scheduled to speak at a large public library to their Library Club, and when I got there, only two elderly ladies showed up. However, I had also learned that it makes no difference if it's two people or twenty thousand people: you give them your best. We had a good time, me and those two ladies, and afterward they wanted to buy several copies of my books. As I was signing one to whomever was dictated to me, one of the ladies observed, "Son, you DO know that you are not selling books, don't you?"

"Oh, yes, Ma'am, I am too selling books! If I don't sell books, I don't eat!" I rejoined.

She smiled knowingly, "No, Son, you're not selling books. You're selling yourself!"

Truth is where you find it.

I had dealt with carrying my books into speaking and signing engagements, and it didn't take me long to realize that most book publishers don't spend a lot of money on packing cases for their products, looking toward long-term toting back and forth. So I looked around for other, sturdier, carrying cases, and found the perfect one.

At that time, we were undergoing several years of abnormal rainfall in the Mississippi Delta, and I owned several hundred acres of swampland that not only was good for hunting, but had what one timber cruiser called, "The best stand of green ash timber in the state!" It was a few years away from cutting, but with all the rainfall, our beaver population suddenly exploded and began damming up the drainage canals. Not only did this make for dying timber, but the beavers loved to gnaw the bark from the flooded trees, girdling the trunk so that it later died. The solution was to dynamite their dams on a regular (like, every other day!) basis, until the rains quit. One summer I used ten cases of dynamite for beaver control.

Dynamite cases are heavy cardboard, impregnated with some chemical that keeps the moisture out of the dynamite – or, the books, if you choose to carry your books around in a dynamite case!

I had been on a book-signing tour up on the east coast, and came back a day before it was mine and Tommy's turn to go into prison for the Wednesday night Prayer and Share Groups that Kairos encourages the formation of. Since it was Tommy's turn to drive, I didn't check my car when it came time to meet him at his house, but when I got there, Rosemary said he had called to say he was running late on a job, and for me to go ahead without him. I said, "Yes, Ma'am," and headed north for the hour drive.

For some reason, at that particular prison, they never checked our vehicles going in. We'd just pull up to the front gate, flash our "Assistant Chaplains Badge" at the guard, announce that we were here for "Kairos in Unit 29," and the guard would wave us in. However, they always checked our vehicles on the way out, especially the trunk, in case an inmate was hitching a ride out. I went to a wonderful P & S grouping in the unit, and left about 9:00 p.m., whistling a little gospel tune as I pulled up to the front gate of the prison farm and punched the trunk release for the lady security officer to check.

Suddenly, lights began to flash, alarm bells began to ring, and a squawking that reminded me of the old Navy "General Quarters" ship's battle alarm began. I rolled out of the car, to find a lady guard aiming a pistol at me in a two-handed grip! "Don't get out of the car!" she ordered.

I was already out of the car. I yelled, "I'm already out of the car!"

She bellowed back, over the alarm noises, "Get your hands against the top of the car and freeze!" She was glaring over an automatic pistol at me, deadly serious. I did as she ordered.

"What's wrong?" I hollered, noticing that two men in flak jackets with automatic rifles had burst from the K-9 quarters a hundred yards down the road, and were sprinting our way.

"You got a case of dynamite in this trunk!" she answered, still aiming my way.

Yikes! I had left my books in the car! "There's no

dynamite in that box!" I rejoined.

"Mister, there BETTER be dynamite in this box! There better not be one stick missing!"

It was apparent that this was an escalating situation that could get serious, as if standing at a prison gate with alarms going off and a woman holding a big pistol aimed at me while two men sprinted toward us with automatic weapons wasn't already serious enough. I carefully raised my hands off the car roof and turned toward the security officer, saying calmly (well, maybe that's not entirely accurate) "Lady, there's no dynamite in that box – it's books. Let me show you," and I took a step in her direction.

She took a corresponding step backwards, still holding that pistol with both hands, now aimed at my head instead of my torso. "Don't move!"

My hands were in the air, and I tried to speak soothingly, "Now, Lady, don't you shoot me. I'm going to show you that there's nothing but books in that box." The two guys in flak vests stopped in the middle of the road and brought their rifles up.

All three armed guards called, "Don't move!"

I shook my head. "Don't you shoot me! I'm going to open the box. There's nothing in there to hurt anyone. Please don't shoot." Probably not the most sane thing I could have done.

Each step I took, the lady gave ground. As I reached into the trunk, one of the men dropped to his belly on the road, presumably to survive the blast, as I slowly grasped the top of the box and lifted it, reached in and grabbed a copy of my book, *THE JAKES*, and held both boxtop and book up for them to see. There was no explosion. I flipped the book open to the back dust jacket flap: "See, here's my picture."

I was grateful that she cut the alarms and flashing lights off. I had to leave autographed copies of each book (at that time I had published six) for each of the security officers into whose night I had injected a little excitement, but that was a cheap fix, for me to get out the gate and head homeward. I did get a phone call from the Prison Security Chief the next day that blistered the whole side of my face.

And, I no longer carry my books in a dynamite case!

"WE'RE GONNA GET THIS STRAIGHT, ABOUT YOU AND MY WIFE!"

Speaking of that Security Chief, my earlier meeting with him, on my first Kairos Team, was somewhat spectacular of itself, and involved loaded pistols again, on the prison grounds. You have to know Lonnie to understand this story.

Midway through the two months of weekly meetings, when I was loosening up and getting to know others on the Team, at the end of a meeting at the prison Spiritual Life Center, a short, barrel-chested, bearded, grizzled man came up to me as the meeting ended, and announced, "I want you to follow me to my house, right down the road about a quarter mile."

This was on the prison grounds, I did not know the man, and he had not delivered that request – well, it wasn't really a request, it was an order – in a particularly friendly manner. Plus I had an hour's drive home myself. "What for?" I asked, in the same tone of voice.

"We're gonna get this straight about you and my wife!" he burst out.

"Mister, I don't know you, and I sure don't know your wife. I'm happily married, and I don't mess around. I'm fixing to get in my car and go home!" I exclaimed.

He squinted menacingly: "Do you have a gun?"

"No! This is a prison." I was getting mad now.

"Well," he jutted his jaw out and leaned toward me, "I got a pistol under my car seat. Now, do you want to walk in front of my car to my house, or would you rather drive your car to my house? We're gonna get this out in the open, between you and my wife!"

I was now scared. "Mister, I don't know your wife!"

"That ain't what I hear," he growled. "Let's go." He shoved me toward the door, and we walked to our vehicles – sure enough, he reached under the seat to produce a pistol – in a prison! "You walkin', or drivin'?" he asked, waving the gun. The other Team members were simply watching from a safe distance, not daring to interfere in our confrontation.

"Drivin'!" I stuttered, and opened my car door.

He called as he got in his car, "And don't think of tryin' to run. I got a radio and they'll hold you at the front gate."

"Mister, I don't even know your wife!" I declared desperately.

"That ain't what I hear," he growled again.

I followed him a few hundred yards and pulled into his back yard, under a huge oak. I tried one more time as I got out. "Mister, please, I don't know your wife!" He just tapped his pistol against his leg and pointed toward the back door. I marched toward it and knocked.

The door was opened by his wife. I did know her!

Cindy had been a bridesmaid in our wedding three decades before. She had been Betsy's best friend and roommate at Ole Miss, as well as sorority sister. We had double-dated, gone to parties together, but then when we got married and left for the Navy a thousand miles away only six weeks after the wedding, we'd lost touch. She had later married and moved off, and when we finally returned from service, we couldn't track her down. No wonder – she lived on the grounds of a prison, was married to the Security Chief, and worked for the prison administration herself. Lonnie had made the connection, and had chosen his own means to reacquaint us. He roared with laughter as I told Cindy how he'd forced me to come to the house.

Then an idea hit me: "Y'all have to come down to see us and surprise Betsy. I'm not gonna tell her about meeting you yet."

Turned out, Lonnie had a speaking engagement at a Leland church the next week, so I invited them to come out for supper afterward. I told Betsy casually, "Oh, by the way, there's a guy on the Kairos Team that will be in town Thursday evening, and I invited him and his wife to eat supper with us. Okay if I pick up a couple of big steaks to throw on the grill?"

"Sure. Do I know them?" my bride asked.

"It's Lonnie and Cindy Herring. Ring a bell?" I replied. She shook her head.

But that Thursday evening, when our doorbell rang, I managed to be occupied with the steaks and called, "Betsy, that's probably them. Can you get the door?"

It worked! In tears, Betsy grabbed Cindy and headed for the living room, calling to me as she passed, "You may as well put the steaks on the back of the grill; we've got thirty years to catch up on, before supper!"

Epilogue: Betsy had told me when I started volunteering for Kairos, "This is not my ministry, it's yours. I will pray for you, I will bake cookies for you, I will pack your bags and kiss you goodbye when you leave for prison, but it's not my ministry. Okay?"

I said, "Yes, Ma'am."

But several years later, when Kairos got permission to hold weekends in the Mississippi Women's Prison, Cindy was the Rector of Women's Kairos # 2 Team, and she told Betsy, "You can't turn me down. You HAVE to serve on my Team." She did, and was hooked, going on to Rector Women's Kairos # 12, then helping to form Mississippi Kairos Outside (a ministry to the female family members of incarcerated people) and leading KO Team # 2.

Yeah, we got it straight about me and Lonnie's wife!

UNCLE BOB RIDES AGAIN!

I have been Uncle Bob for most of my life, sho'nuff. If you don't believe me, go get a copy of my old Leland High School annual for my graduation year, and look at the thumbnail sketch next to my senior picture. It says, in addition to "Booming Bass," and "Prep Boy," as plain as day, "Uncle Bob." That's a long time ago.

In college, I was Uncle Bob to the Pike pledges, and in the Navy, once I made Lt jg, the Ensigns serving under me used Uncle Bob in private. Back home, even my younger brother called me Uncle Bob, and after Adam came along, "Uncling" a host of my buddies (Uncle Dude, Uncle Micky, Uncle Gene, Uncle Beau, etc), they all added me to the list as Uncle Bob. As Youth Minister at our church, a whole generation knew me as such. Several of our tractor drivers called me Uncle Bob, which brought looks of astonishment, since we were clearly of different races. At the office, people who have never met me face to face will call from Noo Yawk and ask for Uncle Bob. My son-in-law John had a hard time with it, having grown up calling me Uncle Bob for five years before he tied the knot to B.C. We were both so obviously uncomfortable with "Papa Neill" that I took him aside for a little talk. However, when he introduces me as his father-in-law Uncle Bob, it raises some eyebrows, as you can imagine!

Yet the most embarrassing Uncle Bob situation has to be from the Kairos Ministry. One weekend I was leading the singing for a group of residents in Unit 29 at Parchman, and during the four-day retreat made a talk. In that speech, I made a reference to a story from my old youth minister days, and quoted one of the kids as saying, "But, Uncle Bob." At the next song session, the rector, Roland Powell, asked, "Uncle Bob, could we have a song?" I have been Uncle Bob in Kairos ever since.

Which is okay. Some of my best friends are in prison.

Anyhoo, several years later I was driving through a large town on a fall day, showing a state tourism official around our part of the Delta. As we approached a major intersection, the light changed to red, and traffic stopped. There were a bunch of men in green-and-white striped britches working the flower gardens around the median. My truck window was down.

Suddenly, a voice boomed out, "Uncle Bob!" I turned to look. This big black guy called again, "Hey, ain't you my Uncle Bob, from Karo?" He was walking across three lanes of stopped traffic to us.

I opened my door and stepped out, recognizing him just as he said, "I'm Big Thunder, from Kairos number four!" He enveloped me in a crushing hug and turned to call to his watching companions (as well as all the folks in the other stopped vehicles, now!) "Hey, you guys! This here is my Uncle Bob, from Karo up in Parchman Prison!"

We did a quick exchange of, "How you been doing?" He had gotten A Custody after Kairos, and had been recently placed in a minimum security pre-release program. Then the light changed to green, and I hurriedly shook his hand good-bye as I got back in the truck. He dodged quickly back to his work station, calling, "Bye, Uncle Bob!" I waved to him, as well as the other green pants, whom he had ordered into a line abreast, hoes and rakes held at attention as they all waved good-bye to Uncle Bob, as well.

As I shifted into gear, I turned to my companion to see him just emerging from under the dashboard, holding my spare baseball cap over his flushed face. Bill declared, "Just get me back to the office, okay? I don't EVEN want to know what all that was about, and don't need to meet any more of your family, Uncle Bob!"

"YOU PAID UP FRONT"

For a dozen years I worked as a news and advertising consultant for a local television station. One year the elderly janitor retired, and the station hired a new younger man to take his place. Joseph was a ball of fire – he cleaned things that hadn't been cleaned for years, and still was finished by Tuesday afternoon with everything that used to take the former janitor the whole week to do, yet you never saw him sitting down, he was always busy doing something.

170

With time on his hands, he then set up a car-washing service out back and took it upon himself to wash all the news cars and vans, even waxing and polishing them. They looked like new, and naturally the sales people desired the same type service, even though they'd have to pay something for it, since they used their personal vehicles for sales. Joseph worked out a deal with the station manager to compensate him for detailing personal vehicles, and soon the sales staff was driving brand-new-looking cars and pickups. With time still left during the week, the new guy made special deals with others who worked at the station to detail their cars, too.

Betsy's Park Avenue Buick was beginning to resemble a car driven by a country girl, so I arranged with Joseph to bring her car in for that special treatment on a Thursday after lunch. Yet when I got ready to go home late that afternoon, he had not even finished the cleaning, much less getting to the waxing and polishing. "Take it on home and bring it back in the morning, Uncle Bob," he commanded. "I just want to do a really good job on this car for Miss Betsy."

I brought it back the next day, and he got right to work on it, yet when I came out at noon, he still wasn't finished with it. "Don't worry," he admonished, "I'll be through by the middle of the afternoon, Uncle Bob."

Had I somehow misunderstood Joseph's pricing? I thought he had told me he charged fifteen bucks for a special job on a car, but this looked like it was getting into real money, for he had spent somewhere around eight hours on it by now, with a couple more to go. Maybe he had said fifty, and I had heard fifteen? Well, too late now, and the Buick was looking like new almost; but I resolved not to pay him any more than fifty bucks.

About 2:00, I stuck my head out the back – he was still working on the Buick.

At 3:00, I checked again – still working on it.

At 3:30, I went outside and interrupted him: "Now,

Joseph, I've got to have this car ready by four, because we've got to go to Winona for a Kairos meeting this evening, and that's an hour and a half drive."

He never stopped polishing. "Yessir, Uncle Bob, I'll be through by then, don't worry."

Just before four, I got two twenties and a ten out of my billfold, folded them up to fit into my palm, and went out the back door. Joseph was shining the driver's side rear-view mirror with a rag, popping it just like a shoeshine man would pop it. When he saw me, he popped the rag again, stepped back and spread his arm like a maestro, and announced, "There she is, Uncle Bob. All ready for you and Miss Betsy. Just in time!"

My eyes popped at a sparkling dark green Buick Park Avenue that looked better than it ever had on the showroom floor. Seeing my look, the entrepreneur broke into a huge grin, then turned to get a cigarette from his shirt pocket, hanging on a pole nearby. He totally ignored my outstretched hand, which held the fifty bucks.

This young man who never relaxed or sat down at the station then took a lighter out of his pocket, tamped the cigarette, stuck it between his lips, lighted it, took a big drag, and then blew a perfect smoke ring. before sitting down on an overturned wash bucket to regard me with squinted eye. He pointed at me with the cigarette after taking another puff. "I been thinkin' this past couple months that I knowed you from somewhere, and then it finally hit me. I met you in the little room across from the law library in the Unit 29 administration building."

It was one of those out-of-place, out-of-time moments, but I connected it up. "Kairos?"

"Right. I used to run with BB and Everette. You're my Uncle Bob, who leads the singing at Karo. I know you now. These folks here at the station don't need to know from where, but I've finally placed you." He leaned back to grin at me, still managing to ignore the extended palm, from which protruded

172

the edge of two twenties and a ten.

Joseph waved at the gleaming Buick: "You take yo' car and go get Miss Betsy, and y'all go 'long to that Karo meetin' in Winona. And next month, when you go into the gym at Unit 29 for that Karo weekend, you tell the rest of those guys that Joseph is doing just fine on the outside."

He stood and popped his rag on the rear fender for effect. "Put yo' money back in yo' pocket, Uncle Bob. You don't owe me nothin'. You paid up front for this a long time ago!"

Healing: The Real Deal

I went all the way through Navy service, combat included, with just a couple of concussions, one pretty severe. Then the year after I came home from the Navy, I hydroplaned a pickup, which flipped several times. I ended up with four broken vertebrae, two of them crushed, though there was no paralysis. Took three years to heal, and the bone doc said to pray for advances in spinal injury research, because I might get twenty good years out of the one I had, and there was nothing then to fix it back right.

He was accurate almost to the month. Twenty years later I had gone to book publishing, and as a corollary, had blossomed out into a storytelling career, listing with the Lewis Grizzard's Speaker's Unlimited Bureau, and getting $3000+ per appearance. That called for a lot of traveling, and I have an oft-ruptured eardrum that does not release pressure, so I don't fly well atall. I got a 3/4-ton custom Chevrolet van to ride in, and when I'd have a speech in Chicago, say, I'd get in the van and drive there. Where I live at Brownspur, Mississippi, if I want to fly to Chicago, it'll take ten hours of driving to and sitting in airports, riding planes, or taxi rides to the speaking place anyway, so why not drive and not burst the eardrum again?

But the traveling to speak brought back the old broke back pain. It had always been present, but you can live with a lot of pain, if you can control the pain, instead of letting the pain control you. I built a mental Pain Box, and managed pretty well, until traveling aggravated the problem, and I had to quit the speaking business, after seeing a bunch of doctors, who all told me that there was nothing doctorial that they could do for me: to put in a rod or fuse stuff, they needed a good bone next to the bad bone, but I had too many busted right together.

I had a speech in New Orleans, so made an appointment with a doc at Oschner's who told me pretty much the same thing, but added, "There's a Dr. Ivester in Charleston, South Carolina, who is doing some interesting work with deadening nerves to control the pain. You might want to see him."

I couldn't believe my ears! Was God watching out for Neill, or what?! My next engagement was in Charleston, at the National Wild Turkey Federation Convention. I wasn't even going back home from New Orleans: I intended to hit I-10 after my Metropolitan Dinner Club speech, and drive to Charleston from south Louisiana. Dr. Whitehorse picked up the phone, got me an appointment with Dr. Ivester (whose son had married my first cousin) and even handed me the Oschner X-rays, saying, "No sense in paying for any more, three days after these were taken." He wished me luck, and the next morning early I hit the road.

Jules, who had married Cuddin Rebecca Furr, had graduated from Medical School and gone into practice with his daddy, so he met me when I got to their office in Charleston and took me back to look at my X-rays right away. Only moments later, his dad opened the door, toweling his hands from an operation, and stepped up to examine the lighted sheets of my back. I was standing almost behind the door, and he hadn't seen me. He pointed at the crucial image and exclaimed, "My Lord! What hospital is this man in?"

Jules nodded my way and said mildly, "He's standing by the door, Daddy."

The senior Dr. Ivester turned to look at me and asked, "Son, do you carry an emergency medical card?" I shook my head, wondering why the question. "Well," he concluded, "You ought to. If you had come in here from a wreck unconscious, I would have assumed from an X-ray that you could not walk, and might have tried to do something before you woke up."

He listened to my story, and why I was there, but shook his head. "I would not recommend cutting the spinal nerves to control your pain. In the first place, if you stepped on a hot coal, you wouldn't know it until you smelled your foot burning. In the second place, your traveling is aggravating the old injury, so if you quit doing what you're doing, the pain will probably be lessened to a controllable degree."

"Doc, I *can't* quit doing what I'm doing. I'm making too much money, and next year they're going to bump me up into the 5000-8000 dollar range. I *have* to go on traveling!"

He nodded wisely, considered briefly, then changed his prescription: "Oh, well, now I understand better, Son, so let me give you different advice: don't buy one wheelchair, buy two. Keep one at home, and the other in that big van of yours, because one day soon you're going to hear something like snapping your fingers softly, and you're not going to work from the waist down any more. Ever. But when that happens, if you're on the road, you can just call room service, give them your keys, and send them down to get your wheelchair out of the van. Then, Son, you can get dressed, and just roll yourself right into the auditorium, and *make that high-priced speech!"*

I was shocked for only a moment, then responded, "Doc, I think you just explained this like I can understand it. Thank you, Sir." I left Charleston the next day, drove to Atlanta and met with the Lewis Grizzard's Speaker's Unlimited Bureau folks to resign, recommended a young man just starting out in the book and speaking business named Jeff Foxworthy to take my place as the Southern Storyteller in their stable, and went home to Mississippi.

Years later, in the summer of 2003, I was leading the music for a Kairos Prison Ministry team rectored by old friend Mickey Plunkett, at the Rankin County prison. A Kairos team meets weekly for two months to prepare for the four days within the prison, and by the week of the last team meeting, I was in severe pain from the four-hour round-trip drives to Jackson. I finally told Betsy that I couldn't go any more: it just hurt too badly. Just so happens that she was also going to Jackson that weekend, as Advising Rector for the first Women's Kairos # 13 team meeting. She offered to drive me to my all-day meeting, go to her half-day meeting, then wait for us to finish, to drive me back. Maybe I could recline on pillows in the passenger seat and the pain would be more bearable.

So I went, though I was hurting. At that last team meeting, we have a prayer circle, and each person on the team prays for, and is prayed for by, every other team member. It is a very moving event to prepare us to head to prison a week later. At the end of the two-hour prayer circle, Mickey gave us a 20-minute break, and a lady who had been sitting across the circle from me walked up and stopped me. "You have a terrible, terrible pain!" she declared.

When I asked how she knew that, she replied, "It's a Gift I have, to sometimes feel another's pain. Would you let me pray for you right now?"

Well, I may be dumb, but I ain't stupid. I nodded, and Joyce stepped to my side, reached around me, and laid her hand right where the broken vertebrae are. "Wow!" she muttered to herself, "it's hot to the touch!" She prayed for maybe five or ten minutes, then said, "I think it's getting better," and turned to walk away.

"Wait!" I called softly, and caught her. "How did you know I hurt, and where?"

She repeated patiently, "It's a Gift from God. When I came into the room today, I knew someone was hurting badly, but I didn't know it was you until in the circle, when you put your hands on my shoulders to pray for me. Then I felt this terrible, terrible pain."

I have been accused of being a skeptic. "How can that

177

be a Gift from God, if you actually hurt as badly as I do?" I asked. Her face just glowed as she smiled up at me.

"Because then God sends this great Light of Love into my body, to drive the pain out of me. And sometimes, I can lay my hands on the person who is hurting, and God will relieve their pain when I pray for them." I had worked many Kairos teams with Joyce, and had never heard anything like this from her, or about her. She was very low-key about this Gift from God, and no one had yet heard us, nor paid any attention to us.

She turned to walk away again, and I called softly, "Thank you, Ma'am."

She turned quickly, a finger pointed upward: "Don't thank me! Thank Him!"

Folks, I led the music on Mickey's Kairos # 9 like I had never led it before. My back did not hurt the whole time, though I had taken liniment and hot pads into prison. It hasn't hurt since then. Oh, the old ruptured hip joint from Rebel football gets out of kerwhackus now and then, but the broke back hasn't hurt, even driving on 2000-mile trips these past three years.

Fast forward to the spring of 2005, when Betsy was Rector of Kairos Outside (a ministry to the female family members of incarcerated people) # 2, which is related in some detail elsewhere in this book. I had caught my toe under a tear in the carpet at the TV station where I worked as a news and advertising consultant, and partially torn a cartilage and ligament in my right knee, which is my good knee – the left one is totally reconstructed from an injury involving a desperate escape from a copperhead's strike. The rug tears aggravated a hamstring pull from a few months before which had been healing, but then backslid from me limping after the knee injury. I finally went to see Dr. O'Mara at the Mississippi Sports Medicine Clinic, and he recommended arthroscopic surgery. "How long will I have to be off of it?" I asked.

"About six weeks, on crutches," he replied.

178

I quickly checked my calendar: Betsy's KO weekend was in less than a month. I explained Kairos to the doctor, and promised to stay off of it as much as possible, but wanted to delay an operation until after her weekend, so I could be on her team. He shook his head, but reluctantly agreed, and got out that big blunt needle to suck the blood out and give me a cortisone shot in the knee joint. The weekend was to be over on a Sunday, so he scheduled me to come back by his office on Thursday before the weekend, then to return the next Thursday afternoon to check into the hospital for early Friday surgery.

When Betsy and I left home for the KO weekend at Camp Henry Jacobs near Utica, we went different ways: she headed down Highway 61, but I detoured down Highway 49, to go through Jackson and see Dr. O'Mara. His examination changed nothing: surgery was still on the schedule for the next week, and he cautioned me to be careful. When I arrived at the camp, deposited my suitcase at the men's cabin, and came back to the main lodge, there was Joyce!

"Joyce!" I exclaimed. "Good to see you, but what are you doing here? You haven't been to the team meetings."

"No," she replied. "But y'all have a handicapped Guest coming for the weekend, and someone called Al to ask if y'all could borrow his golf cart. He was getting ready to tow it over here this morning, and I felt really strongly that someone here needed me to pray over them, so I asked him to wait on me to get dressed, and I rode over with him, but I still don't know who God wants me to pray over. Is it you?"

That's always a good bet: I've had over 22 broken bones, another 15 major joint injuries, 135 or so stitches, five major concussions, been struck three times by lightning and three times by poisonous snakes, in addition to Lyme Disease, gangrene, blood poisoning, salmonella, 3rd degree burns, and various other ailments. But I didn't tell her what my current problem was, I just admitted that I might be her prayer subject, so she motioned me to sit down in a nearby chair and she knelt

179

down – by my right knee – and started to pray, laying her hands on the knee.

In a moment, she looked up: "It isn't just your knee hurting: your pain runs all the way up behind your leg to your hip," she said almost accusingly.

"I didn't even say it was my knee, but yes, Ma'am, the knee aggravated a hamstring pull that's always spasming now, especially at night," I admitted.

"Well, you could have told me," she remarked as she went back to praying. A few minutes later, another lady walked in and without realizing what was going on, exclaimed, "Joyce! I haven't seen you in a coon's age! How are you?" She advanced to hug my prayer warrior, who started to stand, then reacted as if her hands were glued to my knee.

"Just a minute, Patsy," she said, and went back to praying. A few moments later she again tried to stand, but the "God-Glue" still had her stuck. "Wow, what a strong connection!" she murmured, and prayed some more. When she then amened and stood, she actually seemed to have to pull her fingers aloose individually, whispering again, "Wow! That was a strong connection!" She shook her hands as she turned to Patsy, then hugged her and they walked away, leaving me sitting there.

That evening when we menfolks in charge of the kitchen finished setting up for breakfast for the ladies the next morning, our kitchen leader asked, "Okay, who wants to get up at 4:00 a.m. to come down here and cut the coffee pots on?" (We've learned not to trust timers!)

"I will!" I volunteered. "I haven't slept past 3:00 a.m. for a month, with these hamstring spasms and my knee hurting, so I'll be up anyway."

My roommate, Robert Vinson, added, "I'll set my alarm clock just to be sure Uncle Bob is awake." Good thing he did, because I was still snoring away at 4:00 a.m.

The next night, David again asked, "Okay, who wants to

get up at 4:00 a.m. to come cut the coffee pots on?" Once again I raised my hand.

"I will. I ain't slept past 3:00 a.m. but once in the past month." Robert once again set his alarm, just to be sure. Good thing again, for I was still asleep when it went off.

After that wonderful weekend, I drove to Jackson on Thursday afternoon as scheduled, and Dr. O'Mara did a pre-surgery MRI and X-ray. He came into the examination room with the films and pulled up a chair to sit down and eye me suspiciously. "What have you done to your knee?" he demanded.

"I tore the cartilage a month. . . ."

He interrupted almost angrily, "I mean over the weekend!"

"I tried to take care of it, Doc," I protested. "Is it worse than it was? I'm sorry."

"No!" He waved the films. "This is a perfectly normal knee. There's no need for you to have an operation. But it wasn't like this last week – *what have you done to it?!!*"

Well, duuuhhhhh! The only thing different was Joyce praying over it, for God to heal me again, as He did with my back. I proceeded to tell him what had happened, just finishing as his nurse stuck her head in to see what was taking him so long. He waved her away, "Tell whoever is next that I'll be there when I'm finished with Mr. Neill," then he settled back into his chair and declared, "You said this same lady prayed over your back a few years ago? Okay, tell me about that now." So I did, though his nurse glanced through the door window a couple more times.

When I finished, he nodded and reached out to shake my hand. "Okay, go home. And thanks for sharing this with me," he stood, then turned back to say, "You know, sometimes we doctors think we have all the answers. It's nice to realize that God can heal through us, but that He doesn't always need us to do His Healing. I appreciate your time. Come back if I can help you, but you don't need me this time! You got a better deal."

Okay, I realize that some folks are going to have raised eyebrows at this point. I can't help it. I've just related exactly what happened. The Bible talks about healing, as well as people who have that Gift, as Joyce obviously does, although she makes no claim for that herself.

"Okay, then: how come Neill?" is the next obvious question. I don't know. It was not my own faith, I'm supposing, because in neither case was I looking for a genuine God-Healing. Maybe it's because I'm supposed to write about it? Certainly I am not near'bout as worthy of being healed as most folks I know.

We've been here before, remember? "Now we see as through a glass darkly, but then we shall see as face to face. Now I know in part; then I will know fully." I Corinthians 13:12. This is one of those cases where I have to say, "I don't understand this: but I know that my broke back and my right knee don't bother me any more. To God be the Glory – not to Bob, or Joyce."

But in retrospect, I think a lot of it is faith in prayer – both by me and the ones praying, so why don't we check that out next?

Those Praying Hands

I will probably be out of prison by the time you read this, but if not, just wait for a few days, and I will be. Actually, that's one of the best lines we've ever found to deal with those unwanted solicitation calls. If Betsy answers and realizes it's one of those type calls, she just interrupts with, "Oh, yes, my husband always makes these decisions, so could you call back when he gets out of prison next week, please?" They never do. Works just as well if I answer and tell them, "Oh, yes, my wife makes these decisions, so could you call back when she gets out of prison next week, please?"

We spent the 2007 Palm Sunday weekend, Thursday through Sunday, in prison at the Central Mississippi Men's Unit on another Kairos Prison Ministry weekend. I was leading the music, and my former guitar player Jesse Heath was the Leader for Kairos # 16.

But what I wanted to tell you about was the Saturday before we ended up in prison. At the all-day Team meeting, we hold a Prayer Circle, during which (it often takes two hours) every member of the 50-person team prays over, and gets prayed over by, every other member of the Team. It is a very moving, meaningful time, and if your church or Sunday School class or Share Group hasn't tried that, then you belong to consider it.

The way we did it on Jesse's Team is, half of the Team, led by Uncle Bob, stood behind the seated half, and started the rotating Prayer Circle. Since I was first in line standing behind Roy, my keyboard player, I prayed over him, then sat in the vacant chair on his left. Every other Team member then came by and prayed over me before I had a chance to rise and start praying around the circle for them in my turn.

As the Team members passed by me, laying hands on my shoulders and often stooping down to voice their prayers by my good ear, I basked in the Love of the moment, feeling lifted up by a Power I knew but can never fully comprehend. Even though she was not on the Team, I was struck by how many of the veterans also prayed for Betsy, for she has worked in Kairos nearly ten years now, and we are known as a team couple.

Then I got to thinking of, and thanking for, those praying hands.

When you are being prayed over by a bunch of people, for any reason, they will most often put their hands on you. That's Biblical, and it's also a healing of sorts. Jesus did it. I had one lady who told me afterward, "I could sense something hurting you, just at the base of your breastbone, but as I prayed for it to be healed, it just disappeared, so I think you're okay." Healing still works today: not by people, but by the God we serve, who sometimes heals through people, be they licensed physicians or Gifted Prayer Warriors.

But the praying hands that were laid on me for that hour were so different. Some were almost rough – Rusty gave a relaxing back rub while he prayed, and I have been accused of the same technique. "I'll give you a half-hour to stop that," I murmured. Some, like the lady who sensed a hurt, were laid on me so softly I could hardly feel them. The temperature was what was so strange, to me anyway. Some of the hands – men and women – were actually hot. Some were warm. Some were cool. I had no doubt that all were sincere, because I recognized most of the voices, except for a few of the Team rookies. Why the difference in the temperatures of those hands, I wondered? We're all supposed to be about 98 degrees, aren't we? Why did some hands almost burn, and literally made me break a sweat?

Of course, my right hand that was crushed in the cotton gin lint cleaner back when I was thirty has a noticeable temperature coolness from my left in the wintertime, so much so that Betsy often complains when we snuggle up at night. Yet I doubted that anyone else on the Team had crushed hands.

One thing I was certain of: God was in all of them. Those praying hands would carry us through the entire Kairos four days at CMCF the next week, and bring us back home for the Easter weekend better for the experience. What's even better is that most of those 42 residents of CMCF would be better able to celebrate Easter Morning after going through the Kairos weekend. And we would, too.

Then I got to wondering, as the Team had passed by me praying and I stood to now pray over them one by one: what were my own hands like? Rough but relaxing, like Rusty's? Soft and tear-watered, like Gail's? Hot like Willy's, or warm like Mike's, or cool like Al's? Could God use my hands like he had used theirs to comfort, condition, and heal others, me included? I hope so. I sure do hope so.

The above is a column I wrote a few years ago, but it serves to introduce the subject of prayer, which so often is the key to one's life. It was a key to my own life, back in August of 2007. Some newspapers run my syndicated weekly column on Sundays. Some run it on Tuesdays, Wednesdays, or Thursdays. The latter group really appreciates a columnist who sends his musings well before a Monday holiday, since they can better enjoy the holiday if they get most of the holiday week's paper set up early. I set a deadline of getting my column out by Thursday before the Labor Day weekend that was coming up.

This meant writing it Wednesday, or early Thursday. My idea was to deal with a Kairos Prison Ministry International Visioning Committee Conference Call meeting early Wednesday, type up and send out minutes of Monday night's Chamber of Commerce Board meeting, wrap up an estimate for

185

a grant application, then run home for lunch and knock out my column over a cheese & jelly sandwich, since Betsy was making muscadine jelly, and maybe she'd have enough for a pie for dessert. I finished the Conference Call about 9:35, and turned my attention to the Board Minutes. The phone rang about 10:00. It was Betsy.

"I need you to come home right now," she declared with no preamble when I answered. "Something is wrong."

I said "Yessum" and headed for the car. The house is seven miles from the office, and this first thing I looked for when I cleared the City limits was a visible column of smoke, but there was apparently not another house fire. When I rushed in, she was lying on the bed: gray, clammy but wet with sweat, and having chest pains. I asked my bride one question: "Have you taken an aspirin?" She had done so. I quickly scooped her into the car, punched the flashers button, and stomped it. I know, some people would say at this point, "Call 9-1-1," but ever since they took the ambulances away from the funeral homes, whenever anyone who lives in the country calls 9-1-1 nowadays, they tell the EMT, "I'll meet you at the highway west of the Mennonite Church, in a white Mercury." No offense, but the folks who drive the ambulances in these parts just don't know about country roads. That 911 deal works fine if you have time to talk them in to your location, but I didn't feel like I had time, the way Betsy looked.

I cell-called daughter B.C., an Occupational Therapist for the county hospital, mainly to ask where the Emergency Entrance was. She suggested that I call our family doctor, because he has done our physicals for the past decade and the hospital might want a base line. I did that, and Jerry said to bring Betsy to his office first: "To see what's happening and treat her initially, if it's a heart problem." I was there in record time for the fifteen miles. Not one minute after I parked, Betsy was hooked up to a heart machine. The nurse took one look, grabbed Jerry, and pointed.

186

Dr. Cunningham said mildly, "She's having an MI right now! Can you get her to the Emergency Room, or do you want to wait for an ambulance?" I've explained that, so we were out of the office in two minutes flat and at the ER two minutes after that. Not a cop in sight, but there was no traffic and I had my blinkers on again.

Dr. O'Neal met me at the ER ramp with a wheelchair, for Jerry had called ahead to get the action started. Dr. Mansour's heart team was standing by and they wheeled her in as I chunked my insurance card at the registrar lady and answered a few brief questions before a nurse came and grabbed me. I signed a couple of consent forms, and Betsy was in surgery for a stent in the one clogged artery by 11:15. That was one hour and 15 minutes from the first call, and over 30 miles, with two quick stops. She was out of surgery before noon! No permanent damage, no other blockages. Both doctors said that's probably due to the aspirin. Maybe so.

But you know what got me? The prayers and the people. Two church ladies met me in the parking lot as I moved the car from the emergency ramp. Sarah and Maxine were headed in to visit a friend when they saw me, and I hurriedly spilled my news as I ran for the ER door. They both grabbed their cell phones, and right there in the parking lot, Sarah called to start the Calvary Baptist Prayer Chain going, while Maxine, a Kairos Outside Team member, called to get the Mississippi Kairos Prayer Chain activated. Of course, B.C. was there quickly, but not before one Brownspur neighbor dropped by and another had called my cell phone. Two preachers, Park and Ken, came before the OR door was closed, as did a hospital trustee, Billy Schultz, a good friend. The Ex-Mayor's wife, Inge, was there before the doctors got through. Two more ladies awaited me in the parking lot when I left. Janice and Cindy (I still call her "Gifford"; there were three Cindys in one class at the Sonshine House, so we called them Gifford, Pfrimmer, and Pitt – for Pittman) from our old church Youth

Group called or arrived as Betsy was transferred from the OR to ICU.

That night was Calvary's regular Wednesday Night Prayer Meeting, and Benny burst out with, "Praise the Lord for how quickly the Prayer Chain worked to get the word out so we could pray for her!" Chaplain Dave Langdon left a message on our phone that he was getting the word out to our brothers behind bars, as well as the International Kairos folks who knew us. When I got home that night, there were e-mails and phone messages from church friends, family, and Kairos people from South Africa to California, as well as from all over Mississippi. That next weekend, when I visited prison for the regular Kairos Second Saturday Reunion, a whole delegation of Unit 30 and Unit 29 men gathered around to see how Betsy was doing, and to say they had been praying regularly for her, behind bars.

Prayer works, folks. I've seen it myownself, for both me and Betsy.

And then, this past March of 2010, for our younger grandson. This was my column that ran the week before Easter.

EASTER LETTER TO A GRANDSON

Dear Neill Leiton Irwin:

I want you to read this when you are old enough to understand about God and Jesus, okay?

When Yo'Momma called me St. Patrick's Eve to come to the Emergency Room because you had fallen on your head, I called your grandmother Doots first, turned the car around, and headed for Greenville. But my second cell phone call was to activate the Mississippi Kairos Prison Ministry Prayer Chain, so that immediate prayers began going up for you from as many as 1000 people, many of whom relayed the news to their own personal prayer groups. My third call was to our Calvary Baptist Church Prayer Chain, where I lead the music. Then I called your Uncle Adam in North Carolina to get him in on it. So before I even got to the hospital, there were probably 2500 people praying for you, literally around the world.

188

When the CT Scan confirmed your skull fracture, procedure called for you and Yo'Momma to be sent by ambulance to Jackson's University Medical Center two hours away to see a pediatric neurologist, so Doots and I took charge of Big Brudder Sean. Yo'Daddy was piloting an American Eagle airplane that was at the time on the ground in Wichita, so he got a substitute pilot and caught a flight to Memphis, where his pickup was. The EMTs strapped you and Yo'Momma onto a gurney (which REALLY agitated Big Brudder!) and took off, so I called Bryon McIntire (Jake Boateater in my book you should have read by now), as well as the MS Kairos Music Team members – all of whom live in that area – to get someone to meet the ambulance. Bryon welcomed y'all to UMC, and the Music Team got there just a little later to pray over y'all.

All the doctors could see the skull fracture on the X-ray, but you were just smiling and walking around – Bryon said you came right to him right off the ambulance, since he looks a little like Yo'Daddy – acting "Like a normal one-year-old kid." There was no swelling, no dilated eyes or droop to an eyelid, no lethargy, and obviously no pain after the first half-hour or so. They did a few more tests to check things out, and then decided that y'all could go home if you wanted to (by that time Yo'Daddy had driven in from Memphis), or if you wanted to spend the night, they'd give y'all a room. I've never heard of anyone being officially discharged from a major hospital at 11 p.m. before, but you were!

Understand that your grandaddy The Grunk ("Granddaddy Uncle Bob" was too long, so got shortened to "GrandUncle," then "Grunkle", which ended up "Grunk") has had at least five major concussions, two requiring several days in the hospital, two causing weeks of double vision and one when I could not even recall the second half of the football game I was playing in. I know something about head injuries, although no one ever bothered to X-ray my skull to check for fractures, back in those days.

Consider this: you had a fractured skull, confirmed by X-ray; within the hour after that diagnosis, you had literally thousands of Christians praying for you all around the nation and the world; the doctors could see no obvious signs of the usual symptoms of severe head injury – you were just being a "normal one-year-old boy"; you were released by the pediatric neurologist from a major hospital at 11 p.m. to make the two-hour drive back home to sleep in your own bed; at which point a Praise Report was sent to those Prayer Warriors, to the effect that you had been healed and they could begin rejoicing for that.

WHAT A COINCIDENCE!!!

This season of the year we celebrate not only the fact that Jesus died on the Cross, but that He was resurrected from the grave, and left the Holy Ghost here on earth when He ascended into Heaven to sit by God's Throne and to watch that same Spirit operate through people like the ones who prayed for you, plus Bryon McIntire and Mark Propst and Rusty Healy and Mike Lewis who came to the hospital to show you and Yo'Momma that God loves and heals us, even today in these modern times; even little bitty boys.

When you can read this, from the Grunk, I hope you understand Easter just a little better!

This is an aside – well, actually, not really – but when I started a weekly syndicated newspaper column back in 1986, I targeted smaller dailies and weeklies in the South, eventually topping out at over a hundred papers. I had walked into every one of those offices personally to introduce me and my column, as well as into several dozen other offices who did not end up buying my column. I sold the columns as simply rural, small-town, nature-loving writing, with the sole goal that the reader feels better post-Neill than he/she did pre-Neill. There's enough gripey, bitchy writing out there, so that I don't have to do any of that type work. But I also told each editor or publisher toward the end of my interview that the South is known as "The Bible

190

Belt," and to many folks Down Heah, God is just part of our lives, so we talk about Him as we would any Friend – and that I intended to do that in my columns, although not in every one, nor was I trying to lean on anyone about accepting my own brand of religion. But the point was, I wanted them all to know that I was going to at times mention God and Jesus, so if it bothered them to run that in their papers, just say the word and I'd head on down the road. Not a single one objected.

But the best part of all this is, after 25 years of writing columns, I've had a good many editors, publishers, even typesetters(!) call or e-mail me to ask for prayer, or to be put on the prayer chain, when someone dear to them was ailing. I've even had some who volunteered to go to prison with their Uncle Bob, in Kairos!

Back in the late '90s I went for a check-up, and the doctor was somewhat concerned with the throat problems that I had been having for a month or so. He examined me, then decided to take a biopsy by sticking something down my throat and scaping off some tissue to send off to check for cancer. When he finished, late that Wednesday afternoon, he instructed me to not sing or even talk loudly for a couple of weeks, until the results of the lab tests came back. Yet when I got home just before five, I made one call – to Parchman Prison!

"Dave," I asked Chaplain Langdon, "Are you going to Kairos Prayer and Share tonight?" He was. "Then tell the guys that Uncle Bob has this problem" – I told him – "and ask them to pray for me, okay?" He said he would, so I hung up and went to prayer meeting at my own church, as usual, where I revealed the problem and asked for their prayers as well, of course.

Just before midnight, my phone rang, and it was Chap Dave: "Uncle Bob, I know I probably woke you up, but I just wanted to assure you that you do NOT have cancer! The way those guys prayed for you tonight, it may be something else, but it ain't cancer. Good night."

Sure enough, when the lab tests came in, it wasn't cancer. WHAT A COINCIDENCE!

I led a Kairos two-day Retreat once, close to Christmas, which was the natural occasion for not only praying, but also for singing Christmas carols, and those two things combined for a memorable exhibition for me, to guitar accompaniment.

We tend to take Christmas carols for granted in the free world, and I admit I had never given much thought to singing carols in prison. If I had, it might have occurred to me that it's not the usual thing to do in the prison environment, especially with guitars. The guy leading the music waxed enthusiastic: "Joy to the World" was performed with gusto, and it got better when we started "Hark, the Herald Angels Sing." Several more of that same style were enjoyed by all, before Reverend Varnado rose for a brief talk. Willie spoke warmly of God's Love, and how no one was beyond that Love, no matter whether he was in prison or in a duck blind. It was a moving homily, bringing every man there to the realization that the Baby Jesus had come to earth for him personally.

As Willie left the podium, I stepped forward and asked each group of six or so men to quietly join hands and spend a few moments in silent prayer thanking God for His Gift this Christmas season, and for the other blessings in all our lives. As I moved away from the podium, the three guitarists moved forward, gently strumming "Silent Night." No one sang, they weren't supposed to. After the first verse, Ralph left the melody to Jonathan and John, and picked out a tenor harmony part on his instrument. The three of them began to stroll among the groups of inmates, who had their eyes closed, lips moving in prayer and praise. "Silent Night" has never been so beautiful to my ears.

Nor was it just to my hearing: the faces in those groups, uplifted to a Heaven beyond razor-wire fences, began to glow with an unearthly Light. Cross my heart.

Maybe it was a reflection of the florescent lights.

Maybe the sun peeked through the few thick bullet-proof windows just about then. Maybe it was a mass case of heartburn from the lunch taco salad, or perhaps they all had the malaria sweats, like I still do decades later. Maybe the heating thermostat cranked off in the main part of the room just about then.

You believe that if it makes you more comfortable.

"Silent Night" will never be the same for me, after watching those men praying with faces uplifted and glowing – I can still picture that instant, ten years later now.

And I still stand in awe of the Power of Prayer by God's People, in and out of prison.

Memorable Stories of the Way God Works

KIDS IN PRISON AND IN CONGRESS

On Father's Day of the year 2000, I can't help but think of a stat from the Kairos Prison Ministry for this column: only five percent of the men in prison had a positive father figure in their home to guide them.

See, almost any male can be a father biologically, but the responsibility for a kid only starts with conception. Too many homes don't have a father nowadays.

Memorial Day is just past, and as a man who has been in combat, let me make an observation. If we still had a draft in this country today, over half of the guys in prison wouldn't be there. Mind you, I've spent a lot of time in prison the last few years, and have a lot of good friends there. I have the experience to back up my opinion.

See, one of the main problems that gets a kid in trouble with the law is a lack of discipline, which one would normally get from a father. Oh, I know a mother can and does discipline her kids, but when a boy gets a little big for his britches, it's hard for a woman to contend with a strong young man who wants to do things his own way.

Used to be, when a kid got into trouble, a judge might say, "Son, I'll give you a choice: prison, or the Marine Corps?" And the Marines (or Army, Navy, or Air Force) would give that kid the discipline, training, education, and motivation he had failed to pick up at home from an absentee father. (Shoot, I

194

know some fathers who sent their boys to the service anyway!) Mind you, now, I ain't for another shooting war; but why couldn't the military be used as a national reaction force in peacetime, while getting trained in case we did need to go to war again? Fires, hurricanes, earthquakes, floods, and other disasters cry out for a trained force to come to the rescue. Well, I didn't mean to open that box.

What I did mean to tell you was about two boys, neither of them mine. One of them I ran across in the late '80s while on a lobbying trip in Washington DC. I was walking through the House Office Building, when suddenly a voice called in surprise, "Mr. Neill? Coach?"

I turned, and this nicely-dressed young man held out his hand to shake. His parents had once lived in Leland, it seemed. "Don't you remember me? You coached me in Little League."

He now worked for a congressmen from the state his parents had moved to when he was a teenager. He got a faraway look in his eyes as he vowed, "One of these days, my name is going to be on one of these doors!" I congratulated him on setting such a worthy goal, then we caught up on the standard Southern "How's Yo'Momma an' 'nem" routine for just a few minutes.

Then he declared, "You know, I'll never forget something you told me in Little League."

"What could I possibly have told you in baseball worth remembering?" I wondered.

"You remember that we always prayed before each game, and then you had a rule that if we threw our bat, helmet, glove, or cussed, or argued with the ump, you'd take us out of the game?" I did recall that. "Well, we were playing in the championship game, and one of our best hitters came in from the field after an inning when someone had made an error that let in a couple of runs, and he threw his glove at the dugout and cussed. You didn't let him bat that inning when his turn came up with men on base, and you called on me to come off the bench and pinch-hit for him, and I didn't want to."

I still couldn't remember it, so he continued, "You knelt between first and home and asked me why I didn't want to take my bat, and I told you because I was scared of striking out. And you told me, 'Son, don't be afraid of striking out – be afraid of going up there and not doing the best you can do to hit the ball.' So I batted, and I didn't get a hit, but I didn't strike out, either. I'll never forget that!"

That was neat for him to remember that, I thought. We chatted for a few more minutes, shook hands, and parted ways. I've had Lyme Disease, so I have a medically-certified excuse for not recalling his name today.

Nearly a decade later, I was in a Mississippi prison on a Second Saturday Kairos Reunion, and a young man in black-and-white striped britches walked up to me. "Mr. Neill? Coach? You don't remember me, do you? You coached me in Little League baseball."

I didn't recall him, automatically claiming Lyme Disease, so he continued, "I was one of your best players, and you had a stupid rule that we couldn't throw anything when we were mad, or argue with the umpire, or cuss out loud. We were playing for the championship, and someone made an error that cost us the lead, and when I came in at the end of that inning, I threw my glove and cussed – and you jerked me out of the game!"

Well, that rule applied to everyone who played for us, I remarked, and he nodded. "I know it did, and we all knew it. But we lost the championship because the kid you sent up to bat for me with men on base couldn't drive them in, and I told my mom that night that I wasn't going to play for you the next year. So she got me on a team where the coach wouldn't stifle my competitive spirit, and we beat y'all the next year for the championship."

"That the way the ball bounces sometimes," I agreed.

He paused reflectively. "You know, I'm in here because

I got drunk and mad and killed a guy who was drunker than I was. Beat him to death, and he was really a friend of mine when I was sober. I guess I'll spend most of my life here, and I've had a lot of time to think. I never could learn to control my anger, and I've wondered if there was any point in my life at which I might could have turned that around. If so, maybe I wouldn't be in here with striped britches on!" I had to agree with his observation.

Two boys, same situation. I am so grateful for God's having put us together at different times in our lives over three decades!

THE RIDE TO THE WALL & THE MIA BRACELET

As I parked my car in the prison parking lot one day, a big ole motorcycle whipped into an empty space right next to my Buick. I didn't recognize Tony until he pulled off his helmet, and he didn't realize it was me he was parking next to until I got out. We leaned against our vehicles and caught up, not having seen each other for a while, although we had talked several times on the phone. Tony was a Warden at the Central Mississippi Prison where I was scheduled to lead a Kairos weekend in a couple of months, so I had driven down for a meeting with him and the Chaplain, plus my Coordinator, Mickey Plunkett, but hadn't expected to meet in the parking lot with him on a motorcycle, which I had not known he rode.

Tony was getting ready for the annual "Rolling Thunder" Ride To The Wall over Memorial Day weekend. It's a regular event for bikers (as in motorbikes) all over America. "I've seen a quarter million bikes in the Pentagon parking lot," he declared, adding that they then go to the Vietnam Wall to pay respects to comrades whose names adorn that Memorial. He extended his left wrist to show me a black bracelet engraved with the "Rolling Thunder" motto and the date. "It's a moving thing," he testified softly.

It is that. I've been to The Wall myownself, and have wept, noting the names of friends who didn't come home, or came back in a body bag or coffin. We stood in silence for a few moments, contemplating times past.

Then I noticed his other wrist. It had a similar bracelet, but was obviously much older, and more familiar. "Is that an MIA Bracelet?" I asked. "You don't see those very much any more." This was the summer of 2001, twenty-eight years after the USA accepted second place in the Southeast Asian War Games.

He nodded, extending his right wrist. "Jerry hasn't come home yet," he explained. "He was from up there in the Delta close to where you are. But let me tell you a story about that."

"Couple of years ago, a buddy and I were getting ready to make The Run, and I decided to go online to get up a bunch of bikers along the way. There's a web site we use for that, and I just said we were going to leave here on such a date, and were taking such a route, and if anyone wanted to meet us along the way, we'd love the company. Several folks replied, including a lady biker from around St. Louis. We set up places to meet, and left when the day came, picking up comrades along the way, until we had quite a troop of bikers together."

"We pulled into the designated truck stop at St. Louis for lunch, and there were other bikers there to meet us, including the young lady who had replied. We were sitting around the table introducing ourselves, and when her turn came, she said she was originally from Mississippi, which is why she had answered my e-mail. Said her brother had served in Nam as crewman on a chopper that went to the aid of another one that was shot down. He was declared Missing In Action and they had not heard anything about him until years after we pulled out of Nam." We both grimaced over a war that could have been won, and all the lives lost letting politicians fight it instead of generals.

"She said that in 1999 she had succeeded in contacting someone who had been the only survivor of that chopper crash, who had been captured, then later released. A Joint Commission group was organizing a trip to Vietnam to try to find out something about MIAs, and she decided to go along. That survivor led them to the exact spot where the helicopter had crashed that her brother's chopper had landed to try to rescue the crew of, but the second chopper had been driven off by enemy fire before the rescuers could reboard their ship. They even found a couple of the main blades in a nearby village, being used as corner posts for a hogpen. She had brought one of them back, so as to take it to The Wall to leave as a memorial to her brother."

Tony had suspicious moisture in his eyes now. "She said the survivor told her that he had been the only one captured after the crash and botched rescue who was able to walk and keep up with the Viet Cong, so they tied a rope around his neck, and led him away into the jungle, where he ended up in a prison camp." He swallowed. "The guy told her that he had heard shots as soon as he was out of sight of the others, and he just knew that the VC had executed the rest of the Americans, including her brother. But since he didn't actually see that, our Defense Department couldn't legally declare them as Killed In Action."

I interrupted, "Man, what a lick! To go over there and then find out her brother had been dead all those years."

Tony shook his head. "No. She said it was actually a closure for her, and gave her peace about the whole thing." His voice dropped almost to a whisper, "Then I asked her what her brother's name was."

I saw it coming, but couldn't believe it. "Aw, naw, Man! You mean. . . ."

He nodded, and extended his right wrist again. "All those years, I had been wearing her brother's MIA Bracelet. She couldn't believe it either. Nobody in our group was fit to ride anywhere for a while. That was some experience!"

I shook my head in awe. "But now that you know, you

still wear the bracelet? You didn't take it off and put it up, or maybe give it to her, or something?"

He shook his head as well. "Nope. Jerry hasn't come home yet. I gave my word."

The sister and Tony have since become close, as you might expect, with such a common bond. She'd only met one other person who has worn an MIA bracelet with her brother's name.

That was such a touching story that I asked Tony for permission to run it in my syndicated column for the upcoming Fofa July of 2001. He agreed, and I wrote it to send out.

Then Betsy and I left for a week in the mountains, then she flew to New York City to see our daughter for a few days. It was after she got home that I came in one evening and she said a lady had been trying to contact me about that column, leaving phone messages for two weeks.

I've learned that it isn't always good when people want to talk to you about a column, but I called the number she gave me. The lady who answered referred to my MIA column, noted that I hadn't used last names, and asked if I would tell her, if she guessed that MIA's last name. I agreed, and she ventured, "Staff Sergeant Jerry Elliott, from Greenville, Mississippi." I concurred.

Then she softly said, "He was my father." I was stunned.

She followed with, "I was only four months old when he was shot down. He never saw me. My mother was pregnant when he was shipped overseas." Then she almost whispered, "I'd sure like to meet the man who has worn my father's MIA Bracelet for all these years."

Well, I'd have to ask the man if he was willing to meet with her, I opined. Actually, I already had a meeting set up with him, for the following Friday, for my Kairos weekend in Tony's prison was fast approaching.

It worked out fine. I went into his office, he reached for his Kairos file, but first I handed him my column, which he had not yet seen. "Read that," I suggested. He did, straight-faced, and allowed as how it was a good story. Should be – he had told it.

Then I sat back and said, "Now, let me tell you who called me Tuesday: Jerry Elliott's daughter. Gina would like to meet the man who has worn her daddy's bracelet all these years."

A Warden's job demands that he not show much emotion, so he didn't show much. "I never knew he had a daughter," he declared. "His sister never said a word about there being a daughter." Of course, the sister was older, and had already left home for another state a long way off, before her brother went missing. She never went back, had not been around the daughter at all, and had had no occasion to tell Tony about her.

We then went on with the business of the appointment, but at the end of the meeting, Tony took out his card and scribbled his home number on it. "Give this to his daughter, and tell her to call me," he said. I took it, shook hands, and left.

The next week, I met with the lady and explained that Warden Tony was willing to talk to her, then explained his job and why we had been in contact, for me to have gotten that story. She took the card with some trepidation, saying, "Oh, I've got butterflies. This not going to be easy for me to do, but I want to so much. Thank you!"

Two weeks later, Tony called me at home. "Did you give that girl my card yet?" I had. "Well, she hasn't called me yet!" I explained what she had said about having butterflies. "Okay. Can you give me her number? I'll just call her!" I did so. He called to set up a meet with Gina.

The next week, I called the MIA's daughter. "Oh, thank you so much!" she gushed. "That is the kindest man I've ever talked to! We talked for two solid hours, and I feel like I have

201

shed 29 years worth of baggage that I've been carrying around on my back!" Then she said, "It's a God thing: the two of us getting together through your column."

Warden Tony Compton later came to a Kairos Team meeting to speak about the inmates, but then after answering everyone's questions, he asked for more time, so as to tell that story to the Team, ending with, "God put us together, but not just for this Kairos weekend!" Then he pulled on his leather biker's jacket, picked up his motorcycle helmet, shook my hand, and walked across the room. We heard the side door close, and I stood to continue the Team meeting.

Suddenly we heard the door open again, and Tony's boots clicking across the tile floor. Everyone looked up as he appeared once again and entered the circle of chairs, where he walked straight toward me as I stepped around the podium to meet him, wondering what was up.

Tony is a big powerful man. He never said a word. He dropped his helmet to the floor, reached around and grasped me in a bear hug that lifted me clean off the floor – and I ain't no little guy myownself – then he released me, wiped a hand across his face as he bent to pick up his helmet, and marched back across the circle, out of the room, then out of the church. No one spoke until we heard his bike crank up.

That happened, as I said, in 2001, two weeks before the tragic 9/11 events in New York. We had a very successful ("The Best Kairos Ever!") weekend in Tony's prison, and he transferred to another facility soon after that, so I lost track of him.

You may have already read about my youngest grandson's fall and subsequent trip to Jackson in an ambulance, then being proclaimed a normal one-year-old, as a result of prayer, in March of 2010.

One of the emergency room nurses at the Greenville hospital where B.C. had initially taken Leiton to get a CT Scan, where the fractured skull was discovered, came up to me as we were waiting for the ambulance to arrive. "Aren't you Mr. Neill, that writes?" I nodded. "I thought I recognized you. You wrote a column about my step sister's dad several years ago. He was Jerry Elliott, killed in Vietnam, remember?" I did remember.

"That column changed my sister's life," she said softly. "She wears that bracelet all the time now, and it's given her so much peace. Thank you for writing that story."

"What bracelet? You don't mean that Tony. . ?"

She had thought I had known all along, but I hadn't. "Oh yes. That was the nicest man. He had that MIA Bracelet cut off his wrist and gave it to her. You have no idea how that event gave her closure and peace to go on living."

It's a God Thing, as Tony had declared back in 2001!

I was serving as state chairman of the Kairos Ministry during 2007 and 2008, and during a Board meeting at our home at Brownspur, we discussed, then engaged in a long group prayer for, the expansion of that ministry in Mississippi. One week later, I had a call from the Chaplain of the Yazoo City Federal Correctional Complex inquiring about this Kairos ministry. Seems that the mother of a man imprisoned at YC FCC had gotten a call from another son who was housed in the state penitentiary at Parchman. That man had just been through a Kairos weekend in Unit 29, and had accepted Christ. He was so enthusiastic in telling his mom how his life had been changed, that after they hung up, she called the Federal chaplain to see if her son there could have the same opportunity. While we had tried for years to get permission to hold Kairos at Yazoo City, we had not been able to get that door open. Now it was being opened for us!

By God, obviously.

Within another week, Reece Vaughan, who later succeeded me as state chairman, was meeting with the YC FCC chaplain (on the Fofa July!). That next March 1st, Humphreys

McGee was Leader (the terminology changed from Rector, which I still prefer) of YC FCC Kairos # 1. At that Closing ceremony, what had to be one of the funniest statements we've ever heard came forth: one Resident was speaking at the mike, telling how he had been very successful as a drug dealer, but then decided to rob a bank, and "I was a terrible bank robber!" The whole room broke into laughter, but as it died down, a second Resident toward the back row piped up in a somewhat resentful tone, "Y'all don't laugh: bank robbin' ain't near'bout as easy as it looks like it would be!" It should be against the law to laugh that much in prison!

But back to expansion in Mississippi Kairos: after the Fofa July meeting that kicked off our agreement with the Feds, we started Team meetings for Kairos # 22 at Unit 29, Parchman, where Todd Pittman had asked me to lead the music for the last weekend in September. On that Saturday, in walked the Deputy Commissioner of the Department of Corrections. After observing a couple of talks, a song session, a chapel service, and participating in a prayer session with several Team members and Residents, he finally asked someone, "Who would I need to talk to about getting Kairos into Unit 32? We've had some problems there that I think this ministry could help us solve." The Team member pointed out that Uncle Bob was currently state chairman, and when he finished leading this song session, they'd send me over.

I met with the DC, and he told me what his needs were, and I jumped at the chance, although Unit 32 had been named in a recent television special as "The worst prison in America," having experienced at least a dozen major incidents during the past year, four of them fatal. It was a total lockdown unit, and it also housed Death Row. "What's your timeline on this?" I asked. "Are we talking about next spring, or next summer?"

He looked surprised. "I'm talking about next *month*, Man!"

I mused. "Well, we generally have two months of Team meetings for bonding before going for a Kairos weekend, but tell you what: I'll put it to the Team at our meeting tonight, and maybe we can come up with something, okay? I'll let you know tomorrow."

One thing that might make it possible to make his timeline was that the room available for Kairos in U32 was only big enough for four tables, so we'd only be hosting 24 Residents instead of 42, meaning that we would not need a full 50-man Team, we could do it with about 25 men (we try to have a one-to-one ratio). Randy Boren had already been through Kairos Leader Training, so we did have a Leader who could step right in for U32 # 1. At the Team meeting that evening, I stood and told them about the opportunity God had presented us with, and asked if 25 of the men on this U29 # 22 Team would be willing to go right on meeting after this weekend was over, then go into Unit 32 in another month for its first Kairos weekend. Remember, these folks had already been meeting weekly for two months, to be able to put on a Kairos weekend.

Every man in the room stood up, willing to keep right on meeting!

Then the women began standing too, who had been cooking and praying for us this weekend back at the Spiritual Life Center. I held up my hands, "Oh, excuse me: I meant to say, we won't need a cooking team for Unit 32 – regulations say we can't take food in, so their own kitchen will be cooking our food to our specifications and menus."

To which Miss Willie, the head Kitchen Lady, replied, "We're not coming here to cook for y'all. If we're going into Unit 32, we're going to need more prayer than we've ever needed before, so we women are going to be here at the Spiritual Life Center, praying for y'all men."

A second lady opened her Bible and read from Luke 8, where Jesus cast the demons into the herd of swine. Then Susie closed her Bible and asked softly, "Does anyone else know what is the closest building to Unit 32? It's the Parchman Pig Farm, about a half mile west. Well, y'all are gonna need us women to keep those demon-possessed hogs out of the Highway 49 traffic that weekend!" Everyone was either laughing or crying when she finished. Or both.

Since this was the first Kairos weekend at Unit 32, there were some initial problems that always occur in a different Unit, but all that got ironed out, with a great deal of humor, matter of fact. There was some initial resistance to the routine from the 24 incarcerated residents, as can always be expected, for these were the tough guys. There were some mishaps, such as when Our Fearless Leader Randy leaned upon the refreshments table as I stepped by him to start a song session, and the table leg gave way, dumping about six gallons of hot coffee, and five gallons each of tea and lemonade. Since we were at the time in a rather tense atmosphere, both Residents and free-world volunteers were up and running at the considerable noise, although in a prison, there ain't much place to run to!

Then in the middle of a song session that Friday afternoon, suddenly it was like the sun (Son?) came out from behind the clouds and glowed upon the faces of the singers in front of me, when one guy did the splits during "Pharoah, Pharoah," going up and down with no hands, and the whole weekend suddenly turned around. This was my 29th Kairos weekend, and I have never laughed as much! One resident told me the last day, "Uncle Bob, there ain't much laughter in Unit 32, but I have laughed more this weekend than I ever have in my entire life!"

But it wasn't silly funny; just joyous funny, an atmosphere bubbling over with what someone said was "Holy Laughter." Strange to you, maybe, but your Uncle Bob has seen the kind of joy that true freedom brings. Did I say yet that in Kairos, we don't go into prison to get someone out of prison? We go into prison to set people free – in Jesus Christ! Maybe it's hard for some folks to realize that God loves all of His

Children: even the ones who took a wrong road in their lives.

Kairos is also organized to minister to the people who work with the incarcerated folks we usually deal with, and two Kairos Outside ladies, Carol Dowdy and Kathi Coleman, were given a Vision from God for a Chaplain's Retreat, to renew the Spiritual Swords of a group of God's Servants who often are underpaid, overworked, and under-appreciated. They sought the state board's blessings, pitched in to organize a Team, and the first Machaira-Chadash (which means "Re-sharpening their swords") was held, and it was successful even beyond Carol's original Vision. "McKaro" will not only inspire Chaplains, Wardens, Administrators, and Security Officers for years to come in many places, but it will cement Kairos-DOC relations throughout the world, is what we believe. The second McKaro invited prison Wardens and their spouses, and was unbelievably powerful.

We're still talking expansion in Kairos, right? Darryl McElrath challenged the board to let him recruit a Unit 32 Team to work back-to-back weekends for that # 3 Kairos, his reasoning being that, if we couldn't take but 24 Residents each time, why not do it twice with one Team, and introduce 48 Residents to Christ? Warden Morris enthusiastically agreed, and it was a first for Kairos anywhere, holding # 3-A and 3-B weekends with one Team!

Then Randy Boren and Skip Jack were given a vision to do just the opposite: in the Unit 29 gym, there is room for many more than the usual seven tables, or 42 Residents. Skip recruited a big enough Team for U29 # 24, and had 48 Residents, then Ben Boren recruited an even bigger Team the next spring and had 54 Residents! (We belatedly learned that a state needs special permission from the KPMI High Muckety-Mucks to add tables, however.)

All those were answers to our prayer for expansion in MS Kairos, but God wasn't through yet. He'd saved the best for later, and once again, put the pieces together to make it happen.

For years, we had been trying to get permission to take Kairos into the only Youth Correctional Facility in our state, at Walnut Grove, for which KPMI has a special weekend Manual for juvenile offenders, called Kairos Torch. However, our one attempt got called off by new MDOC regulations at the last minute, and since that one failed, the Torch leadership had gone elsewhere, which often happens after a major disappointment like that which one has no control over. We had been praying for God to raise up someone to take Torch leadership again.

About a year after that inspired board prayer session at Brownspur, I had a call, on my cell phone, a number I seldom give out. It was a lady from east Mississippi, whose son had been involved in a vehicle accident in which alcohol was present, and there had been a fatality. Her son was scheduled to be sent to Walnut Grove, and she wanted to know if there was a Kairos program there for him to take advantage of. "How did you get my number?" I asked.

All Mississippi convicts are initially sent to the Central Mississippi Correctional Facility for check-in, orientation, and reassignment to the other prisons for confinement during their sentences. Her son was no exception, and she had gone to the CMCF website to see who to contact about Kairos programs in other facilities. "Your name and number are on that website," she declared, "so I called you."

I had not known that. We went on with our conversation, me telling her that we had as yet been unsuccessful in our efforts to introduce Kairos Torch into the Walnut Grove YCF, but that I would keep her number in case that changed. She was very emotional during our talk, which is tee-totally understandable, for a mother whose son has just been sent to prison, more or less because he was in the wrong place at the wrong time. I sympathized, and after we hung up, got to wondering whereabouts on the CMCF website was I listed, and how did they get my cell phone number? I'm not particularly computer-literate, but I went on-line to that site.

I searched it for almost an hour, going to every link, but could not find my name or number. So, I called the lady back and asked her to walk me through the process. She obligingly went on-line while we were on the phone, to guide me as requested.

It was not there.

"Let me call you back," she said, and we hung up.

A couple of hours later, she did so, mystified. She had not been able to find my information there either. "Maybe it was another website?" I asked. "Did you go to the Mississippi Kairos website, or the Kairos International website, maybe?" She had never been to either of those. She insisted that she had gotten my number from the CMCF website.

I began to get that little creepy-crawly feeling. "Ah, Sheila? I'm getting the notion that God may be putting us together for a reason here. Let me tell you about the Kairos Torch program, and our efforts and prayers to get that into Walnut Grove." I did so. Then I added, "We have been praying for God to inspire someone to take the leadership in establishing this program. How about if you pray about that, and see if God is raising you up in response to our requests for this ministry?"

She did. God affirmed that He had indeed called her to lead Torch. At the next state board meeting, I asked for Sheila Coleman to be approved to head an Ad Hoc Committee to start Torch at Walnut Grove, telling that story. She was speedily approved, and Manuals ordered.

One month later, I had a meeting with the head MDOC Chaplain, Eugene Wigelsworth in Jackson. This is an aside, but I met him for coffee at a mall in north Jackson early Saturday morning, but first I had to be fitted for a tuxedo to wear in my son's wedding later that summer. I arrived before the tux store opened, walking up to try the door just as a large black guy walked up from the other direction. He peered through the glass, and an attendant saw us, coming over to open up even though we were a few minutes early. He needed to be fitted for a tux, too. The fitter came over and asked, "Which of you gentlemen wants to go first?" I piped up, "Well, the Prison Chaplain is waiting outside for me." And the big black guy backed up, saying, "Oh, you go ahead, Mister!" I did, but later enlightened him!

Anyhoo, Chaplain Gene in our meeting advised me that now might be a good time to try to get Kairos Torch into Walnut Grove, because a new warden and chaplain had just been transferred to that facility. And one of the first calls Warden Brick Tripp had made to him was to learn who to contact about getting a Kairos program into that facility! Sure enough, that next week I got a call from Warden Tripp, and put Sheila in touch with him. We signed the Institutional Agreement in early December: me, Sheila and Kathi Coleman (friends, not related), and Linda Jack, Skip's wife. That was a great meeting, but let me tell you how it started.

Warden Tripp began the meeting with prayer, then addressed Sheila, our Torch Bearer: "Sheila, I've just come from visiting Josh, your son. I want him to be on this first Torch weekend, as I know you do." She nodded, in tears (Sheila cries a lot!). The Warden continued, "You know that there is a regulation forbidding you from being in the same place with your son except for formal visitation, so I want to get this right out front: I hate it, but if he's going to be on this weekend, you can't come into our facility at all that weekend. Do you understand?" The Warden had tears in his eyes, as well: this was empathy, not just sympathy!

In another chapter, I'm going to acquaint you with the Kairos Cantata music, but I'm going to preview that by introducing you to the last song I wrote for that program. It's entitled "Take This Piece of My Heart," and was inspired by Sheila during that first Torch weekend, co-Led by Danny and Marilyn Brunt. Each morning we would meet at the host church before car-pooling to head for the WG YCF. We'd pray up the day, get our Leaders' instructions, then leave the family life center. The Kitchen Team was cooking at the prison (they turned a double kitchen completely over to us for the weekend) so they all went in with the rest of the Team.

Except Sheila, the lady who was in charge of Kairos Torch in Mississippi. She had to stay at the church by herself, and just pray. One day her husband Danny came to keep her company, another day chairman Reece drove in with his wife Diane; sometimes the church's pastor would come to pray with her, but mostly she was by herself.

And the look on her face when we left the church to head to prison, where her son was going through the Torch weekend, was like she was clutching a piece of her own heart in her fist, then handing it to us as we walked toward the parking lot, saying, "Take this piece of my heart with you, please!"

So on the three-hour drive home after the Sunday afternoon Closing for Torch # 1, I wrote these words, and the accompanying tune:

"Take this piece of my heart;
Ttake this piece of my soul;
Take it with you to prison,
Whene'er you go."
For every boy who's in prison,
Has a mother who cries:
"Take this piece of my heart,
Take this piece of my soul,
For my love never dies!"
When a boy goes to prison, when a son's sent to jail;
There's a mother who's willing,
To give her heart for his bail.
But a judge can't consider, her heart or soul.
How can Love enter in, to the hearts of young men,
In all this darkness and cold?

repeat Chorus

211

There's a Light for this darkness,
There's a warmth for this cold;
There's a hope for the hopeless,
There's a Christ-light to hold;
Love will enter this prison, hold your Torch up high,
Jesus Christ gives us wings,
Teaches young men to sing,
In His Name, they can fly!

repeat Chorus

A postscript: for some reason, I was the first Team member to arrive back at the church after the Closing, and as I walked across the parking lot, Sheila emerged from the church, talking on her cell phone, face shining like the sun (Son?). When I finally reached her, she was saying that his time was up, she loved him, was glad that he'd had such a wonderful weekend, and would see him at the next visitation. Her son had called her as soon as he could get to a phone (I have always believed it was either Warden Tripp's or Chaplain Chaney's!) to tell her about the weekend in the allotted five minutes.

"I've just got one question for you," I declared as she hung up. "Was that call worth all you've done this past year to get Torch started?"

"I didn't do a thing," she wept. "God did it all; you know that better than anyone else!"

That Mighty Rushing Wind

Once I had the pleasure of listening to some really fine music in two different places, only a week apart, presented so enthusiastically that the audience was caught up in it as much as the performers. The singers were mostly young black men and boys. The performance halls were maybe 25 miles from each other.

One was a state of the art Performing Arts Center, engineered for the most dramatic acoustics, and for the comfort of the audience. Those performers wore tuxedoes. The other place was an old rundown gym, where the performers wore striped britches. It was a prison.

I love music, and am fairly omnivorous about it. I mean, I like classical, semi-classical, pop, rock, gospel, folk, blues, near'bout all of it but rap and heavy metal. I even sing along when I can, and can lead the music if called upon, if it's familiar. Those two performances last month, I participated in! They were great.

The leader of the more formal performance, the Harlem Boys Choir at Bologna Performing Arts Center in Cleveland, Mississippi, made the point several times that his charges "were not angels," yet were required to meet high academic, musical, and character standards. If they did not, they were counseled by professionals, and if they still were judged deficient, they could be dismissed from the school. I was struck by the boys' discipline during the performance: they did not take their eyes from Dr. Turnbull as he conducted, even if one of their comrades had a lengthy solo, or a couple had a duet. Kids as young as maybe eight or nine stayed focused on him for the full two-hour program. I saw one kid wipe away either sweat or a tear from his cheek, and one other either scratch his ear, or perhaps wipe sweat away, too. The others, if they sweated or itched or wept, simply let it go.

Dr. Turnbull described his curriculum as "Teaching these kids to be the best that they can be!" It was easy to see that they were on their way to that. My hat is off to him.

The second group of mostly young black men singers were, as I say, in prison. It's obvious that many of them had at some point in their lives been on the road to the exact opposite curriculum: being the worst that they could be. I came in contact with them through the Kairos International Prison Ministry, which both Betsy and I have worked in for years. We have seen many men and women dramatically turn their lives around, though they still must serve their sentences. One saying in Kairos is, "We don't go in there to get them out of prison; we go in to set them free." Obviously, free in Jesus Christ!

In most cases, and I am going to be dogmatic here, what the latter group lacked is exactly what the Boys Choir focuses on: discipline and inspiration. Being the best that one can be requires an ongoing vision, and early in one's life that vision must be inspired and established by someone older: a parent, a teacher, a sibling, a mentor of some kind. The discipline required to reach that goal must almost always be enforced by a mentor. The statistic is that, of the group in prison, only five percent had a positive father figure early in life, like Dr. Turnbull and his associates are for their boys.

This is an aside, but it is my opinion that, if we still had a draft in this country, fully half the people in prison wouldn't be there. Oh, I'm not for another shooting war; don't misunderstand me. I've been there, and wouldn't wish it on anyone. Yet the military in those days provided the discipline and motivation that turned many a wayward kid into a fine young man. Check how the prison population has mushroomed since the draft ended.

The commonality between these two groups is spiritual. Whether it is called Christianity or not, these singers were for the most part offering up praises to God, and obviously depending on Him for their direction in life. I realize that one can get caught up in the strictly musical part of gospel singing and not be touched by the spirituality, but for the most part, continually singing gospel songs, spirituals, hymns, and praise songs cannot help but affect the belief of the singers, whether in prison or on a free world stage.

The Boys Choir also did a number that was not gospel, but it was the "gospel truth," as the old saying goes. It was about black heroes. Maybe that seems like a strange point to bring up in a column written by a white guy, which will be published close to Mother's Day. But Mothers need to make sure their boys have heroes – the right kind, men who provide discipline, inspiration, and some spiritual guidance. Give them tuxedoes instead of stripes.

And make sure they grow up praising a God who doesn't care what color or denomination they are.

I went to a funeral recently, at the Catholic church. While Betsy and I are Baptists, we have a varied denominational background, as previously stated. My mother was an Episcopalian, my daddy was Presbyterian, her mother was Methodist, and her daddy was a Catholic. In Kairos we worship and work closely with Christians of all denominations.

So, although I am familiar with the practices and procedures of many churches, I saw something at the beginning of this funeral that puzzled me. I was standing at the back of the church -- there was standing room only -- and as some folks came in, they stopped at a little table in the back, picked up a set of silver tongs, and transferred something from one dish to another on the table. I made a mental note to ask someone about that after the service.

I didn't know any of the chants or songs during the service, for us standers didn't have hymnbooks, so I pretty well just kept my mouth shut, until they did the hymn after Holy Communion. I knew it because we sing it a lot in Kairos. It's entitled "I Am the Bread of Life," and the chorus goes, "And I will raise Him up, and I will raise Him up, and I will raise Him up on the last day!" It's a real moving song when it's done enthusiastically, and since I lead the music in prison a lot, I know how to do it thataway!

After the funeral, I caught the guy next to me, whom I had seen using the silver tongs, and asked him what that meant. He looked at me kind of funny and I added, "I'm a Baptist, and we don't use tongs for much of anything, as far as I know."

He cocked an eyebrow and asked, "You're not Catholic? Why, the way you sang that last song, 'I Am the Bread of Life,' I thought you were. That's not a Baptist song, I know."

I confessed, "Oh, no, it's not a Baptist song. I learned that song in prison."

He left quickly, without telling me the significance of the silver tongs. I had to wait and catch a high school classmate, to learn the answer.

"Bread of Life" is a special song to me, and I wanted to share why. If you haven't worked in a prison ministry you cannot imagine the intensity of the singing there. Imagine that you are in prison and are not allowed to sing for a decade or so. Then a group of men comes into the prison for most of four days, and they bring guitar players and songbooks, and they encourage you to sing God's praises -- loudly and enthusiastically. And you know that they are going to leave, so you'd better cram another decade's worth of singing into these four days. In Kairos, we go back at least once every month, but the 42 inmates don't realize that until the last day of the four-day weekend.

Tell you how great their singing is: I learned this on

"Bread of Life." See, I'm pretty much deaf in the right ear, so when I lead the music, I have to keep one of the guitar players on my left. Ralph McGee and Jerry Ford were my guitarists for a Parchman weekend, and one song session, Ralph was on my left. We did several songs, then went into "Bread of Life." On that chorus, those guys had the prison gym shaking. There are about six verses, so the intensity just keeps building. Then, on about the fifth verse, I suddenly lost Ralph -- I mean, I couldn't hear the guitar on my left.

Without stopping singing or leading music, I turned to look for Ralph.

Afterward, I sure did feel stupid -- but this illustrates how great the singing was.

Because, I turned and looked over my left shoulder -- but I looked UP! Into the rafters of the Unit 29 gymnasium in the Parchman Mississippi State Prison!

That's how spiritually all those men were singing -- my initial assumption was just naturally that my lead guitarist had been Raised Up hisownself!!!!

No, he had not levitated -- though, seriously, in another song session on that Kairos, five different people (three free worlders and two Residents) told me that I had actually levitated a foot or so on a couple of songs. Ralph had merely just stepped over to a nearby table of men who were improvising on a tenor harmony, and was helping them out a little bit. No one noticed but me, I'm sure.

Yet I will never forget that moment in that song on that day in that prison. You want to hear singing that will really Raise Him Up? Come to prison with your Uncle Bob sometime!

At a Men's Team meeting, one of the guitar players asked me to teach him the words for the "Fried Chicken Song," written by Jimmy Phillips, that the McGee Brothers made famous in Kairos. While we were doing that, I noticed that Doug wasn't strumming with his usual enthusiasm. When I asked, he held up a maimed, still-healing hand, on which the middle finger was newly-shortened. "Well, I usually strum with three fingers, but one doesn't reach the strings anymore," he confessed.

Now, over the years of leading music in prison, I have seen guitar players wounded in many ways. I've seen Ralph's, Jesse's, or Jerry's fingers bleed from too much fretting (not the worry kind), even though a couple had gone through finger-toughening exercises in anticipation of playing so much over the four days. One used sand in an ashtray next to his chair, repeatedly jamming his fingertips into the sand as he watched TV or read in the evenings for a few weeks before Team meetings started. The other said he kept a wide-mouthed jar of pickle juice next to his chair to soak his fingers in and make them toughen up. Jerry's fingers went from bleeding to being infected on one Kairos, and oozed pus when he played. But he kept playing! On CMCF Men's # 9, Jesse's fingers were oozing pus, but Linda Smith had prayed over me and given me a small vial of healing oil before I left for the weekend, so I took him into the chapel, prayed over his fingers, and anointed them with oil that morning early. At the very next song session, he held out his hand: the fingers were callused!

WHAT A COINCIDENCE!!

I've seen pickers bust guitar strings while playing, and get struck by the recoiling wire, one in the cheek, one in the neck, and Randy Coghlan's string once stuck Rusty Healy in the chest, right through a white sweater! They each continued playing, blood showing where they'd been cut.

I once saw Jerry plug his instrument into the sound system while standing in a damp spot where water had leaked from the prison gym roof. It was obviously a shocking experience, and if his partner Doug Deweese hadn't been standing close enough to jerk the plug out, no telling how high a note that guy would have hit!

After one Kairos, I decided to learn to play guitar

myownself, and got an instrument that came with an instruction book. I was doing pretty good on "Red River Valley" and "Bury Me Not On The Lone Prairie" until the day I walked out into the garage and a wasp buzzed me. I'm terrified of wasps, and swung at it in panic. I missed the insect, but connected with the door facing and broke the hand. End of guitar playing for me.

Yet I had never before seen a guitar player plumb wear one finger plumb off before, and told Doug that. "Oh, I didn't wear it off playing," he admitted. "I was working on an airplane with a jack to get two holes to line up and slide a pin in. The pin wouldn't quite go in, so I stuck my finger into the hole to see whether it needed jacking up or down a little, when the jack slipped out. I'm lucky I only lost the tip."

Some of us offered to help him solve the problem. The most popular suggestion was that, seeing as how he braced his guitar on the protrusion above his belt while he played, he could perhaps grow that good-sized bracing mound a little larger, so that the guitar would extend closer to the finger in question. In reply, he extended the injured member itself out, for our closer inspection, I suppose. Well, you try to help some people, and they just can't be helped.

But be careful playing guitars. They are wonderful instruments and give a lot of pleasure to those of us singing along, but those things can be dangerous!

Since I've led the music for years in Kairos, and get asked to speak a lot on that subject, I've sometimes twisted the arm of one of our local guitar players to come play and sing prison songs in church with me on Sunday morning -- I mean, even High Church! Of course, it's not as exciting as singing with a roomful of guys in striped britches, but it works anyway.

I've called on Ralph McGee most often, for we've known each other since we were kids together in the same church, and he only lives a few miles from Brownspur, therefore we can get together for practice easily. I just counted up, and there are at least four dozen guitar players who have been to prison and played for me leading the music, over the past two decades.

I once sang with a young lady guitarist, and another girl singer, at First Baptist Church on a Sunday morning -- a prison song, at that, though neither of them has been to prison yet. At practice, I noticed that Brantley eyed me with a little exasperation during the song, and I knew where she was coming from. When we finished the last chorus, I tried to explain: "Look, I move around a little bit when I sing."

Layne snorted, "Uncle Bob, you move around a LOT when you sing!"

"Okay, maybe so," I confessed. "I can either sing or I can stand still, but I can't do both at the same time. Can't we just coordinate when Brantley sways with the guitar, and I'll sway the same way?" We tried it in practice, and it worked, but that Sunday morning, I was lucky to have great peripheral vision, because I caught a glimpse of her guitar neck coming my way during the first verse, and barely missed getting a knot on my head, until we got our rhythms synchronized.

Ralph and I have sung together so much that we just naturally coordinate our rhythms, but we were in the midst of a song one morning in a church, when I noticed that he was really getting caught up in the Spirit of the Song. I mean, he was bouncing and swaying to literally beat the band! I noticed that the whole congregation on that side of the church was grinning, even chuckling, an unusual reaction. We finished the song to an enthusiastic round of applause, before I found out what had happened.

During the first chorus, with me standing on the right side of the pulpit, where the music was, and Ralph on the left side, his guitar strap had broken clean in two! Of course, this is an enthusiastic guitar player, who often breaks the guitar strings during his strumming. Yet I had never before seen him break the whole strap. And since I don't play a guitar, I never really appreciated the duty of the strap -- I mean, it holds the guitar up, so the player can strum or pick with one hand, while he frets with the other hand. Generally, if the strap breaks, the player has to quit, or at least sit down so he can hold it on his lap and play.

Not Ralph! When that strap broke that morning, we were in the middle of a great song, so he jerked up one leg, to brace the instrument upon his knee. He never missed a beat, balancing on one foot until we completed the song! God held him up!

Ever since then, he's been known as the Kairos Flamingo Guitar Player!

Ralph and I worked together on U29 Kairos # 5, which for various reasons started and stayed hours behind time, throughout the weekend. Everyone was running on adrenalin, and sleep was precious. We had gotten to bed in the Training Center after 1:00 a.m. Saturday night, and were going to have to rise about 5:00, so one can imagine my state of mind when at 3:00 a.m. I was suddenly awakened by a chorus of voices singing, "Alleluia, He Is Coming," and then they went into "Lights of the City." I was enraged (though the music was wonderful!) and rolled back the covers to sit up and order the singers to shut up so we could get some shuteye.

When I sat up, it was dark, and no one was awake besides me.

I lay back down, and the chorus continued, song after song, wonderful harmony and instrumentation – apparently all for me, because everyone else was snoring. I rested until get-up time, listening to the Heavenly voices – that's all I can figure they were – but was completely relaxed and rested during the day, in spite of only two hours of sleep.

I know, you're going to say that I dreamt it, right? No, I'm a Lyme Disease victim, and Lyme Disease victims never reach REM (rapid eye movement) sleep after the tick gets through with you. I have not had a dream (well, there's one type cough medicine that induces weird flashes during the night) since 1978.

I choose to believe that it was Heavenly Choir Practice, and God piped it into my ears.

Once when I led the music for a Kairos weekend, one of our Team members commented on the Spirit with which the Residents were singing, as well as the free world volunteers. Andrew remarked, "It's like, when God sings, everybody sings!"

God does sing, I believe that. Sometimes He sings through the wind of a thunderstorm or even a hurricane at sea. Sometimes He sings through the voice of a mockingbird or wren at Brownspur early in the morning. I've heard Him sing in the voices of a pod of whales, on sonar – at least, that was my own interpretation. He's sung to me through the whistle of wings in a flight of mile-high pintails, or in the chorus of bullfrogs (basses) and tree frogs (tenors) in a swamp at night. There are few Heavenly songs as sweet as the chorus of hounds behind a deer, or beagles behind a rabbit: voices of Jupiter Pluvius, Bellowin' Buford, Trouble, Belle, and Miss Adventure. I've even heard God singing through a pack of coyotes at night.

He also sings through people – doesn't necessarily have to, He just does it to bless us thataway. Some people He gives beautiful voices to, and they lift up His praises in those voices. Some of us, He just gives the Gift of musical enthusiasm to, and we try to worship through that in music. Then there are the folks to whom He gives the Gift of playing musical instruments: pianos, organs, guitars, drums, harmonicas – all types of instruments upon which to play His praises. Put all that talent together, and sometimes it literally lifts you up in praises of Him corporately.

I've recently been blessed to be a part of that type lifting up. The Mississippi Kairos Music Team, composed of me, Rusty Healy, Mike Lewis, Stephen Stuart, Mark Propst, and Reece Vaughan currently, most from the Jackson area, who play drums, guitars, and mouth harps, as well as sing in harmony, got invited to the Grand Opening of our town's Studio 61, the last weekend of March 2009. We opened up the Gospel Music time on Sunday afternoon for an hour, then they stayed to do a Kairos Concert at Calvary Baptist in Greenville. I kid you not: by the time we hit that last song at Calvary, the hair on the back of my neck and my forearms was literally standing up. What a blessing, to be a part of that worship!

But I had been doubly blessed that day: between the two Kairos Music Team concerts, I had snuk in a practice for a Joint Choir Easter Cantata that I was directing with Calvary and Parkview Baptist, for Palm Sunday presentation. I wanted to try to put into words, the feeling a music leader sometimes gets.

When one is privileged to stand before such a company of singers and players who are intent on offering up their talents in praises to the God who bestowed those Gifts upon them, it's like that "Mighty Rushing Wind" that is described in the Book of Acts. One knows that the Mighty Rushing Wind is going straight up to the Throne of God, and that God Himself is pleased with that sound.

Yet that beautiful uplifting musical enthusiasm on its way to the Throne must go right by – maybe through is a better word there – the person who is standing out front waving his arms – even though sometimes the singers all have their eyes closed in worship!

I have stood on the decks of ships at sea in strong storms, and I know from experience that a 40-knot wind will actually hold me up when I lean into it. When standing in front of that Acts-like Mighty Rushing Wind of singers praising God, I can actually feel that same support of my physical body. Does that make any sense atall? Am I communicating this, or mis-communicating this? Does it matter?

I think it matters only to the One who sits upon that Throne, to whom the praise is directed. Yet to be betwixt and between is a tee-total blessing, and your Uncle Bob has been in that place, and as Betsy says, it has "Blessed my socks off!"

The Way To A Man's Soul

I had just gotten home from one of the most entertaining, satisfactory, and spiritual weeks of my life. A group of Mississippi musicians were invited to attend the Kairos International Prison Ministry Winter Conference, for the purpose of leading the praise and worship sessions. Calvary Baptist Church in Greenville, where I currently lead the music, provided the church van for our 1007-mile trip, and St. Matthews Methodist Church in Madison, where Rusty Healy, one of the guitar players, worships, provided trip funds from their mission budget. Guitarists Jesse Heath, Mike Lewis, and Stephen Stuart, plus harmonica player Mark Propst, joined us on the Atlanta-bound van in Jackson, beginning with a group prayer.

Thursday evening, we led a couple of hundred Kairos volunteers in a program that told the story of the music progression on a typical Mississippi Kairos weekend. Most of the audience was familiar with most of the songs, so they enthusiastically joined in as we explained how a music team in prison begins with familiar songs that the inmates – we call them residents – might remember from their childhood, like "Swing Low, Sweet Chariot" or "Down by the Riverside," then moves into fun, active songs that tell stories, as in "Pharoah, Pharoah" about the Hebrew Children's Flight from Egypt (No, Virginia, Pharoah's army did not drown in water only knee-deep to their horses!) to the Kairos National Anthem "Lights of the City." As the weekend moves along, we gradually get into songs that mention the Savior: "Jesus on the Mainline" and "Jesus is the Rock." By the end of the first day we say goodnight to our Heavenly Father with "Abba, Father" and "Yahweh," then greet the residents the second morning with "Woke Up This Mornin' with My Mind Stayed on Jesus" and "Somebody Touched Me." Soon we're doing "Come, Now is the Time to Worship" and "Alleluia, He Is Coming."

We led the always-with-us audience through the Kairos Experience until they were deep into meaningful, closed-eyes, palms-up worshiping while I stood singing and waving my hand, in front of the strumming, harmonicing, harmonizing accompanists. Then that thought hit me once again: I was right in between the strummers and the people, and their Praise, like unto the "Mighty Rushing Wind" of the Holy Spirit's coming in the Book of Acts, was going straight upward toward the Throne of God. But I was in the middle, so it had to go by me first. It was like getting caught between two tornadoes: I felt uplifted physically, and it effectively drained – no, more like sucked out – my own body's life-juices. Can you imagine sweat pouring off of you, yet flowing upward? A sensation of all the hairs on your body standing upward, maybe like stepping on a city sidewalk grating that vents hot air?

Perhaps I'm not expressing myself well this close to the event, and maybe I should wait a few more years before writing about it. Yet I wanted you to try to get the feel of it, being in the middle of this much worshipful expression of praise.

Have you ever felt that you were, for a time, exactly where God had placed you, doing exactly what God would have you do at that exact time? That you were being used; indeed, almost being used up? That your Life's Forces were not really drained, which implies going downward, but were certainly completely poured out for the moment, leaving you trembling with the sensation of being carried away by a Force beyond your imagination, yet still being held upright by that same

Force?

It was thataway for us Mis'sippi boys at the KPMI Conference in Atlanta.

A lady later stopped me to say how much she had enjoyed the Praise and Worship Service. "You know, you were right in that the residents initially come to eat cookies and good food: 'The way to a man's heart is through his stomach'," she quoted. Then she added: "But God is using y'all, and He blesses you through your ministry. I want you to always remember that sometimes the way to a man's SOUL is through music. God bless you!"

He did that!

Truth is where you find it.

That was the first of several trips to lead the music for the KPMI Winter meetings, and the travel back and forth brought home to me that, as another old saying goes, "You can take the boy out of the country, but you can't take the country out of the boy." We Mis'sippi boys had a hard time navigating on concrete for some of those trips.

"WE DON'T NEED NO STINKIN' MAP!"

The next year we led the praise and worship at the KPMI Conference for two days in Orlando, Florida, where the automatic sprinklers came on each morning, and iced over the shrubs, flowers, and sidewalks. Sunny, but cold, in early February!

We drove the Calvary Baptist van again and left Jackson at daybreak on Wednesday. I had purchased an up-to-date Rand McNally Atlas, and a couple of the guys had printed out compooter directions, just in case. I want to get it in the record early that we did have those things in the van, okay?

No problem getting to Orlando: across Mississippi, lower Alabama, the panhandle of Florida, and down the Florida Turnpike (with toll booths every few miles, it seemed like) to the city we sought, where the convention was to be held at the Airport Holiday Inn. Though it was well after dark when we got there, we considered it a no-brainer that an accommodation thusly named would be quite near the airport. What we had not anticipated was that the road to said airport went right through the airport, just as if we had wanted to catch a plane.

I have an oft-ruptured eardrum which doesn't release pressure well atall, so I am tee-totally unfamiliar with driving nearunto airports. As the designated driver, I panicked. It did not help that my wife, three guitar players and a harmonicaist were all offering directions, one even with a compooter-generated map, which later turned out to be a map to the Orlando airport, when examined in daylight. We went around and around that location – I was reminded of the old Kingston Trio song about "Poor Charlie on the MTA," whose wife brought him a sandwich each day, "as the train comes rumbling through!" Charlie never returned home, poor guy. "And his fate is still unknown."

Yet we did finally make it to the designated hotel, though when we pulled into the parking lot, everything was darked out – even the lobby! We spent another half hour trying to find a lighted entrance, then sent out a scout, like unto Noah's dove from the Ark.

Rusty returned with a figurative olive branch. It was indeed the right place; we entered, got our keys, and crashed for the night, intending to set up the band Thursday morning, and did so. Next on the agenda was to get Betsy to the Orlando train station, for an AmTrak trip to Fort Lauderdale to visit Christie. Again, we had compooter-generated directions, which were confirmed by the hotel manager: "Take a right out of the parking lot, go six lights to Michigan Avenue, take a left, and it goes within a couple of blocks of AmTrak."

I am a prejudiced person, though it's not racial. My great-grandmother's home was sacked and the contents burnt by yankees under General Sherman. I should have suspected Michigan Avenue would do me wrong. We were rolling right along this divided four-lane street, when all at once it ended without warning, long before the train station. One could turn left or right, neither narrow street labeled as Michigan, both lazily meandering through neighborhoods. After a few blocks, I caught a straight side street, hung a left, and within three blocks, Michigan Avenue reappeared, just like it had never disappeared in the first place. Did the same durn thing on my return trip, too, then took us smack dab back to our usual airport orbit again!

We left at daylight Saturday for the trip home, again trusting the directions of the hotel manager to get back to the Florida Turnpike without touring the airport again. We were so overjoyed at missing the airport, that my passengers chose to doze whilst I tooled along the Turnpike-looking highway. It was when I saw the sign proclaiming that Tampa was only 43 miles that I awoke them.

Yea, verily, we had gone the wrong way – I suspected that when the sun came up on my left, actually. Took 45 minutes to cut across country to I-75 N.

We stayed found until Pensacola, when we got off of I-10 to eat a late lunch. Then the waitress directed us, "Go four blocks to Garden Street, and you'll see the signs for the Interstate." Maybe we didn't leave her enough tip. We filled up at a Tom Thumb station, then passed it four more times before we found I-10 going west.

We're composing a new song: "I am a man! I don't need no stinkin' map!"

GOD, PLEASE GUIDE US OUT OF ORLANDO

For the third year in a row, the Mississippi Kairos Music Team was asked to lead the Praise & Worship Music at the Annual Winter Conference of the Kairos Prison Ministry International. The MKMT is composed of leader Uncle Bob from rural Brownspur, Reece Vaughan from rural Benton, but Mike, Mark, Rusty, and Stephen were all from the urban Jackson area. Reece not only played guitar and sang lead, but he had succeeded me as State Chairman of Kairos the year before. Since my Official Title is The Grunk (Granddaddy Uncle Bob got shortened to GrandUncle, to Grunkle, to Grunk, and my State Board conferred that upon me as my Title: The Grunk – ain't but one!) Reece had acquired an Unofficial Title from my granddaddy's days as a Shriner: the Grand High Muckety-Muck, we called him.

Since three Kairos Ladies were accompanying us, we made the 2010 trip in two vehicles, and because of The Grunk's navigation foibles last year, other drivers assumed command of Karo 1 & Karo 2, armed with maps, and a plug-in super-sized GPS system. The G stands for Global, remember?

With The Grunk driving, our 2009 trip included a half-dozen ground orbits of the Orlando International Airport, two trips to investigate the disappearance of three blocks of Michigan Avenue, plus a different escape route from Orlando, the key to which was a road sign proclaiming "Tampa: 45 miles," although the non-sleeping driver later stated under oath that the sun rising on his left gave him an initial clue as to his wrong direction. Therefore, The Grunk was not allowed to drive within 200 miles of Orlando on this 2010 Concert Tour. As a further precaution, I was replaced by the Grand High Muckety-Muck, whose wife came along to read maps. An Official Navigator was the new GHMM's first appointment, since that lady owned a laptop GPS – the G standing for Global, of course. This new GHMM was also a self-proclaimed expert in the art of Dead Reckoning, to boot.

We departed Orlando on a DR course, the driver pointing out to The Grunk that the descending sun being on our left was an assurance of a northerly course, in spite of the fact that our Karo 1 vehicle, driven by those Urban Dudes, had immediately disappeared from our sight upon departure from the Airport Hotel. "Aw, they probably wanted to circle the Airport a couple of times before they left, just for old times sake," was the answer to this observation. When Karo 2 occupants noted, "We've never seen that landmark(s) on our earlier trips," their doubts were dismissed by the GHMM as negative thoughts, like unto the Hebrew Children's Spy Reports of Giants in the Land.

However, the announcement of a road sign, "John F. Kennedy Space Center: 45 miles," called for a re-plugging-in of the GPS, G standing for Global, remember?

While that machine was "booting," the driver/GHMM pulled into a nearby gas station and grabbed the first person out the door to ask, "Say, Podnuh, how do we get to Interstate 75 from here?" Podnuh deposited his extra-tall beer can in his vehicle and bent over the map on our hood, which allowed those of us inside to suddenly recognize that he was a twin to our own Chap Dave, who is notorious for his "short cuts" and mismatched directions in the MS Delta. Then Diane, wife of our GHMM, exclaimed, "Lordee! Look at his pickup: the whole back fender's gone, he's got a super-sized beer can on his dashboard, and the truck's got a Connecticut license tag! And my husband, our Leader for the whole state Kairos organization, is asking HIM for directions??!!"

But Grand High bounded back into his seat, infused with confidence: "We got to double back a few miles, but my Dead Reckoning will get us right back on track." The re-booted Global PS at that point announced, "Turn around," echoed by the Official Karo Navigator and five of the six occupants.

Florida is naming their new east-to-west highway "The Mississippi Karo Turnpike," in honor of our adventures, as well as the fact that we paid for the construction of said roadway with visits to friendly Florida tollbooths. One booth manager even offered us their "Frequent Toll Flyer" Discount, during our hour and 32-minute departure from Orlando. The cry from the back of the van, "Tell them we've already paid!" echoed at each request for additional quarters.

All this was punctuated by periodic calls of concern from vehicle Karo 1, which was now approaching Pensacola. Then we suddenly heard the cry from their vehicle phone,

"Pascagoula! Hey, you guys let me miss our turnoff, back at Mobile!"

Motto from our 2009 trip: "We're men! We don't need no stinkin' map!"

2010 Motto: even a Lady with a GPS ("Global") can't help some men get out of Orlando.

Let us now sing Hymn number 462: "Guide Me, Oh, Thou Great Jehovah!"

As you might have guessed by now, I love music. And it got even better.

God has given many of us the Gift of Music (and I know that isn't specifically mentioned in the Gifts of the Spirit) in both voice and instruments, and my hat is off to the ones who use those talents in praise to the One who creates and parcels out Gifts and Talents. Why some of y'all get them and some of us don't will remain a mystery to me until whatever time I get to the Pearly Gates myownself, but I intend to ask that question once I do get there. I've often declared that if God was to tell me, "Neill, I'll give you a Do-Over, but you can't change but one thing, so what'll it be, Bubba?" I wouldn't even hesitate: "Lord, let me play a guitar, please, Sir!"

He did give me a fair voice, and more importantly maybe, the enthusiasm to use that in praising Him (though the folks next to me might think differently). As one Choir Director told me somewhat sarcastically, "Enthusiasm counts for a lot, Neill." For some reason, I am less inhibited in leading music with Prison Ministry teams that I regularly serve on several times a year in prisons around the state. However, when a local church – Calvary Baptist – called on me to lead their music in 2003, I warned the committee, "Now, I can either stand still, or I can lead the music, but I can't do both of them at the same time. If it bothers you for me to move around some, tell me now, and I'll leave, no hurt feelings." That Easter Sunday, in conducting a joint Choir Cantata of "God With Us" with Calvary and Second Baptist, Betsy said the poinsettias on the stage were really shaking behind me. I told her that the Bible says Little David danced when he sang praises, too.

Incidentally, when I started leading the music at Calvary, it was because their interim pastor, Park Neff, a farmer friend from Arcola, had asked me to come lead their music one Sunday morning as a favor. I just assumed the regular music guy was on vacation in August. Then they asked me to come back that evening, which was logical, so I did. I saw Park at a funeral that Tuesday, and he asked if I could come back on Wednesday night for prayer meeting, so I did, then they asked me to stay and lead a song for choir practice afterward, then asked me to come back Sunday and direct that, plus lead congregational singing again. Right after church, their committee buttonholed me and asked me to come as Calvary's Music Director. Their's had resigned several months before, it turned out.

I laughed, turned them down flat, agreed to come back that night, and went home to tell Betsy, "You know what those crazy people asked me to do?" I told her, chuckling.

"And?" my bride prompted.

"Well, I told them no, that I didn't even read music," I declared.

"Let me get this straight: you can go into prison and lead Spirit-filled singing for murderers, rapists, robbers, druggies – but you cannot do that for free-world Christians in a church?" Betsy has a way with words.

"Well, I'm just not qualified to lead music for a choir, especially. I mean, you know that I don't even read music," I reiterated.

At the time, I had just been Associational Moderator for two years, and had made a point of trying to preach (or, to speak from the pulpit) in every one of the two dozen Washington County Southern Baptist churches. I kept all my sermons in a little black notebook. My wife excused herself, walked out of the den, and returned with that little black book, flipping through it until she found what she was looking for.

"Ah-hem!" she announced. "See if this sounds familiar, because it looks like it's actually in your own hand writing: 'God does not call the Qualified; God Qualifies the Called!' Does that sound even remotely familiar to you?"

Truth is where you find it, even if you have to get beaten over the head with it.

You guessed it. I took the job. They even paid for me to go to a New Orleans Baptist Seminary Music Leader's Course, from which I earned my degree in two years.

What I wanted to share with you is a different musical experience I have had recently as a Gift, no doubt from all this intense musical education and experience. In mid-July of 2008, I attended a Kairos team meeting, actually a "McKaro" Team meeting, which I have told you about. When I left driving home, I began to hear a song in my head: words, tune, and all. I grabbed a notebook, and by the time I got home – hour and a half – I had written the chorus and four verses to "The Sword Song." I called a Kairos Music Team member in Jackson, and sang it to Mikey, so he could figure out the chords on his guitar. That was on a Saturday. I called the Team Leaders, Carol and Kathi, and sang it to them, and they agreed that it fit the ministry completely, asking me to have it printed up for the next meeting.

On Thursday afternoon, mowing the pasture, I heard another song, this one about a man in prison who had been included on a Kairos weekend that changed his life. I had to go to the house for a notebook and pencil, which I laid on the picnic table by the Swimming Hole. Every couple of rounds, I'd stop and write down another verse. Friday morning about 2:00 a.m., another song woke me up, about a letter an inmate had received from a little girl. I went to the den and wrote it.

This happened over a dozen times during the next few months. The songs come complete with tunes, but on one, "The

233

Prayer Chain Gang," Rusty, one of the Jackson guitar players, read the words that I had e-mailed to the Music Team, and came up with his own tune, which turned out to be really close to mine – which he had not heard at the time!

You guessed where I'm going with this: God has given that MS Kairos Music Team a Kairos Cantata. All these dozen songs are from the viewpoint of someone who has come to know God's Love through a Kairos or Kairos Outside weekend retreat. I've written a dozen books so far, have written a weekly syndicated newspaper column for 25 years now, have written probably 1500 magazine articles, plus have written my share of poetry in my time. But never had I written songs before. Well, actually I didn't originate these songs – God gave them to me, and I just had to put the words on paper and call the tune in to Mikey, Mark, Stephen, & Rusty!

Now we're into the recording business, this past year: we've finished our second CD this summer of 2010, and who knows where this Singing Gift from God will take us next?!!

God Speaks!

I was serving on an Emmaus Walk Team a few years ago, and while Emmaus doesn't require as many Team meetings as Kairos does, we did have three scheduled, one of which was a Friday night and Saturday meeting at the North Mississippi Christian Camp at Grenada. At noon we were in the chapel for the final service, and the preacher was really getting het-up about the Great Commandment: "Thou shalt love the Lord thy God with all thy heart and soul and mind."

It was the week of my 33rd Anniversary.

I was really having a hard time with this subject: Betsy is beautiful; I can fall in love all over again when she walks in a room; I can hug her, kiss her, make love to her; we can cuddle up on the sofa and watch a movie at night. How can I love a God whom I cannot feel or see, like I love my own wife?

I know, you figured out the answer a long time ago. I had not, and was really agonizing over it. And the preacher finished preaching before I got finished listening, the which doesn't happen very often.

He then started right into the Communion service, which required his audience, the Team, to get up and come to the front to take the bread and wine. Since I had a front row seat, I was one of the first in line, but then couldn't get back to my seat because of the folks still in line behind me. I walked over to the side of the chapel and sat on a prayer bench, with my head in my hands, still worrying about how could I love a God I couldn't feel or see as much as I did Betsy, whom I could?

Some merciful soul realized my problem, and leaned down to impart to me the answer: "You love God, by loving God's people."

Duuhhh, Neill! I could have slapped my forehead. It says that right in the Bible, in red letters just like Jesus wrote it in: "People will know that you are My disciples because you LOVE ONE ANOTHER!"

That was it! I shook my head in wonder at the wisdom imparted unto me, and looked up to thank my benefactor.

There was not another person within twenty feet! No one was even looking my way.

It's the only time that I KNOW that God has spoken audibly to me, and He said, "The way you love God, is by loving God's people."

I could not wait to get home and tell Betsy about this Revelation which I had personally received, and when I got home she was in the kitchen fixing supper. I burst in, grabbed her, hugged and kissed her, and declared, "Let me tell you what happened to me today! God spoke to me!" And I told her that story, so she could marvel with me.

She declared, "You knew that," and turned back to the stove, frying eggplant.

I tugged her back around, "No, I didn't know that! If I had, I wouldn't have been. . . ."

"Yes, you did!" she interrupted.

"No, I didn't!" I stated firmly.

"Yes, you did!" she insisted. "Where have you been?"

That threw me off-base for a moment. "I've been to an Emmaus Team meeting, Betsy. You knew that."

"That's right! And what time was it over?" she demanded.

"About one," I said, wondering where she was going with this.

"And it's seven o'clock now," she pointed. "Grenada is

an hour and a half drive, right? So, where have you been?"

"Oh," I was relieved. "This is Second Saturday. I had told you that I was going to try to make the Kairos Reunion at Unit 29, Parchman, if I could. I made it just in time to go in with the rest of the guys, had a great time at Prayer and Share, then came on back home."

And she turned back to flipping eggplant. "You see," she observed gently, "You did know that, didn't you?"

Truth is where you find it. She's pretty good at that kind of thing.

However, what bowled me over was that God had actually spoken out loud to me, in a human-like voice that I could understand and recognize as having come from Him.

You don't believe that? I don't care. I've told that story many a time in print and in person, and have been surprised at how many people smile and softly say that God has spoken audibly to them, too. It's not a Neill exclusive, nor was I ever minded to claim that. It's just that until I started telling people how God spoke audibly to me, no one had ever told me that He had done so to them too.

May I say right here that there's no Blessing like the Blessing of working in Christian service with your spouse. While I understood Betsy's early declaration that Kairos was not her ministry, though she'd support me if I felt it was mine, I was unprepared for the way that she embraced it as her own once Cindy Herring convinced her to try a weekend. It was the very next Kairos weekend when I realized how much of a Blessing it could be.

She was working on Women's Kairos # 3, at the CMCF prison near Jackson, two hours south of Brownspur. I was working on Kairos # 6 at Unit 29, Parchman, an hour north of Brownspur. They were the same weekend, which was really unusual, but it meant that I'd be leaving Thursday morning headed north to prison, while she'd be leaving headed south to prison. We huddled up in the garage next to my packed pickup,

237

prayed over each other, kissed good-bye passionately, and then I got in the truck and drove away, headed north, while she went back in to pack her make-up bag before leaving.

I got almost three miles away from home before that durn pickup turned around and went home. She was amazed when I walked in the door and hugged her. She actually did not believe that the truck had done it to me itsownself!

We prayed over each other again, kissed passionately again, and I drove away again. That doggone truck didn't make it to the county line this time, before turning around. She was just getting into her Buick when I drove up behind her. Still didn't believe it was the truck's fault, but she prayed over me again as I did the same to her, then we kissed passionately again.

Then she walked me to my truck and declared, "The house is locked, and I'm driving out of this driveway right behind you, heading south to prison. Now you go north to prison, and stay there for the weekend! I'll see you Sunday night."

Lordee, it was hard to keep that pickup in the road headed north toward Parchman!

I was leading the singing for that Kairos, and early Saturday after a song session, the aforesaid prison Security Chief grabbed my arm and headed toward the prison office in the back of the gym. "You come with me, Mister!" Lonnie ordered.

"What have I done now?" I asked plaintively. He just shook his head and forged on into the office, flinging me into a chair.

"Now, you sit down and shut up and let me make a phone call to get you straight and out of trouble, if I can," he ground out. I started to speak, but he waved me roughly to silence as he picked up the phone and punched buttons. Seconds later he was talking Official Prison Talk with someone. I tried to remember what rules I had broken this weekend.

Finally, he seemed to get the person on the phone whom he wanted to deal with Neill. I got up tentatively as he beckoned, then handed the phone across the desk to me, bellowing to whoever was on the other end, "I got a lovesick puppy up here who ain't smiled in three days, so FIX IT!"

I took the receiver. Betsy was on the other end. Lonnie had called CMCF, gotten the Security Officer in the Karo room to go get Betsy during a break, and put her on the phone to get a smile on the face of "this lovesick puppy!" I could have kissed him, and he knew it, too, the way he ran out of that office!

A couple of years later, on another Emmaus Walk weekend, I was listening to a speaker who seemed intent on upsetting my applecart. He worked up to this point by talking about setting priorities in our lives, then asked us to take a piece of paper and list our top five priorities in our own lives right then. Well, that ain't so hard. I nailed down my five pretty swiftly.

The guy talked a while longer, then asked us to cross out one of those priorities. Well, that wasn't too hard, so I did that.

He talked a few minutes longer, than asked us to cross out another, leaving three.

Still not too hard. I did that.

He took off again, and I was about ready for him to get to the end, when he said to cross off one more. Now he was starting to meddle, but I whittled my list down to just two: God and Betsy. Time for him to sit down, I figured.

Not to be. That sucker kept on bearing down, and finally asked us to cross out one more, leaving only one.

Well, it's a Christian Retreat, for goodness sakes. I knew that I was supposed to end up with just God on my list. Duuuhhh!!

But it's not an easy thing to do, to cross off the name of the lady you love. Knowing that I was supposed to line through Betsy, I could not make the pencil move to do that. The guy got to agitating, giving us thirty seconds to make a decision that maybe some others were also struggling with. I couldn't move that doggone pencil. "Fifteen seconds," the guy warned. Still couldn't move it. "Ten seconds," he counted down. Was it just me, holding things up? "Okay, you got five seconds!" he grated out. "What's your priority?"

I could not cross out the word "Betsy." With seconds to go, I moved the pencil up and started to draw a line through the word "God."

And a voice infinitely kind and gentle said – not audibly, but just as clearly in my head as if I'd had on earphones: "Bob, wait. What if I told you that My first priority for your life, is for you to love Betsy? Could you trust Me enough to cross her name off then?"

What a relief flooded over me! I thanked Him for coming to my rescue, moved my pencil down, and drew a line through "Betsy," knowing that God wanted me to love her!

I've read many adjectives for God in my life, but never have I seen Him referred to as "sweet." Yet it was so sweet of Him to see through my predicament, and enlighten me as to how to set my priorities and honor Him by that.

Perhaps a year later, I was working another Team, and at the overnight meeting, all three of the preachers in attendance had to go home late Friday evening, leaving us with no clergy to conduct a Communion on Saturday, much less lead the devotional prior to that. For some reason, I felt moved to ask the Team Leader for permission to give the devotional, and used that "God's Priority" story for the theme. A couple of weeks later we had a very successful weekend, and the Leader called me a week later to see if I wanted to ride with him to that Saturday's Reunion. I said that'd be great, and he picked me up early that morning. We drove along, laughing and joyous as we remembered the things that God had done over that weekend.

When the conversation lagged for a moment, I wondered out loud, "You know that I mainly work Kairos weekends now, but on every Emmaus Walk weekend that I've worked, there has

240

always been an 'Aha!' moment, when I knew exactly why God had moved me to serve on that Team. Yet that never happened on this weekend, for some reason, and I can't figure out why." Again the conversation lapsed for a few moments, then I heard a suspicious snuffle from the driver's side of the pickup. I looked, and my companion had huge tears trickling down his cheeks. "What's wrong?" I asked, offering my bandana handkerchief.

He wiped his eyes, blew his nose, and shook his head. "Maybe you weren't even supposed to serve on the weekend," he mused. "Remember that devotional you did on the overnight Team meeting?" I nodded. "Well, the night before, my wife and oldest daughter and I had a real knockdown dragout about a boy she was dating, and I finally cussed them out, told them that I wasn't speaking to them, and stormed out of the room. I stomped back in to tell them that I didn't even want them to be on the Team, and left home that next morning without speaking to them. They drove over to the meeting by themselves, but I didn't acknowledge them at all, mad as a hornet that they had come.

"Then you got up and gave a devotional about God's priority for you was for you to love your wife. After everyone else left, I cried and asked their forgiveness, and my marriage has been better since that weekend, than it's ever been. Like I say, you didn't even need to go on the actual weekend with the Team. God placed you there just for me, at the overnight Team meeting. You could have stayed home and gone hunting that weekend."

God still speaks to us today. He can use people to speak through, and most often does. I have "seen Him in the lightning, heard Him in the thunder, and felt Him in the rain," as the song says. I have heard kids, adults, preachers, and regular folks obviously speaking His Word.

At a recent hometown concert of that Kairos Music Team, my grandson Sean Robert Irwin walked up to observe and listen at close range. He was only three years old, but we had already noticed that he was developing musical talent, or at least an appreciation of music. We took a break and got some water, and Sean walked over to Mark Propst, the harmonica player, to ask about the lyrics of one of the songs, "Lights of the City." Mark explained that it was a picture of Heaven, and when Sean obviously didn't grasp that concept, Mark tried to go one step further: "You know, Heaven, where Jesus lives?"

Instant understanding shown in the three year-old's eyes, and he confidently corrected Mark: "No, Jesus lives here," he tapped his little chest, "in my heart!"

Mark had a McKaro # 1 Cross around his neck. He burst out into tears and laughter, and pulled off that Cross, then hung it over Sean's neck and hugged the boy.

Truth is where you find it. It can be spoken even by a three-year-old.

But He ain't got to use people to speak for Him – He can certainly do it directly, when He chooses to, even today.

It's just like healing: He can use people: doctors, nurses, folks to whom He has given the Gift of Healing – but He can just do it Hisownself, if He chooses.

God has healed me; God has spoken to me directly, and through others. Why me, Lord?

Final Arrangements

My favorite Aun-tee called one Sunday afternoon for the annual update of her Final Arrangement Plans. She had a new song that she wanted me and Betsy to sing at her funeral, "And it'll go so well with the one that Cuddin Polly Sue is going to do now. She's singing a new one that I like a lot, with the theme of Heaven being all aglow, and this one that I now want y'all to sing will fit perfectly."

"I thought we were going to sing 'Jesus Will Outshine Them All' for you?" I replied.

"That was last year. I'm revising my plans, to go with this new theme. Cuddin Dexter will also be doing a different song, and his daughter is taking violin lessons in college now, so she's going to play 'Ave Maria' while all the family comes in. It's going to be such a beautiful service!"

"Do you have a date set for this beautiful service?" I joked. "I'm going to be doing a lot of traveling, what with my new book coming out next month, and our new CD coming out last month. If I could put your funeral's date on my calendar ahead of time, it'd sure help me plan around it."

Aun-tee (not the one you're thinking about: if you don't know the difference between an Aunt and an Aun-tee, ask a Southerner) laughed, "Of course not! You know we've got the genes to make it to a hundred, so this might be twenty-five years away. What new CD? I haven't heard it. Bring me one."

"I'll do that, because there's a song on it that would work

just right with your new funeral theme. It's called 'Lights of the City,' and I bet you'll want to revise your plans again after you hear it."

"Oh, I just can't wait to hear it, then!" Aun-tee enthused. "This is going to be such a beautiful service. Wish I was going to be able to hear the whole thing myself."

I have a book by the great outdoor humorist Ed Zern, which includes a chapter that is entitled something like, "The Pre-Funeralization of Charlie Gunn." I recalled that tome, and the thought struck me: why shouldn't Aun-tee get to enjoy these beautiful funeral services that she revises annually? I promptly told her about Zern's Pre-Funeralization concept.

"What a marvelous idea!" she immediately grasped the potential. "I could hold one each year, and then revise it for the next year, so no one would get bored. Everyone would get to enjoy the good time, and we could have an old-fashioned dinner on the grounds afterward, with fried chicken and all the trimmings. Cuddin Rosemary could whip up her delicious burnt sugar cakes each year, and May-May would bring a big pan of her banana pudding."

A thought struck her: "Do you think folks will get tired of coming to my funeral every year? Most folks only have one funeral, you know."

I considered judiciously before replying, "No, Ma'am, I don't think they'd get tired of it. Matter of fact. . ." the thought struck both of us at the same time: "We could commercialize this concept!"

I personally favor cremation, as noted, though have not set a date for that myownself, and that type Final Arrangements doesn't lend itself so much to traditional Southern funerals, so the idea of Pre-Funeralization fits in well with my own plans. Aun-tee wasn't so inclined: "I don't want ANY fires around when I kick the bucket, thank you!" she declared firmly. "But I know I'm going to Heaven, because I believe in Jesus, so I don't want folks to be really sad when I pass away. I want them to

244

celebrate, and it'd be nice to get in on the celebration myself, if that's possible with this Pre-Funeralization concept."

Aun-tee and I are working on it, okay? First thing is, I've got to see if Mr. Zern, who I understand has already been Funeralized hisownself, has a copyright on this process. I'm like Aun-tee: as the song says, Jesus is going to take me to Heaven when I die, so I'm hoping folks will celebrate then, and I'll sure hate to miss the party when that time comes!

So I'm cogitating now on my own Pre-Funeralization, and my own family has enthusiastically joined in on that, as well as even going Beyond (so to speak) the original concept, bless their hearts.

I had been in a big store that specialized in non-run-of-the-mill merchandise, and a sort of regal-looking vase caught my eye, it being the week before daughter B.C.'s birthday. It even had a little top on it, and it wasn't expensive, so I bought it for her present. I have had Lyme Disease, so have acquired a terrible history and reputation for buying gifts early, then hiding them, then forgetting either that I had bought them, or where they were hidden, so I took the vase back to the TV station with me and set it on my desk, where I wouldn't forget it. At the next desk, my colleague Lorraine smiled sort of dubiously and remarked, "That's a nice urn. Who is it for?"

My vase turned out to resemble an urn in which one keeps the ashes of dearly departed loved ones, apparently. I still thought it would look fine with flowers in it, though, so announced that it was a vase, thank you, and it was a birthday present for B.C. next week.

I got some grief from my co-workers, all of whom I came to suspect must have closets full of their departed ancestors. I had never encountered such a custom before, though after I considered how much good cotton land is taken up in cemeteries, I began to lean toward that method of Final Arrangements myownself. It was reputed to be cheaper, too.

I had burnt my hand checking a welding job the week

before, and the resulting scab was just beginning to work off as I scratched it, so when I finally worried it aloose, I thought, well, here's a natural place to put it. If this was truly an urn, then why not start the repository process with Dear Old Dad's burnt scab. Sort of an Initial Deposit of Dad; maybe B.C. could think of it compared to an add-a-pearl necklace: I mean, things have eternally been getting burnt off, or chopped off, or broken off of me my whole life – why not start collecting them?

We had all the kids out to the house for the birthday party, and I presented the urn with my best wishes, as well as the add-a-pearl concept I had come up with, explaining that I had thoughtfully already started that process for our youngest child. B.C. took the top off the urn, gingerly sniffed the opening, and wrinkled her nose: "Ugh! Your Initial Deposit of Dad stinks! Did you think about adding some rose petals or flowers?"

We were on the back screen porch, and Adam was grilling dove breasts on the patio, well within hearing. He asked, "Well, did you marinate the Initial DOD before you burnt it? I bet soaking it in Dale's Sauce or Wishbone overnight would have done wonders for it. We'll try that on the next Deposit of Dad, okay?"

Son-in-law John went one better: "Hey, if we marinate Uncle Bob before his Final Entry Into The Urn, we might could use him to season stuff we grill. Can we fill up a couple of salt shakers with Deposits Of Dad to sprinkle on the spareribs, reckon?"

Well, good-smelling and good-tasting stuff from the fire is Biblical, I had to agree, so maybe the boys were on to something. B.C. concurred: "Oh, marination would make a lot more sense than putting flower petals in with the Deposits of Dad, all right. He just isn't a floweredy sort of guy, is he?" I really had to agree with her character assessment.

John chimed in again, "Y'all know, all of Uncle Bob ain't gonna combust very well, like those pins he's got holding him together."

Adam was right there: "Yeah! I can take the pin metal and cast it into bullets! Why, 'Going hunting with Uncle Bob' will take on a whole new meaning, won't it?"

"Better not miss, or you won't be able to take him hunting with you the next deer season," Christie cautioned.

"Right you are," John declared. "Better go for neck shots, too, so the Uncle Bob Bullet won't go all the way through the buck and into a tree trunk somewhere. See, we can recover Uncle Bob when we cut the deer up, re-cast him into another bullet, and take him hunting again every year!"

"I don't want to kill any does, okay?" I volunteered. "Save my shots for the big bucks."

Betsy was beginning to get enthusiastic, too. "Y'all do know that he's got all those lead shot in his appendix, don't you? Plus several pellets or so in his hand. Y'all can reload him into shotgun shells and take Uncle Bob duck and dove hunting, as well."

"Again, no misses," John warned. "Nothing but sure shots, so we can recover the lead and take him hunting again next time."

"Can't take Uncle Bob Shells duck hunting, Mom," Adam shook his head. "It's against the law to shoot lead shot at ducks now."

John snorted, "When has Uncle Bob paid any attention to that law? Y'all know how he hates shooting a duck with steel shot, then watching it fly off, when he knows it would have been dead if he'd been shooting lead."

"Yeah, but you don't want to get an Uncle Bob Shell confiscated by the Game Warden, do you?" Adam asked. "I mean, I know he spends a lot of time in prison now, but I don't think he'd want to be on a jailhouse shelf as evidence permanently, do you?"

"True," Betsy conceded. "Better just use the Uncle Bob Shells for doves – or maybe squirrel and rabbits? You know how he loves to hear those beagles run rabbits. I think he'd enjoy going on rabbit hunts."

They all agreed that I had come up with a great gift idea, and were eager to participate in my Final Arrangements!

I have a good friend in Nashville who hails from New York originally. Charlie Flood has been my longtime publishing consultant and agent for literary efforts, and he once told me of the Final Arrangements for his aunt and his father, who passed away within a week of each other.

He is one of five brothers, all big men, who served as pallbearers for both funerals. Auntie was a small lady who had lived a long fruitful life, and had wasted away to almost nothing, in her last days.

The week before, bearing their father, the brothers discovered that the difference in height between sidewalk and hearse required lifting the casket to shoulder level in order to slide it into the hearse. Papa Flood was a big man, so that demanded considerable muscle.

They were set to lift Auntie the same way, but she was to be cremated, so her casket was a light burnable one, and her weight was considerably less than their father's had been. At the hearse, the lead brother stopped and whispered, "Okay, ready? Lift!" They did so, unprepared for how little Auntie weighed, compared to Papa .

To their horror, the coffin almost flew into the air with the mighty lift! Two shorter brothers went to tiptoes to retain their hold on the handles. Adding to their horror, they felt Auntie float upward within the box. The same thought hit them all: "What if she busts through the bottom of this thing when she comes back down?!" Without a word, each brother reached beneath the lightweight casket to brace the bottom with one hand. It held, though it bent, when Auntie hit bottom. Their collective sigh was taken to be one of grief.

The week before, at a wake for Papa Flood, the brothers had agreed to bring items that their father had loved to deposit

248

in the casket (unbeknownst to the undertaker). Papa had been an avid golfer, so Charlie brought two golf balls. On his visit to the coffin, he slipped the balls under his dad's crossed hands. His brothers brought other items to sneak in. When viewing time was over, the undertaker closed the casket. The funeral began, with brother Jimmy playing the bagpipes. After the service, the bier was wheeled to the front of St. Patrick's Cathedral, to be carried down ten steps, across a flat landing of ten feet, then ten steps down again to another landing, repeated several times before street level and the waiting hearse.

Of course, each ten steps down required the casket to be slanting downward. On the first set of steps, the golf balls slipped out of Papa's hands and rolled downhill.

Suddenly the pallbearers, as well as the undertaker, heard a sound which might be described as "Klunk, klunk!" However, such a noise within a casket sounds remarkably like, "Knock, knock!" The mortician hesitated briefly. The brothers, knowing about the golf balls, managed straight faces as they hit the first landing, and the coffin leveled out. Charlie and Jimmy, in front, raised their end slightly, to cause the balls to roll backwards slowly.

Going down the next steps, the coffin tilted again: "Knock, knock!" This time the undertaker stopped, and the brothers almost ran over him. Once more, they managed to keep straight faces, and the procession started again, the mortician frowning in deep thought.

Another landing, another surreptitious tilt back, then another downward flight. This time, the undertaker stepped to the side as the brothers went ahead. Sure enough, there it was again: "Knock, knock!" Panic seized the funeral director, and he spurted ahead of the pallbearers to the hearse, there to go into frenzied conversation with his assistants.

The team of undertakers took extra care easing the casket into the hearse, but as they started to close the door, Jimmy wiped a tear from his eye, and asked to be allowed to ride in the hearse. The funeral director refused, which seemed to distress all five brothers, four of whom turned away with shaking shoulders as Jimmy pleaded his case, evoking his father's wish to be piped off on this final journey. The rest of the family, unaware of any knocking sounds from within the casket, were in their cars, ready to proceed to the graveyard. Finally a policeman came over to see what the holdup was, and affirmed the funeral director's claim that custom at least, if not law, dictated that no one but morticians and the recently deceased were allowed to ride in the hearse. With poor grace, Jimmy shook his head and joined his brothers in the pallbearer limousine.

It was reported that strange sounds of grief, remarkably like hysterical mirth, emanated from that limo for the whole drive, but all the pallbearers were under control at the graveside service, though understandably red-faced and teary-eyed.

So, if you hear knocking sounds from within a golfer's casket, rest easy, knowing that at least one golfer's casket was surely opened during transport to the cemetery, and there were no signs of life.

No disrespect intended here, for funerals are almost invariably sorrowful occasions. However, when someone who is a Christian has passed away, it is to enter a better world, a place where, to paraphrase the Bible in the words of a John Peterson song, there's "no more tears when we get to Heaven. . .no more pain when we get to Heaven. . .no more war when we get to Heaven. . .no more death when we get to Heaven! This is the Good Life!" So many times I have been to the memorial service for a longtime Christian, and the occasion has been a joyous celebration of a life spent with Jesus, that I've come away from the cemetery smiling and thanking God for having known such a Saint as the dearly departed. It should be thataway for all of us, really.

At a recent Calvary Baptist staff meeting, we got on the subject of being there when a Christian friend has passed away,

250

and in many instances the departee just before dying took on almost a glow, smiling and pointing at something the others in the room could not see, perhaps exclaiming, "I see Jesus!" or "Angels!" One lady reportedly whispered, "What beautiful music!" I've never been present at such an encounter, but I've not heard of any instances of that type experience in combat deaths, some of which I've been present for, unfortunately.

One the other side of the coin, literally, is the type encounter that friend Gene Drake related to me. A deckhand had fallen overboard from one of his towboats in the New Orleans area. This man was not of the highest social strata, a rough-edged working man given to much profanity, and fond of the bottle, reputedly.

My mother was from Arkansas, and her prejudicial view when I was growing up was not racial by any means, but more cultural. In descending order, the lower caste of her Order of Society were termed, "White Trash," "Poor White Trash," "River Rats," "Peckerwoods," and finally "Hoop Roobins," a term I've never heard except in Arkansas. Not even sure it's two words, matter of fact. But I grew up secure in the knowledge that some folks were better than other folks in her estimation, and that Peckerwoods were not tree-pecking feathered birds.

Gene's employee was, from his description, a River Rat from south Louisiana.

Fortunately, he slipped into the water almost across from a Coast Guard station along the Mighty Muddy, and someone saw him go over and sounded the "Man Overboard" alarm. He was underwater for nearly ten minutes, but they brought him up, resuscitated him, and got him on oxygen, then to the hospital in time. There seemed to be no obvious brain damage, they told Gene when he got to the hospital himself within a half an hour. He walked into the River Rat's room, and the guy grasped his arm, pulled the oxygen mask aside, and exclaimed, "Skipper, get me a priest!"

Gene shook his head: "You're gonna be okay. You don't need Last Rites."

The guy insisted, "No! Get me a priest!"

Gene demurred again, "Listen, you didn't die. You didn't drown. You're alive, and you're going to be okay, do you understand?"

And the man replied forcefully, "No, YOU don't understand! I DID die – and I went to hell! Now I'm back, but I need for you to get me a priest right now, so I can get my life straight with Jesus!"

Gene got him a priest. The man accepted Christ, quit his job, and the last time my friend heard of him, he was speaking actively in the Charismatic Catholic movement!

When I had the wreck that broke my back so long ago, I had one of those "out-of-body" experiences that one can read books about nowadays, but back then, if I had told about it, every one would have considered that I was crazy. It wasn't until the first book on that subject came out decades later – was it entitled something like, "Life After Life"? – that I related, mainly to Betsy, the sensation of watching myself through the rolling pickup windshield, even as the first cracks appeared in the glass, then the image of myself grimacing as the windshield and cab crushed and were torn off in another roll, then seeing myself projected from the tumbling wreck, to regain consciousness lying face-up in a soybean field in the rain, with four broken vertebrae (two crushed), a crushed chest, and collapsed lungs – yet no paralysis. Nor will I forget the guy who stopped to call out, "Is he dead yet?" I will never forget, but don't ever discuss, the darkness before consciousness and the sensation of swimming through what seemed like sorghum molasses toward a speck of light; until the pain began and brought me back to earth, as it were.

With that type injury, aggravated by a total of over 23 broken bones as well as fifteen more major joint injuries, plus Lyme Disease arthritis, I have experienced a great deal of pain throughout the years, of course. (I say "over 23" because when I crushed my right hand between the rollers of a cotton gin lint cleaner 1/16th of an inch apart, it was midnight before I got to the small town hospital – I drove myself – and Dr. Nichols observed that since the skin had been stripped off when I slammed my feet into the front of the machine and straightened my back out to drag my hand out, that he would have to treat the injury like a burn, so there was no sense in waking up the X-ray technician fifteen miles away. Therefore I just count the hand as one break, not knowing how many of those 20 bones were actually fractured.) As self-help therapy, I built me a Pain Box: it's framed up with 2 X 2s, covered by cypress 1 X 4s, with a hinged lid, then a hasp that's locked by one of those old-timey brass swinging-gate padlocks. That's a mental box, by the way. Then I pack in all of the pain that I can expect during the course of a regular day, and lock the box. That much pain is normal, and is not allowed to affect detrimentally my daily demeanor. Sometimes it gets out of the box, and then I have to cope with the extra pain, but it's only the overflow that I have to deal with then. Does that make sense? I built the same type box for combat memories, and another one for those Rural Crisis Committee Farm Suicide Hotline experiences. If I want to unlock those boxes and re-live the contents, I can, but then I pack them back up and lock the box again, so they don't have permission to roam around in my head. The key to living with bad experiences or major-league pain, is to control that, not let it control you, understand? I've had a psychologist shake her head and admit that my method made perfect sense, although she's never read about that technique anywhere else before.

An annual overflow from the Pain Box is when the first real cold front comes through each late fall. Every broken bone hurts extra then, all of them together for about 48 hours, but after a couple of days I can get it locked back into the Box again, and go on with my day normally. One fall, after that first cold front had hit, I recall telling Betsy that I wasn't planning on going there just yet, but that "When I get to Heaven, I ain't gonna hurt any more!" That is a promise from the Bible to depend on! No more pain when I get to Heaven, as the song says.

Son Adam is tee-totally color blind, and used to throw an 88-mile-a-day paper route when he was a teenager, making about $600 a month profit! I'd get up with him at 3:00 a.m. on Sunday mornings, to roll the larger editions as he threw. One morning there was a cloud bank coming over from the west, just as the sun was coming to the eastern horizon, and when he turned the car east, it revealed such a glorious sunrise that I exclaimed in awe, "Wow! What a beautiful sight!"

And Adam asked, "What?"

It's hard to describe a sunrise to a colorblind person, and when I finally quit trying, he declared with certainty, "Daddy, when I get to Heaven, God's gonna give me a new set of eyes, and let me come back to just mirate over sunrises and sunsets for a few thousand years!" That sounded like a reasonable prophecy to me, not looking forward to death, but certainly to Heaven!

So in many circumstances, a departure from this Vale of Tears is a cause for joyous celebration although there has to be a lingering sorrow that we won't be able to see our dearly departed any more, until we join him or her in that Land Beyond the River ourselves.

Assuming that you have already made your post-mortem arrangements, of course.

When my first book, *THE FLAMING TURKEY,* came out in what used to be called the "blue-line proofs," as the last chance to correct or change something before it was printed and bound, I told my then-agent that I wanted to add an "Afterthought." The book ended with the death of my father, Big Robert, and afterward I had written a letter to most of my friends and hunting companions who had enjoyed Daddy's company, and whose company he had enjoyed as well. I wanted to include that letter, edited of course.

She read my "Afterthought," and protested, "You can't add this. It changes the direction of the entire book."

"I feel led to do it thisaway, Joanne," I declared.

She shook her head. "I can't go along with this."

I was paying for the book anyway, so rejoined, "Fine. But it's going into the book."

That book was a small press best seller, and the "Afterthought" was the most-commented-upon part of it! That was 24 years ago, and *TFT* was one of the titles that we lost in the fire, so it's been out of print for a long time. I felt led to end this book by editing and reprinting that final chapter once more.

Religion is a personal matter, and it's hard to talk to some folks about it. There's also some folks you know don't need talking to, and others whom you wish would share with you about how their religion seems to be so joyful. This letter is not an attempt to meddle, nor to be Big Bobby Better'nYou. It is simply friendship.

Sometimes you strike up an acquaintance with someone whom you figure you'd like to be friends with for a few years. You've made other friends you've enjoyed for decades. There are some folks whom you consider to be life-long friends.

Then there are the ones whom you want to be friends with Forever.

I suddenly came to the realization that I have a good many of the latter brand, more than most folks do. And that I had not shared my concept of Forever with all of them. If you have a friend of this caliber, you belong to at least make him or her aware that Forever is longer than life here on this planet, and that you don't want distance and temperature to one day ruin a beautiful relationship. 'Course, he may be better prepared than you are, too.

I ain't arguing with anybody about religion. Like I said, it's a personal thing, and if you don't believe like I do, that's your little red wagon and you can pull it like you want to. This is simply my belief. It is not a theological statement.

I have concluded, after many years' research on both subjects, that religion is a lot like wild turkey hunting:

"The sooner you realize you don't know all there is to know about the subject, the better chance you have of being successful in the practice of it."

Dear Reader:

I wanted to write and thank you for coming here to share my joy and sorrow. . . .

Which brings me to a subject that's hard to talk about, especially to friends. Maybe it will be easier thisaway, or maybe I'm just striking while the iron is hot. At any rate, in conjunction with Big Robert's passing, I wanted to tell you something I believe and ask you to think about it.

He and I had never talked much about things like this, but enough had been said that I have to believe he went to Heaven. I'm not sure what it's like, but I can't help imagining that it'll be even better than opening weekend of Dove season, deer season on Woodstock Island, and turkey season on Woodstock, all rolled into one. The old Indians may have had a good concept with their Happy Hunting Grounds theory. Can you imagine the turkeys always having twelve-inch beards, gobbling at every third step, coming up in less than an hour, and never appearing behind your gun shoulder?

Point of talking like this is that I don't want to get up there myownself and find out that someone with whom I would enjoy spending Forever failed to make the barge. So I've screwed up my courage this one time to say that I believe there is a Heaven, and some folks will go there and some won't be going. I think you can know for sure one way or t'other. I don't believe that it depends on what church you go to, or whether you even go to church. I think it depends on what you believe, and that belief has to include a personal acceptance of Jesus Christ as your Savior.

There are a bunch of folks in this world who believe in other saviors, and I think that they are going to find out too late that they have made a mistake. There will also be some preachers and deacons who thought that they knew everything about religion, and I believe that they are going to be unfortunately surprised when their time comes.

I ain't leaning on you atall, 'cause I know that I don't know it all, and for all I know, the whole bunch of you may have gotten your tickets punched for the Pearly Gates years before I did myownself. So if you never mention this again, probably I won't either.

Well, there it is, and if I bothered or embarrassed you, I apologize. I ain't keeping a list, and don't need an answer. I just wanted you to know that Big Robert's already working on a lease for some big timber deer and turkey woods with milo, millet, and sunflower fields around three sides. There's a couple of flooded rice fields on the same side as the cypress brake lake, which is stocked with Eden bass – from which the Florida strain was derived. The old clubhouse he's got located is in the edge of the woods next to the lakebank, with a good-sized bunkroom in the back. I just want to be sure that one of those bunks has your name on it.

Thanks for the friends and the memories,
Uncle Bob

I have been blessed by many wonderful friends and memories, as you have understood if you have read this far. I figure on going to Heaven, myownself. Sure would love to see the rest of y'all Up There.

But be sure that you have taken care of your own Final Arrangements before that day arrives, okay?

LaVergne, TN USA
04 March 2011
218787LV00001B/2/P